Life in the Medieval Town

Life in the Medieval Town

Kathryn Warner

First published in Great Britain in 2025 by
Pen & Sword History
An imprint of Pen & Sword Books Limited
Yorkshire – Philadelphia

ISBN 978 1 39904 210 9

A CIP catalogue record for this book is available from the British Library.

Typeset by Mac Style
Printed in the UK by CPI Group (UK) Ltd, Croydon, CR0 4YY.

The Publisher's authorised representative in the EU for product safety is Authorised Rep Compliance Ltd., Ground Floor, 71 Lower Baggot Street, Dublin D02 P593, Ireland.
www.arccompliance.com

For a complete list of Pen & Sword titles please contact

PEN & SWORD BOOKS LIMITED
47 Church Street, Barnsley, South Yorkshire, S70 2AS, England
E-mail: enquiries@pen-and-sword.co.uk
Website: www.pen-and-sword.co.uk
or
PEN AND SWORD BOOKS
1950 Lawrence Road, Havertown, PA 19083, USA
E-mail: uspen-and-sword@casematepublishers.com
Website: www.penandswordbooks.com

Contents

Introduction		vii
Chapter 1	Arriving in a Medieval Town	1
Chapter 2	Vagrant Pigs and Obnoxious Fumes	11
Chapter 3	Godday, Ich Highte Johan (Hello, I'm Called John)	23
Chapter 4	Common Nightwalkers and Curfews	34
Chapter 5	At Whiche Hande Shall I Take My Way? Travelling	41
Chapter 6	Faitours, Bocardo and the Thewe: Crime and Punishment	52
Chapter 7	Tallow Candles and Penny Loaves: Sleeping, Washing and Eating	70
Chapter 8	Water, Wine and Ale: Drink and Taverns	84
Chapter 9	Surcotes and Scrimpyn: Clothes	91
Chapter 10	Eme, Mome and Cousyns Germain: Family Relations	97
Chapter 11	Midovernone and Right Grete Gramercy: Time and Talking to People	106
Chapter 12	Tisik, Apostomes and Quinsy: Health	117
Chapter 13	Foteball and Penypryk: Having Fun (1)	127

Chapter 14	Wrastleng, Mommyng and Romanse: Having Fun (2)	131
Chapter 15	How Moche Cometh It To? Going Shopping	139
Chapter 16	Medieval Misteries: Working	144
Chapter 17	Olifaunts, Sothseyers and Storms: Oddities and Intense Weather	154
Chapter 18	Frenzy and Next Friends: Medieval Kindness	163

Abbreviations 174
Notes 175
Bibliography 191

Introduction

Imagine the darkness of a world many centuries before the invention of electric light. In the late Middle Ages, wax candles cost as much as 5 shillings each, and as this amounts to several weeks' wages for most people, they can only be afforded by the well-off. Everyone else must make do with smelly candles made of tallow, i.e. rendered animal fat which costs only 2d a pound, or rushlights, dried rush plants covered with tallow or grease and set alight.[1] Think of the long, dark evenings and nights of winter. You are illiterate, and even if you could read, there are no newspapers or magazines, which will not be invented until hundreds of years later. While books do exist, they are rare, all copied by hand until the middle of the fifteenth century, and so costly that they are beyond the means of all but a few. Furthermore, trying to read by the dim, smoky, guttering light of your tallow candle would strain your eyes intolerably. When you step outside your home to use your latrine, the darkness is, even in the middle of a town – and even in the middle of London – absolute. With no light pollution whatsoever, the Milky Way arches vividly above you, and you see untold thousands of stars twinkling brightly in the sky.

Imagine the almost total silence of a world without machinery. The bellowing of oxen and the neighing of horses, the screaming of a woman in labour or the yelling of a person in a rage, the creaking of cartwheels or the local mill wheel as the miller turns it to grind corn, the bells of your nearby parish church, a minstrel playing a kettledrum, thunder and torrential rain during a storm, the sound of iron being hammered in the blacksmith's forge as he crafts a horseshoe; these are the loudest noises that will ever reach your ears. You will never hear a humming fridge, the drone of a lawnmower, a pounding bass line from your neighbour's window, a power drill, the wailing siren of an emergency vehicle, a motorbike being revved, a car or house alarm going off in the middle of the night, the ringing of a phone, the whirring of a sewing machine, or the clacking of someone typing. You will never see the vapour trail of an aeroplane passing overhead or a train speeding past or a line of cars waiting at traffic lights or electricity pylons stretching into the distance. You will only be able to listen to music or watch any kind of entertainment if minstrels perform it near you.

You live in a world where everything around you, including the cart or ladder or bucket or hand tools you use in your daily job, was made with human hands, as was the house in which you live, which is made of wood and was built by carpenters. The clothes and shoes you wear were all stitched by hand. When your clothes become dirty, you will have to wash them in a stream or river or pay someone to do it for you, and you will have to get used to washing your hair and body with cold or tepid water from a jug or basin, or in a stream or river when the weather permits. You will have to draw your own water from a well, and if it dries up in hot weather, you will have to go instead to your nearest lake or stream and fill buckets, then carry them home. If you live in London, you have the option of using the Great Conduit at the junction of Cheapside and Poultry, a marvellous thirteenth-century invention which brings fresh water into the city centre from the River Tyburn several miles away, though this will still require carrying the water to your home.

Imagine how it feels to exist in a world where you live hand to mouth, and if the local harvest fails, you and your family risk hunger, malnutrition and even starvation. A world where every stage of the rearing and slaughtering of animals and the preparation of their carcasses for food and other products are far more present and visible than selecting a wrapped and labelled cut of meat in a supermarket. A world where the temperature scales of Fahrenheit and Celsius will not be invented until the eighteenth century, hundreds of years later, and accurate weather forecasts not until the nineteenth, so you have no reliable means of knowing when it will be bitterly cold or blazing hot or snowing or blowing a gale and planning your week accordingly. Without newspapers, television news or radio, and without the ability to read a letter or a public notice, the only way you have of knowing what is going on in your world, both at a local and a national level, is when other people tell you in person.

Imagine a world where there are no maps, no grid references and no house numbers, and to find your way to a place which you do not know, you will have to ask people for directions, or pay a guide to take you. You will never travel faster than a horse can gallop or a team of mariners can pull their oars, and even in a country as relatively small as England, it will take you days to get anywhere. If you wish to travel to Santiago de Compostela in northern Spain as a pilgrim – and plenty of English people do – you will need to set aside several months to get there and back. When Robert Westbech from Kent makes a pilgrimage to both Santiago and the Holy Land in the early 1340s, he is away from England for a year and eight months.

Imagine a world where Christianity dominates everything, and marks the daily and yearly rhythms of your life. Your parish church's bells will ring out the canonical hours that form the routine of your day. It is a world where pigs roam the streets of your town, some people urinate or throw wastewater out of their upper-storey window regardless of anyone passing below, and the streets are often so narrow, with the upper storeys cantilevered and jutting out, that you could shake hands with your neighbour on the opposite side through your windows. On the other hand, while your town may be filled with the ripe smells of dung, the tanning process, rotting animal remains, and unwashed bodies, the air is, compared to the modern era, fresh; there are no industrial processes to pollute it, and no smog or choking London peasoupers.

In a world long before reliable contraception exists, you will most probably have a sizeable number of siblings, some of whom will die before they reach adulthood. Perhaps many of them will, and the shockingly high child mortality rate is no respecter of rank: Leonor of Castile, Edward I's Spanish queen, gives birth to at least fourteen and perhaps as many as sixteen children between 1255 and 1284, and only six of them live past the age of 10. Only four outlive their father. There is a reasonable chance that your mother or aunt or sister or wife died during childbirth or shortly afterwards, and also a reasonable chance that a male relative was killed or maimed while fighting in the king of England's wars in Wales, Scotland or France. You live in a much younger society than your modern descendants do; in England in the twenty-first century, the median age is almost 40, but in the fourteenth century is about half that.[2]

You live in a world that is hyper-violent, with a murder rate barely seen in the modern era except in war zones. You will almost certainly know of a homicide victim, as in the fourteenth century the average English urban dweller has a less than 1 in 1,000 chance of being murdered in any year. Your descendants seven centuries later are much safer, with only a 1 in 100,000 chance. You will almost certainly know of someone who died of gangrene after breaking a bone or died of tetanus or an infection after sustaining a wound. Although cholera does not exist in medieval England, typhus does, as does the horrifying disease of smallpox, and the first terrible pandemic of the Black Death scythes through England and the rest of Europe in the late 1340s. You know of epilepsy, though you call it the falling sickness, you know of dysentery, though you call it the flux or bloody flux, and you know of tuberculosis, though you call it *tisik*. If you live in or have visited one of the low-lying marshy areas of eastern England, you might have suffered from malaria, though you will call it tertian fever or quartan fever.

Other than herbal remedies – which can, to be fair, be very effective if you have the good fortune to be treated by an apothecary who knows what he is doing – there is little anyone can do for your ailment. If you break a limb, there is a reasonable chance that you will die a few weeks later, and if you suffer a bad head injury, death is all but certain. There is no social welfare, and if by misfortune you fall ill or suffer an accident, and consequently cannot work, you have no other choice but to depend on family or to take to the streets begging. If you are imprisoned, and have no family or friends to bring you food or have no money to pay the guards to give you some, they will simply let you starve to death.

Your teeth are better than modern people might imagine, as sugar is a rare treat, though eventually you will wear them down by eating coarse-grained bread, and if you suffer from terrible toothache the only real solution is to pull the tooth out. Your diet is monotonous, and in winter you face a constant battle to stay warm and dry.

You know most people in your town by sight, and are aware in which family or mistery (guild) or household they live and work. In your world, strangers are regarded with suspicion, and it is vitally important to belong somewhere, to have your face known, and to have painstakingly constructed a reputation as someone trustworthy and reliable. Your memory is excellent because you cannot write anything down to remind yourself, though you know some people who are able to read and write and can calculate with numbers. In a world many hundreds of years before photography exists, your recall of faces is superb.

You do not care much about the landscape outside your town except insofar as it might be utilised to feed you and your family, and the modern way of enjoying a view of hills or the sea would leave you somewhat baffled, but you find beauty in practical, well-made objects that are fit for purpose and will last a long time. You own very little; in 1321, the only things that belong to Isabel Pampesworth of London are a blanket, an 'old sheet' and a chest, and the following year, William of Grimsby owns two small pigs, a piece of timber, a broken chest and table, a pair of worn linen sheets, a worn linen cloth, and a blanket. In 1393, Henry Whitley of Nottingham owns an old chair, an old barrel, an old chest, two old and broken skillets of brass, several broken boards, a coverlet and some cushions, and not much else.[3] The items you do own, therefore, and the tools you use to earn a living, are precious to you, and as you cannot easily afford to replace them, you find a sort of beauty in their utility and longevity. Because most people are poor and own so little, theft is viewed as one of the worst crimes anyone can commit, and the death penalty is imposed on those who steal items worth more than 12½d.

You are the resident of a medieval English town.

Kings of England

Henry III reigned 1216–1272 m. Alienor of Provence
Edward I (aka Longshanks) 1272–1307 m. (1) Leonor of Castile (2) Marguerite of France
Edward II (aka Edward of Caernarfon) 1307–1327 m. Isabella of France
Edward III 1327–1377 m. Philippa of Hainault
Richard II 1377–1399 m. (1) Anne of Bohemia (2) Isabelle de Valois
Henry IV 1399–1413 m. (1) Mary de Bohun (2) Juana of Navarre
Henry V 1413–1422 m. Katherine de Valois
Henry VI 1422–1461 m. Marguerite of Anjou

Money

A pound consisted of 240 pennies, written as 240d (the 'd' stands for *denarius*); a shilling (*shiling*, *sheling* or *shellyng* in Middle English and abbreviated as 's') was 12d; and 20 shillings made one pound sterling (*pund of sterlinges*). Another unit of accounting used in medieval England was the mark (*marc* or *marke*), which was two-thirds of a pound, i.e. 160d or 13s and 4d. For much of the Middle Ages, the only coin in general circulation in England was the silver penny (*peni* or *peny*), though the groat (*grot* or *grote*), a coin with a value of 4d, was sometimes also used. Three groats (*grotes* or *grotis*) made one shilling. A penny coin was often cut into two to make a half-penny (*halpeni*) or into quarters to make a farthing (*ferthing* or *ferding*), and the lowest possible denomination was a *mite* or *myte*, which had the value of half a farthing, i.e. an eighth of a penny. As an unskilled labourer earned 1½d or 2d per day and a master craftsman 6d a day, the concept of pounds and marks was of minor relevance to the lives of most medieval people, in the same way that most modern people are unlikely to find much use for banknotes with a value of £20,000.

In the middle of the fourteenth century, Edward III issued a coin called the noble, worth half a mark (6 shillings and 8d, or 80d), and in 1489 Henry VII issued the sovereign, worth one pound sterling. For most of the later medieval period, however, if a person was lucky enough to be wealthy, they needed to use barrels whenever they transported the many thousands of silver pennies that they possessed, and also needed to have plenty of carts and carthorses as well as a few carters on hand to drive them.

Chapter 1

Arriving in a Medieval Town

On a warm spring day in the twenty-first century, you stand in Parliament Square near Westminster Abbey. The Prime Minister's residence at 10 Downing Street and St James's Park are several minutes' walk away, as are the Cenotaph and the seventeenth-century Banqueting House. Near where you stand, Big Ben looms over the Houses of Parliament, and beyond it is Westminster Bridge. On the other side of the Thames, the London Eye glints in the sunshine. As you take in your surroundings, crowds of tourists talking in countless different languages pass by, people sit on patches of grass and benches to eat their lunch, a man does a brisk trade selling burgers and coffee from a van, and car horns from numerous vehicles navigating the clogged streets are an endless cacophony in the air. You are in the middle of the great cosmopolitan city that is modern London.

Now imagine that you close your eyes, and when you open them, you are standing in the same place in the early 1300s. You are now two miles outside the walled city of London and in the entirely separate settlement of Westminster. It is an island formed by the Thames on one side and narrow tributaries of the River Tyburn on the other sides, and is known as Thorney Island. Westminster Abbey is there, and you recognise the abbey church from your own era as the location of Elizabeth II's funeral, her son Charles III's coronation, and other events you have watched on television. It is, however, now surrounded by buildings and spaces that no longer exist in your own time: the monks' dormitories, a refectory, an infirmary hall, a cloister, herb gardens. Where the Houses of Parliament and Big Ben stand centuries later is a huge walled palace, entered via a great gateway and dominated by Westminster Hall, which you also recognise because it still exists in the twenty-first century. The endless urban sprawl of modern London on the other side of the Thames is now marshland and moorland, with the archbishop of Canterbury's palace of Lambeth and the nearby church of St-Mary-at-Lambeth the only buildings in sight. Westminster Bridge has also disappeared and will not exist for another four and a half centuries, while you will have to wait five and a half centuries until Lambeth Bridge, the next bridge upriver, is built in 1862. The Thames is wider and slower than it will be hundreds of years later and sometimes freezes solidly in winter. Although at low tide the river is just about fordable at Westminster, it is safer to hire the local *ferymon* (ferryman) if you wish to cross.

It is the morning of Sunday, 22 May 1306, the feast of Whitsun, and you are one of several thousand people lining the streets to cheer on the procession of more than 250 young men invited by the elderly king, Edward Longshanks, to be knighted in Westminster Abbey. The men have spent all night awake in temporary accommodation within the grounds of the New Temple on Fletestrete (Fleet Street), where they were meant to while away the hours in prayerful contemplation but instead passed a raucous night yelling, laughing, and blowing trumpets. They have walked a mile and a half to Westminster from the Temple, with joyous crowds applauding them all the way. As you wait for them to come past where you stand, you see a man with a tray of pasties filled with capon or rabbit, which he sells to hungry spectators for half a penny each, and another man selling eels out of a bucket.[1]

A happy, festive atmosphere prevails, and some of the minstrels hired by the king to perform for the new knights in Westminster Hall after the ceremony are out and about in public, entertaining and interacting with the waiting crowds. You see the renowned acrobat Matilda Makejoy, whose somersaults make spectators gasp with awe, the blind musician *Perle in the Eghe* or 'Pearl in the Eye', who has cataracts and is helped about by his assistant, Reynald the storyteller holding a group spellbound as he recites a fable, and two German musicians called Heinrich and Konrad chatting to Lambyn Clay, a taborer (drummer). Several Kings of Heralds, highly experienced and prodigiously talented performers, have also been hired for this momentous occasion: the famous Scottish harper James Cowpen, whose stage name is King Capenny; King Druett, who plays the vielle, a stringed instrument similar to a fiddle; William 'Gillot' Morley, another harper, who hails from Pontefract in Yorkshire and is known as the King of the North; and King Robert, also called Little Robert, a short and highly skilled performer who is splendidly attired in a red overtunic trimmed with lamb's fur and is both a trumpeter and a taborer.[2]

The young men about to be knighted, wearing cloaks embroidered with gold thread over tunics, linen shirts, breeches and boots, yawning but enjoying all the attention, pass by you and head into the abbey. After the long ceremony, they will enjoy a banquet in the massive splendour of Westminster Hall, and cooks have cleverly constructed two swans encased in gold thread as 'subtleties' to form the showpiece of the feast. The Hall looks much as it does many hundreds of years later, only without its famous hammerbeam roof, which is constructed in the late 1300s. Just nine months before your visit, on 23 August 1305, the sham trial of the Scottish patriot Sir William Wallace of *Braveheart* fame took place in the Hall. Inevitably found guilty, he was dragged by horses to the Elms at Smithfield, several miles away, and put to a gruesome death. The day after he was killed, the paternostrer (maker of paternosters, i.e. prayer beads) Roger Southcote went to 'look at the head of William le Waleys' on Neugatestrete or Newgate Street, where Southcote was arrested for 'making a disturbance'. Wallace's head was eventually spiked on the southern gatehouse of London Bridge, though the fact that Roger Southcote went to look at it on Newgate Street the day after Wallace's execution implies that his head and perhaps the four quarters of his body were first taken through London for residents to gawp at.[3]

As you are not invited to the knighting ceremony or the banquet, you decide to follow the knights' route back towards London. Before you leave the Westminster complex, a grim sight reminds you that you are in the Middle Ages. Wooden gallows stand stark against the sky, and swinging from one of them are the decaying remains of a man.

He is Richard Pudlicote, who stole much of the royal treasure from a crypt under Westminster Abbey chapterhouse in April 1303, and was hanged in November 1305 after being brought to Westminster from the Tower of London in a wheelbarrow.[4] The corpses of executed people are frequently displayed in public for months, even years, on end, and Sir William Wallace's remains are also still on display in London. On 7 November 1306, a few months after your visit, another Scottish nobleman will be executed in London and his remains publicly displayed: John Strathbogie, earl of Atholl.

To leave Thorney Island and Westminster, you cross a footbridge over the stream that is a tributary of the Tyburn, and come to King Street, later called Whitehall. The road is, thankfully, reasonably dry in late May, albeit with deep ruts in the mud caused by cartwheels, as well as numerous hoofprints. As you walk along the road and come around the river bend, London gradually comes into view in the distance; you see high stone walls encircling the city, and the spire of St Paul's – *Seint Pool*, as it is called by contemporaries – rising above everything. This is not, of course, the Christopher Wren-designed building with which you are familiar, but Old St Paul's, which will stand for another 360 years until consumed in the Great Fire of London in 1666. Although you cannot see them at this distance, men are hard at work building an extension to the east side of the cathedral, which was begun in 1255 and will finally be completed in 1314. In June that year, eight years after your visit, some precious old relics will be discovered in the belfry of St Paul's, including bones of the 11,000 Virgins, part of the True Cross, a stone from Mount Calvary, and 'a stone of the Sepulchre of Our Lord'. They are shown to the public and replaced the following month.[5]

At the junction called Charing Cross you bear right into the Strand, or *Cherryngcrouch* and *Straunde* as they are usually called by contemporaries, noticing the large and elaborate stone cross built in honour of the late Spanish queen of England, the king's first wife Leonor of Castile, after her death in 1290. In the 2000s, the Strand is back from the river because of the embankments built in the nineteenth century, but in the Middle Ages it is on the riverfront and is where numerous noble people and bishops build their London palaces. You pass a mansion called the Savoy, named after its thirteenth-century builder and owner Peter of Savoy (d. 1268), count of Savoy in the western Alps and great-uncle of the present king, Edward Longshanks. In the mid-fourteenth century, Henry of Grosmont, first duke of Lancaster, inherits the Savoy and rebuilds it as a huge and luxurious palace, and it will be destroyed during the Peasants' Revolt of 1381 because it then belongs to Henry's detested son-in-law John of Gaunt. Five hundred years later, an opulent hotel called the Savoy will be built on the site. On your left as you walk along the Strand are arable fields, gardens, and orchards full of fruit trees. Four decades after your visit, Edward Longshanks' grandson Edward III will order that 'all those who have the taint of leprosy shall abandon the highways and field ways between the city of London and the town of Westminster', a reminder that the two places are separate and that much of the space between them consists of fields.[6]

Another reminder of this occurs when you pass the church of St Martin-in-the-Fields, which in the twentieth and twenty-first centuries stands close to Trafalgar Square and Charing Cross railway station. You realise that this is not its name because it is a pleasantly bucolic thing to call a church in the middle of a large city, but because it is, literally, in the fields. Trafalgar Square is, of course, not there; the battle after which it is named will not be fought until 499 years later. At the end of the Strand, you see Temple Bar, which marks the city limits on the road between London and Westminster. London has begun to spread beyond its walls and gates, and on the roads out of the city, 'bars' indicate where it starts and stops. Later built as an elaborate gateway, in the early 1300s Temple Bar is little more than a chain across the road. Past Temple Bar, you walk along Fleet Street, catching a glimpse of the church that belongs to the military monastic order the Knights Templar and is where the crowd of new knights stayed awake last night being rowdy. Although they do not know it yet, the Knights Templar, an organisation which has existed for almost 200 years by 1306, will soon be destroyed by King Philip IV of France and Pope Clement V, beginning in October 1307 when the Templars in France are suddenly arrested on charges of heresy and idolatry, imprisoned, and tortured.

You cross the bridge over the narrow, smelly River Fleet, which is one of the small rivers that flow through medieval London. In the twenty-first century, these rivers – Fleet, Tyburn, Walbrook and others – are culverted over and run entirely underground. In November 1307, the new king of England, Longshanks' and Leonor of Castile's son Edward of Caernarfon, complains that the Fleet's course is obstructed by all the filth that is thrown into it. It is not the only waterway in London used for such purposes: in 1314, the London Assize of Nuisance orders William Fourneis to remove a privy he has built over the River Walbrook.[7] Londoners are meant to throw their muck into the Thames rather than one of the city's much smaller rivers, though this hardly seems like a sensible solution either, and by 1345 the Thames has become well and truly 'corrupted by dung and other filth'.[8]

To your left as you walk along Fleet Street are the stone walls of the Fleet prison, which is surrounded by a ten-foot-wide ditch into which the prisoners' latrines empty. Three tanneries, i.e. workshops where animal skins are treated and turned into leather, are also located nearby. The tanning of leather, and the next stage in the process, curing it with rendered animal fat – herring oil is often used for this purpose in the late Middle Ages – are collectively called a *foul crafte* that *stynketh* in the fifteenth century. The stench is indescribable, and in the 1340s Edward III declares that the Fleet prisoners are afflicted with 'grievous maladies' owing to the 'infection of the air' in the vicinity.[9] In later centuries Fleet Street will be the centre of the British media, but in 1306, it is, despite the appalling smell nearby, a residential area with fields beyond it. The inhabitants of Fleet Street in the early 1300s include Stephen Auverne, who pays 96d a year to rent the house nearest to the reeking River Fleet, Nicholas Beaubelot, a spurrier (a person who makes spurs), and his apprentice Robert Fraunceys from Maltby in Yorkshire, Richard and Margery Latymer, Henry Brewere, Alice Stockyngge, Nicholas Lockyer, Hugh Armurer, John of Paris, who works as a corder (maker of cord), William Enefeld, Alexander and

Maud Newerk and their daughter Maud junior, and John and Emma Hattere and their sons Ralph, Giles and Thomas. A knight called Sir Fraunceys Vilers, or Francis Villiers in later spelling, owns a large house with a gate and a stable on Fleet Street, next door to Henry Brewere. Next to Nicholas Lockyer's house stands a brothel, whose clients include a pair of disreputable chancers who call themselves Credo and Falwey, while Hugh and Sarra Strubby run a tavern next to Stephen Auverne's house. Hugh inherited the tavern and ten small shops in the area from his parents Robert Strubby and Alice Odyham, who moved to London from Lincolnshire and Hampshire respectively. Hugh and Sarra bequeath their property to the church of St Bride on Fleet Street, as they have no children. Later in the fourteenth century, and possibly already in the early part of the century, their tavern is called the *Swerd in the Hope* ('Sword in the Hoop' in modern spelling).[10]

You cross another footbridge over the wide city ditch, which is, like the River Fleet and prison ditch, so smelly that you have to hold your nose, and you do not dare look down at it too closely; dead animals are among the things that inhabitants of the city throw in there, and there is a good historical reason why the name of a street in modern London is 'Houndsditch'. The imposing stone walls, 35 feet high, that enclose the city are now looming over you, and you stand in front of Ludgate, one of the seven massive oak gates that lead in and out of the city. Like all these other gates, Ludgate is high and wide enough to allow groups of people riding abreast as well as heavily laden carts to pass through it. The gate has a portcullis, wickets – two much smaller, narrower passageways for the use of pedestrians on either side of the main gate – and a heavy iron chain to secure it at night after the bells ring for curfew. As it is morning, though, Ludgate stands open to allow pedestrians, riders, and merchants to pass through, and it is bustling with people, animals and wares. Half an hour after you left Westminster, you have finally arrived in London.

It seems almost unfathomable in modern times that Westminster Abbey lies so far outside London, and it is almost beyond the stretch of the imagination to visualise just how tiny the capital city is in the late Middle Ages. Around 1300, London has the same population that provincial English towns such as Aylesbury, Nuneaton, Crewe, and Redditch will have in the twenty-first century: about 80,000 or 90,000 people.[11] Its population in the 2000s is 100 times greater. The modern cities of the north of England – Manchester, Liverpool, Leeds, Sheffield, Bradford, Newcastle-upon-Tyne – are mere villages in the Middle Ages and will remain so until the Industrial Revolution, and the only settlement of any size in the entire north is York, with about 10,000 or 15,000 inhabitants in the thirteenth and fourteenth centuries. Bristol, Norwich, and Coventry, which are, after London and York, the largest towns in medieval England, also have somewhere between 10,000 and 20,000 people each in the thirteenth century.[12] The pandemics of the Black Death in the fourteenth century, particularly the first and worst one in 1348/49, reduce these already tiny numbers considerably. The largest towns in medieval England are about the same size as towns in modern England that are so small and obscure many people will never even have heard of them, such as Uckfield, Leek, Yarm and Gerrards Cross.

In the south-east corner of tiny medieval London stands the Tower. When the king is not in residence at the Tower of London, and he only rarely stays there, the drawbridge is down, and you can wander in and out as you please. Blacksmiths, carpenters, and armourers have workshops there, though be careful of the water-filled ditches surrounding the complex, as people have drowned in them.[13] Just outside the sprawling fortification, Tower Hill is an unpleasant, smelly place to be in the late Middle Ages, because for untold decades, numerous people take carts full of their refuse and dump it there. By the early 1370s, the authorities have had enough of 'the accumulation of refuse, filth and other fetid matter' which has 'foully corrupted' the air of Tower Hill and, they say, endangers the lives of those who dwell close by.[14] On the opposite side of the Thames to the Tower, on the river's south bank, lies the suburb of Southwark, often called *Stewysside* or 'stew-side' because it is the red-light district of medieval London.[15] The word 'stew' really means a hot bath or a steam bath, but is employed euphemistically to mean a brothel, functioning in much the same way as the expression 'massage parlour' does a few centuries later. The brothel madams of Southwark are called the *wyf of the stewes* (in Middle English, *wyf* or 'wife' means a woman in general, not only a married woman).[16]

On the subject of red-light districts, many medieval English towns have a road called Gropecuntlane, which means exactly what you think it means. London, Bristol, Northampton, Oxford, Cambridge, Banbury, Norwich, Reading and Shrewsbury all have one, even tiny Wells in Somerset has one, and the earliest recorded one dates to about 1230. The three words in the name, 'grope', 'cunt' and 'lane', have not changed for 800 years. In the 1320s, Cecilie Tavernere runs a tavern on Gropecuntelane in Bristol, and fisherman Robert White and his wife Christine Grave own a garden there. William Brodwode and his wife Agnes Canun rent out part of their tenement in Gropecountelane in Wells to William Ferrur in the early 1300s.[17] Throughout the Middle Ages, town authorities try, without notable success, to banish brothels and the existence of prostitution outside the town walls.

Somewhat to your surprise, you hear many different languages besides English in the London streets of 1306, as you would a few hundred years later as well. The city is already home to numerous residents from other countries, Italians being particularly well represented. There are also many German, French, Spanish and Portuguese inhabitants, as well as people from further afield, such as Adam of Antioch and Bidan of 'Araby'. In Middle English, people from Portugal are called *portingalers*; Germans are *alemayns* (as in modern French, *Allemands*); French people are *frenchemen*; Spanish people are *spaynardys*. Italians are usually referred to by the area from where they come, e.g. *lombardis* from Lombardy and *ienewys* from Genoa.[18]

Even in provincial English towns, the residents are sometimes more diverse than you might imagine. A resident of Twycross, Leicestershire in the 1320s and 1330s, who moves to London, bears the name Ralph Sarasyn, meaning 'Saracen'.[19] This is a word often used in medieval England to refer to a Muslim, or a person of Arab or North African origin more generally, and probably indicates Ralph's origins. Even if it is only a nickname and he is in fact English, the name shows that his contemporaries have some awareness of non-Christian and non-European people, and perhaps indicates that something about Ralph's appearance lends itself to the name. An apprentice spurrier on Fleet Street in the early 1300s is called Robert Fraunceys, which means 'Frenchman' in medieval French (the word is *Français* in modern French). Robert comes from Maltby in Yorkshire, and though he was almost certainly born in England, one of his recent ancestors, probably his father, grandfather, or great-grandfather, must have moved to England from France and settled in Yorkshire. A resident of London in the early 1300s is Katherine la Frаunceyse, 'the Frenchwoman', and she has lived in England since at least 1292.[20] Another London resident, who makes his will in 1349, the year of the Black Death, is Richard Alwy. He calls himself *Tolousere*, meaning that he comes from Toulouse, and raises five English children – Isabella, Alice, Katherine, Richard and Thomas – with his English wife. Richard leaves his children several houses and land 'in the vill and fields of Iseledon', now called Islington.[21] In his will of May 1349, John Northall of London mentions his grandson John, son of his late daughter Wymarca and her late husband Bonaventure Bonentente of Florence. The half-English, half-Italian John Bonaventure is also mentioned in his grandmother Alice Northall's will of May 1361.[22] Wymarca and Bonaventure marry in or before early 1336, and John is said to be 8 years old when Wymarca dies in August 1345.[23]

Chapter 2

Vagrant Pigs and Obnoxious Fumes

Most English towns in the Middle Ages have more or less the same name that they still bear centuries later, sometimes spelt rather differently, though Boston in Lincolnshire is called 'the town of Saint Botolph', and Lincoln is Nicol, Nicole or Nicholl. King's Lynn is Lenne or Bishop's Lenne; Bury St Edmunds is Burgh Seint Esmon; Ipswich is Gippewiz or Gippewich; Warwick is Warrewyk; Norwich is Norwyz; Cambridge is Cantebrigge or Grantebrigge; Canterbury is often spelt Caunterberi; Great Yarmouth is Gernemuth; Uxbridge is Woxebregg or Woxebrugge; Coventry is Coventre or Covyntre; Derby is often written Derebye or Derebeye; Barking is Berkyngge. Oxford is called Oxenford, and over the centuries loses its middle syllable. As medieval documents, especially in the thirteenth and fourteenth centuries, are often composed in French, English placenames are sometimes written in that language, e.g. Newcastle-upon-Tyne is Noef Chastel sur Tyne and Westminster is Westmoster or Westmouster, or occasionally Westmestre. There is no one correct way to spell anything in the Middle Ages, let alone the names of towns, and in one document of 1322, the name 'Grimsby' is spelt in four different ways in five sentences: Grymysby, Grymyby, Grymisby, Grymesby.[1]

As you walk through the streets of any medieval English town, your senses are assaulted by the various smells, sights, and sounds. The first thing you notice is that medieval streets are often remarkably narrow: in fourteenth-century London, some lanes leading to the Thames are only 45 inches wide at the river end, though 7 feet wide at the other end.[2] The lack of light caused by the looming, tightly squeezed buildings in the confined streets makes it difficult to see where you are stepping.

Difficult though it is, you do need to watch your feet: the streets and pavements are likely to be full of mud, muck, and manure. In Chester in 1421, the authorities remind residents of the importance of keeping the street in front of their house clean and tidy, and in Leicester several decades later, residents are instructed to clean the streets and remove all the filth in front of their house, using a cart if necessary. They are told that in future, they must not throw dirt outside their door into the street, including the muck of horses, pigs, dogs or cats.[3] Fourteenth-century Londoners are threatened with large fines for throwing muck into the streets rather than dumping it into the Thames as they are meant to do, and people who sneakily leave their refuse outside their neighbours' houses instead of their own are hit with a double fine. In 1357, Edward III complains about the 'fumes and other abominable stenches' arising from the filth in the London streets. Inevitably, given that throwing refuse and muck into the city's main waterway is also a very bad idea, the king declares fifteen years later that the Thames is obstructed by filth and ships cannot navigate it properly. The mayor and aldermen of London investigate who is responsible for throwing dead animals 'and other filthy and putrid matter from the slaughtering of beasts' into the Thames, 'whereby the water was rendered corrupt and generated fetid smells'. The habit of transporting slaughtered animals to the Thames means that the streets and alleys leading to the river are also full of blood and animal remains that fall from carts, 'making a foul corruption and abominable sight and nuisance to all dwelling near or using those streets or lanes'. Edward III states in 1371 that the slaughtering of animals in London has led to the streets of the city running with blood and has caused the air to become 'greatly corrupted and infected, whereby the worst of abominations and stenches have been generated, and sicknesses and many other maladies have befallen persons dwelling' in the city. He therefore orders that animals should only be slaughtered in two places: Stratford-le-Bow to the east of the city, and to the west, of all places, Knightsbridge, which will become one of the most expensive and desirable areas of London in the twentieth and twenty-first centuries. In the fourteenth century, it is called 'the village of Knyghtebrugge'.[4]

In the late Middle Ages, there is a widespread belief that 'bad air' is hazardous to health, and killing, skinning and burying animals is forbidden within the walls of towns and cities because it is thought to corrupt the air and endanger residents (this prohibition is, however, frequently repeated to little effect). Partly as a result of the muck in town and city streets, John Tygre loses his life during a deadly brawl at the beginning of 1322: while being pursued by a gang of men armed with swords, cudgels and knives, he 'fell over a heap of dung' and is caught and stabbed to death.[5] One important job, in the centuries before rubbish collections and automated street cleaners exist, is the *rakiere* or 'raker', meaning a muck-raker, who rakes out the streets and latrines.

Broken pavements are another hazard and endanger pedestrians and riders alike, and residents are responsible for repairing and maintaining the pavements outside their homes.[6] You also need to watch your head, especially if you are on horseback rather than on foot: pentices, i.e. solars (upper-storey rooms), the extended eaves of a house that jut out over the street, or a roof that provides a covered walkway, are another potential hazard. Not everyone abides by the rule, issued after numerous complaints that pentices built across narrow streets impede riders, that they must be at least 9 feet above the ground.[7] Thomas Ryver is reprimanded in 1313 for building a solar on his house in Scarborough, 18 feet long and 3 feet wide, that is so low above the ground people cannot walk underneath it.[8] There is a good chance that you can shake hands with your neighbour across the way, given how narrow the streets are and that upper storeys jut out even farther. And another reason why you need to watch out overhead is that some people throw wastewater out of their upper-storey windows, and even worse, some men have a habit of urinating out of them into the street.[9]

In the twenty-first century, you look both ways when crossing the road to make sure that no vehicles are coming, and sometimes, cyclists seem to swoop out of nowhere. In the late Middle Ages, you need to watch out for wandering pigs instead. Numerous orders to remove 'vagrant pigs' from the streets are issued in London, while in Leicester it is ordained that 'no man latt no swyne ne neet go a brode' (no man let swine or livestock go abroad), and no *dukkes* or ducks are to be 'letyn abrode' either.[10] In Canterbury in 1348, J. Morys and J. Upton, whose given names are probably John, or perhaps Joan, are reprimanded for keeping pigs which smell and are unsanitary, while the marketplace at the 'Bulstake' (i.e. bull-stake, now called the Buttermarket) is 'blocked up with filth and excrement'.[11] In Nottingham, it is a long-established custom that pigs must be kept in a pigsty or in their owner's house. In the 1390s, Robert Hayward's pig, which he has unlawfully allowed to wander around, finds its way onto John Bank's property and eats one of John's chickens.[12]

As well as the problem of hygiene, pigs can be genuinely dangerous to small children. In Westminster one March evening in 1290, a sow 'entered the house of Geoffrey Paneterye while Lucy the wife of Geoffrey was looking for milk for her son Simon, dragged the child forth from his cradle and killed him'. In the spring of 1254, 1-year-old Amice Soper is bitten by a sow and dies, and in May 1322, a 1-month-old baby named Joan is bitten by a sow as she lies in her cradle in her father's shop and dies a day and a half later. Agnes Perone, half a year old, is another infant killed by a sow in Oxford in May 1392. Disturbingly, the animal starts to eat her head while she is still alive.[13] The frequent proclamations issued in medieval English towns against pigs roaming around demonstrate that their doing so is a common problem, but also that it is deemed unacceptable and dangerous, and that the authorities try their best to prevent it from happening.

The vast majority of houses you pass are made of wood, and many of the older ones will have thatched roofs. As these represent a major fire hazard, however, roofs made of tile, lead or stone are much preferred, though implements to pull down burning thatch during a fire exist.[14] Tilers and *sclatteres* (roofers, slate-layers) are kept very busy throughout the later Middle Ages, and in London in early 1362, some tilers attempt to charge more than usual owing to the massive demand after a terrible storm destroys the roofs of numerous dwellings in the city.[15] In London, it is prohibited to have roofs made of straw, reeds, rushes or stubble specifically because they are all a fire hazard, and they should be made of tiles, shingles or boards instead. This regulation is not always obeyed, however, and in late 1376 seven men are ordered to remove the straw from the roofs of their houses and replace it with one of the permitted materials. This must be carried out within forty days 'on pain of having the work done for them at their expense and paying the sheriffs 40s for their trouble'.[16]

A house is built by the carpenter Simon of Canterbury for the skinner William Hanington between 16 November 1308 and 30 March 1309, and costs William £9, 5s and 4d. It has a hall and a room with a fireplace, with a larder between them; a solar over the room and larder; an *oriole* (gallery or porch) at the end of the hall 'beyond the high bench' (i.e. dais); a covered step from the ground outside into the hall; two cellars beneath the hall; one enclosure for a sewer, with two pipes leading to the sewer; a separate kitchen (kitchens are built apart from the rest of the house wherever possible to minimise the risk of fire spreading); and a stable 12 feet wide between the hall and the kitchen, with a solar above and a garret above the solar.[17] An inquisition is held by the sheriff of Gloucestershire in 1253 regarding houses built on a place that King John (d. 1216) gave to a man whose name is recorded as Gwibert Rue. The houses, on East Street in Gloucester, are made of boards and plaster and are covered with tiles, and they each have 'one small hall', one chamber and a kitchen.[18]

Front doors have bolts for security, and many houses have cellars, often called *colceler* or 'coal-cellar'. In the early 1300s, Thomas Cattewith inherits two houses with cellars on Wollemongorestrete in Northampton – i.e. Woolmonger Street, which is still there – and a few decades later Margery Walpole owns a tavern in the Bread Street ward of London with a cellar for wood and coal.[19] In London in 1333, William Thorneye states that his and his landlady or lover Joan Armenters' neighbours, Andrew and Joan Aubrey, have made a hole in the floor of their house above William and Joan's cellar and are able to spy on his 'secret business'.[20] This shows how medieval houses tend to be a bit higgledy-piggledy; part of the Aubreys' house lies above William and Joan's cellar.

You may not have expected to see that many houses in late medieval English towns have glass windows as early as the thirteenth and fourteenth centuries. In Ipswich at the beginning of 1297, a group of vandals throw stones at the windows in Maud Pedham's house and break them, and the same thing happens at the home of Henry Steward in Market Rasen, Lincolnshire, in 1301 and in London the same year.[21] The nuns' dormitory at Wilton Abbey in Wiltshire has glass windows fortified with iron bars in 1277, though this does not deter one John Romayn from breaking in and abducting Cecily Walesse, one of the nuns.[22] In the 1340s in London, John Thorp, a skinner, has four glass windows in his home, John Hadham, a potter, has six in his, John and Juliane Wroth have ten in theirs, and in the 1350s and 1360s Roger and Margaret Lachebrok have no fewer than twenty windows in their London house, as well as two doors and a solar. The habit which many London residents have of shooting pigeons with catapults and crossbows is prohibited in 1327 on the grounds that the missiles break numerous windows.[23]

When modern people think of medieval England, they tend to visualise castles, but of course most people do not live in castles, and certainly the overwhelming majority of townspeople do not. While modern people often think of medieval houses as being dark and dingy, this is, at least ideally, not always the case; it is in fact considered very important to have as much light as possible in one's house. In the fifteenth century, it is stated that 'the house well ordained ought to be well windowed of diverse windows, by which it has great light'.[24] There are a few examples of fourteenth-century Londoners complaining about their neighbours blocking the light into their houses. In August 1321, Thomas Berkyngge, a goldsmith, states that Henry atte More, another goldsmith, has prohibited him from building a new house on the east side of Henry's own house. Henry explains that the plot where Thomas wishes to build his property has a condition attached to it that no building on it should 'obscure the light from two glazed windows' in Henry's property and should not stand within 10 feet of his home. He produces deeds dating back to 1263/64 in support of his claim.[25]

A similar example dates to October 1278, when Reynald Cantebrege (i.e. Cambridge) leaves various houses in London to his seven sons, 'on condition that one brother does not shut out the window light of another', and Rohese Farndone asserts in September 1343 that, as the occupant of 'a tenement abutting on a street or lane', she is entitled to light through her windows, according to London custom. The building work of her neighbour Hugh Brandon is, however, obscuring the light.[26] Isabel Godchep (d. 1349) goes to the Assize of Nuisance in London in July 1331 to complain that her neighbour John Ruddok piles his firewood against the window in the west gable of her house, so high that it covers the window and Isabel's 'light, view, air and clarity' are entirely impeded. She produces a deed dated 1 April 1299, granting her father Richard Wolmar the right to have 'the view, opening, light, air and clarity' from the window. Nearly a hundred years later in 1426, Margaret Curteys also produces a deed proving that 'nothing should be done to obstruct the light' from three of her windows facing her neighbours' house, but they are building a new *shedde* which blocks her light.[27]

Glass windows consist of several small pieces of glass rather than one large pane. When a new chapel is built near Guildford in Surrey in 1326, its twelve windows are made from fifty-seven pieces of glass, and it also has thirty-six iron bars, three for each window. The cost is 19 shillings (228d) for the glass plus 2s 3d for the bars and another 2s in wages to the man who measures the frames and inserts the windows.[28] Chimneys are recorded as early as the thirteenth century, and in the mid-1200s, there is a reference to a man in Oxford building 'a chimney for the smoke to go out of his house, as is the custom of the whole town'. Isabella Worstede of London sues William Grene, a plasterer, in 1373 for making a chimney in her house that falls in, and poor William is having a bad year; he is also sued by his neighbours for burning plaster of Paris in his house, 'so that the fumes were obnoxious'.[29]

As well as being surprised by the number of glass windows, the importance of having light in one's house, and the existence of chimneys and cellars, you may also be surprised to discover that medieval people value their privacy and do not appreciate their neighbours being able to see into their house or garden. The right to a private life in one's own home and garden is zealously maintained, and people are ordered to block up any windows that look out over somebody else's space. It is the custom in London that windows can only be built overlooking someone else's house if they are at least 8 feet above the ground and 'glazed with thick glass or barred with iron'. If they are not, they must be blocked up. In 1369, John Haukyn complains that his neighbour Alice Bury has six windows in her house from where Alice and her tenants can look into John's garden and 'see his private business and that of his tenants'. She is ordered to block up the windows within forty days.[30] Isabel Luter keeps the London Assize of Nuisance in 1341 busy with complaints about her neighbours. Firstly, the skinner John Thorp, whose tenement adjoins her garden, has four windows with broken glass in his tenement, through which he and his servants can see into her garden. Secondly, John Thorp has another seven windows in his tenement and can see into Isabel's own tenement. Thirdly, Henry Ware has four apertures in his tenement overlooking her own, through which the stench from his cesspit penetrates. Fourthly, Joan Corp has twelve apertures overlooking Isabel's tenement. Fifthly and lastly, the fishmonger John Leche has a 'leaden watchtower' on the wall of his tenement, and he and his household stand there daily watching Isabel and her servants. The Assize finds in Isabel's favour in all these matters. By December 1341, five months after Isabel makes her complaints, John Thorp and Joan Corp have not yet complied with the order to block up their windows, and are each fined £2 (480d).[31] This is a massive sum that is equivalent to a few months' income for most people.

And even in crowded towns and cities, another surprise awaits you: numerous people have their own gardens, including herb gardens, which are called *herber* in Middle English. William and Felicia Chaloner own a house on Faytereslane (now called Fetter Lane) in London in the

1370s which has a garden 120 feet long. Grass and fruit trees grow there.[32] In Nottingham in the 1310s, William Sporoun owns several houses with gardens on a street called Milneholes ('milne' means mill), and in 1340, Stephen Pychermaker gives two gardens in Bodmin, Cornwall to William Scarlet.[33] In Wantage, Berkshire in the late 1300s and early 1400s, Fulk and Anne FitzWarin have a *lytulgardyn* (little garden) accessed via the hall of their house, as well as a pantry, buttery, larder and a kitchen with a tiled roof, while their hall is roofed with thatch.[34] A pantry is where dry goods such as bread, flour and spices are kept, and a buttery is for drinks and other liquids.

It is likely that your latrine or privy will be outside, not in your house, and you will probably have to share it with other people who live nearby. Near Cripplegate in London in the early 1300s, a saddler named John of Paris and his wife Alice share their privy with their neighbours John and Agnes Lung and Gillotin Sautreour, aka William Grey, a minstrel who plays a psaltery (a stringed instrument with a resonating wooden box). Latrines cause more disputes among neighbours than almost anything else. Robert Asshecombe complains in 1400 that his neighbours Gilbert and Mazera Accon own several privies for themselves and their tenants, and that 'foul odours' issue from the latrines which bother him. In 1357, the fishmonger Adam Pykeman complains bitterly that sewage from the latrine belonging to his neighbours, Hugh and Isabel Sadelyngstanes, which is 12 feet long and 12 feet deep, seeps into the foundations of his home. Three years later, Thomas and Idoine St Edmunds have a latrine with two pipes that stands on the land of their neighbour, Nicholas Hotot. Nicholas is unhappy about this, but Thomas and Idoine produce a document dating back to 1298 which proves that the latrine on Nicholas's land has always been part of their property. It is the custom in London that the cesspits of latrines must be encased in a stone wall 2½ feet thick or an earthen wall 3½ feet thick.[35]

As well as private latrines shared between several houses, public conveniences also exist in medieval towns. Several, for example, are located on and close to London Bridge, and one of them, which has at least two entrances, is first mentioned in 1306. By 1377, the London Bridge latrines are in a 'dangerous state of disrepair', and locals complain about them. There is another public latrine at Queenhithe.[36] In 1344, the royal and elderly Henry of Lancaster, earl of Lancaster and Leicester, gives the town of Leicester 'a waste place in the town on the water of the [River] Soar' on which to build 'a privy for the ease of all the community'.[37]

Using a medieval latrine will be a rather unpleasant experience for a person used to modern flush toilets, though on the other hand, medieval plumbing is often better than you might imagine. Gutters already exist in late medieval English towns, though are much wider than they will be centuries later, between about 1½ feet and 3 feet. Some of them are up to 100 feet long.[38] Inadequate guttering and failure to remove wastewater or rainwater properly is frequently another bitter complaint between neighbours. In 1314, the neighbours of Alice Wade in London state that 'a gutter running under certain of the houses was provided to receive the rainwater and other water draining from the houses, gutters and street, so that the flow might cleanse the privy'. Alice, however, 'has made a wooden pipe connecting the seat of the privy in her solar with the gutter, which is frequently stopped up by the filth therefrom, and the neighbours under whose houses the gutter runs are greatly inconvenienced by the stench'.[39] This reveals that not only is Alice ingenious in being able to devise and construct a wooden pipe which carries away her waste, but that she has a privy in her solar, i.e. an upper room of her home. In addition to guttering that carries away rainwater, many towns have a channel, gutter or open drain, *canellum* in Latin, in the middle of streets and lanes to carry away wastewater and rainwater to the nearest stream, river or ditch.

You might buy a property or rent one. Orlandino Podeo, an Italian, buys a house in London in the late 1200s, and in the early 1300s a house in the parish of St Michael on Cornhill also in London is purchased by, successively, Peter Waltham, Stephen atte Holte, John Bekles, and Nicholas and Alice Chaundeler. In September 1386, the pie-baker John Pygeon buys a house in the London parish of St Andrew by the

Wardrobe for 100 marks (£66.66) which he intends to let out for 20 marks (£13.33) a year.[40] In the 1310s and 1320s, Thomas Fairfax rents out two houses he owns on Micklegate in York at a massively cheaper 24d and 12d a year, and also owns eight cellars by the Ouse bridge.[41] Joan Goldcorn pays 120d a year for a house near Ludgate in London in 1298, and a few years later, Richard Bakere, who really is a baker, pays his landlord Walter Taillour 80d annually for a property on Aldgate. He also bakes a *penitourte*, a loaf of brown bread which costs a penny, for Walter every week.[42] As noted above, Stephen Auverne pays 96d a year in the early 1300s to rent a house on Fleet Street next to the River Fleet, though several decades later, Adam and Auncilia Aspal pay 60 shillings (720d) annually for a house in the London parish of St Mary Woolchurch Haw. Sixty shillings is a considerable amount to pay in annual rent in the fourteenth century, even in expensive London, so the Aspals' house would seem to be a large and well-appointed one.[43] John Pygeon's house, which he believes to be worth 3,200d a year in rent in 1386, must be particularly huge, and few people would be able to pay such an amount.

Rent is paid quarterly and will fall due on feast days; these will usually be Christmas, Easter, the feast of the Nativity of St John the Baptist on 24 June, and the feast of St Michael on 29 September. You have up to six weeks after the due date to pay the rent.[44] When renting a property, you are, as in later centuries, not allowed to alter it too much without the permission of your landlord or landlady, and will have to pay them damages if you do. This happens to a butcher named John Parker in London in 1374 when he rents a house from Clement Spray, a mercer, for a year. Clement takes John to court and accuses him of removing two partition walls, three doors and doorposts, a seat, and the kitchen hearth and mantelpiece. At the same time, William Burdeyn, a goldsmith, sues his former tenant Thomas Bermyngham for doing damage to the fixtures of his house, and for leaving twenty cartloads of dung in and next to the house after he moves out.[45]

Sometimes, rent is purely nominal, such as presenting the landlord or landlady with a rose every Midsummer or giving them a peppercorn annually. The requested rent is often rather unusual. In the 1300s, the manor of Mears Ashby in Northamptonshire is held 'by service of lifting [your] right hand yearly on Christmas Day towards the king, wherever he may be in England', and if you rent the Norfolk manor of East Carlton, you must 'carry to the king wherever he should be in England 100 fresh herrings in twenty-four pasties' once a year (twenty-four, not twenty-five, which would be much easier and would make more sense).[46] Simon Ruggeleye rents a fishpond near Stafford called *Kyngespole*, or 'king's pool' in modern spelling, 'by service of holding the king's currycomb on his first mounting his palfrey, every time of his coming to the town of Stafford'.[47] A manor in Shropshire is held 'by service of finding a man with a bow, two arrows and a bolt in the king's army against Wales, who on seeing the king's enemies shall shoot his arrows at them and straightaway return home with the bow and bolt'.[48] In Henry II's reign in the twelfth century, the famous – or infamous – Roland the Farter ('Roulandus le Fartere') holds his land by service of making 'a jump, a whistle and a fart' at the king's Christmas court every year.[49] And in the 1300s, the Scilly Isles off the coast of Cornwall are held 'by service of rendering yearly 300 puffins' to Edward III's son the prince of Wales. Three hundred puffins are still the annual rent in 1508, on the eve of Henry VIII's reign.[50]

Chapter 3

Godday, Ich Highte Johan (Hello, I'm Called John)

The chances are high that couples you meet will be called John and Joan or Thomas and Agnes, and that they will have children called John, Joan, Thomas and Agnes. Quite possibly, they will have two sons called John. Modern novelists often give their medieval characters implausibly exotic monikers, and though a handful of people with unusual names do exist in late medieval England – stand up, Laderana Byker, Scholastica Mewes, Grimbald Pauncefot, Anabilia Grapefige, Sampson Strelley and Pentecoste Karshalton – in reality, there is a paucity of given names. A massive percentage of the male population is called either John, Thomas, William, Robert, or Richard. In a subsidy roll – a record of people whose movable goods are to be taxed – taken in London in the late 1200s, 423 of the 814 men listed have one of these five names, and in another taken in 1319, 1,070 men, well over half the total, have one of the five. The name John alone is borne by 431 men in 1319.[1] Walter, Roger, Henry, Gilbert, Simon, Adam, Hugh, Geoffrey, and Nicholas are also common male names. By far the most common female names are Joan, Agnes, Margaret or Margery, Alice, and Isabel, while Emma, Katherine, Maud, Juliane, Beatrice, Mary, and Mabel are also often used. The name Joan occurs as frequently among women as John does among men, and if you stand in the street of a late medieval English town and call out 'Joan!', every third or fourth woman will turn her head.

Many given names are spelt the same way as in modern English, though John is Johan, Joan is Johane or Johanne, Agnes is Anneis or Anneys, Alice is Alis, Alys or Aleise, Peter is Peres or Pieres, Mary is

Marye or Marie, Margaret is usually Margarete, Emma is Emme, Ralph is Rauf, Nicholas is often Nichol, Matthew is Mayhew, Bartholomew is Bertelmew, Geoffrey is Geffrei, and Benedict is Benet. Philip, Edmund, Alan and Alexander, names that are neither particularly common nor rare, are spelt Phelip, Esmon, Aleyn and Alisaundre. In most cases, you will be named after one of your parents, grandparents, aunts, or uncles; or after one of your godparents; or after the saint on whose feast day you were born. Unusual names cause confusion. Drew Barentyn is mayor of London in 1398/99 and 1408/09, and dies in 1415. When he becomes an apprentice goldsmith in 1364, a clerk, unfamiliar with his name, wrongly assumes that he must be called 'Andrew' and records it as such, and this erroneous variant is perpetuated over the years. Decades later, Drew has to request that 'everything done or to be done by him in that name [Andrew] might stand good'.[2] French scribes wrestle with the peculiar Anglo-Saxon name 'Edward' borne by three kings of England between 1272 and 1377 which they have never heard before, and which in medieval England is almost always spelt in the same way that it is in modern times. They write it 'Oudouart' or 'Edduvars'. For their part, English scribes puzzle over Welsh names such as Llewelyn and Gwenllian, and spell them 'Thwellin' or 'Thoellin' and 'Wenthliane' respectively. The name of a Welsh archer of the 1320s, Gruffudd Llwyd, is written 'Griffith Thloyt' in England.[3] There is no such thing as correct spelling in the late Middle Ages, and if even there were, there is no way of checking the correct spelling of a name which is foreign or unfamiliar to you. People therefore write a name the way it sounds to them, and English scribes who do not know the 'll' sound of Welsh hear it as 'th'.

Two ways of differentiating the many people with the same given name develop: diminutives and surnames. For the extraordinarily common name John, spelt Johan, at least a dozen diminutives exist: Jack (or Jak or Jakke), Jake, Jakyn (or Jakin), Jaket, Jakinet, Jakemyn, Janyn (or Janin), Jankyn, Janot, Jancok, Hancok, and Hankyn. They all reflect the fact that the name John contains an A in late medieval England, though hundreds of years later it is not at all obvious that the modern surname Hancock originated as a byname for men called John. Men with the name William are often known as Wille, Willekyn, Willok, Willecok or Willekot, while minstrels named William often use Gillot or Gillotin instead; men called Robert are Robin or Robyn, Robynet, Hobbe, Hobekyn or Robechon; Thomases are Thomme, Thomelyn or Thomasyn; Rogers are Hogge (pronounced 'Hodge') or Hoggekyn; Gilberts are Gibbe, Gibon or Gilkyn; Nicholases are Colle, Colet, Colin or Colinet; Walters are Watte or Wattekyn; men called Mayhew (now Matthew) are Maykin; men called Paul, often spelt Pool or Poule, are Paulyn; men called Edmund are Monde; and men with the name David, a comparatively rare name in late medieval England though much more common in Scotland and Wales, are sometimes called Dawe.

Joans are known as Jonete, Johanette or Jony, Isabels are Bele, Ibote, Isode, Sibbe or Sibille, women called Agnes are often known as Annet, Annot or Annote, women called Juliane are Julkyn, and women called Maud are sometimes nicknamed Mold. Another diminutive of the name Maud, Malkyn, is used pejoratively for a servant woman, a young woman of the lower classes, or a woman believed to be of loose morals.[4] The second name of William Moldesone or Moldesson of Cublington in Buckinghamshire, who escapes from Aylesbury gaol in October 1353 (see Chapter 6 below), means 'Mold's son', i.e. he is the son of a woman called Maud. A man in Sussex in 1327 named Walter Malkynesone is also the son of a woman called Maud, while John Belesone is the son of Isabel, John and Richard Sibbesone are also sons of Isabel, Richard Emmesone is the son of Emma, and Robert Julkynsone is the son of Juliane.[5] In almost all cases, men who are identified in this way, as the son of a woman, are born out of wedlock.

The suffixes -yn, -kyn, -lyn, -cok, -et, -ot and -on are often used in pet forms of male given names. Examples are Adecok, Adekyn, and Adinet for Adam; Syme, Simcok, and Simkyn for Simon; Hick, Hichecok, Diccon or Dycon, and Richardyn for Richard; Huchon and Hughelyn for Hugh; and Raulyn for Rauf (Ralph). The suffix -ot gives us Eliot as a pet form of Elis, Henriot for Henry, Perot for Peres or Peter, Bertelot for Bertelmew or Bartholomew, and Phelipot for Philip. For women, the suffix -ote is often used: Annote for Anneis or Agnes, Mariote for Mary/Marie, Magote (usually spelt Magota or Megotta in Latin) for Margaret, Emmote for Emma, and Alisote for Eleanor, which is spelt Alianore or Alienor. Another suffix, -on, gives us Alison, a pet form of Alis or Alice, and Marion, a pet form of Mary/Marie. The -on suffix is often spelt -oun, so the name Alison sometimes appears as Alisoun. The name Philippa is vanishingly rare in England until Edward III marries Philippa of Hainault in 1328, whereafter it becomes reasonably common. It is spelt Phelipe or Philippe in late medieval England, and, in the same way that men with the name Philip/Phelip are known as Phelipot, Philippas are known as Phelipote or Philipote. Many of the medieval pet forms of given names survive as modern surnames, such as Eliot, Philpot, Wilcox, Tomlinson, Hicks, Hitchcock, Hobson, Hodgkinson, Gibson, Watkins, Dawson, Rawlinson, Simcox, Simkins, Sibson (son of Sibbe or Isabel), and Ibbotson (son of Ibote or Isabel).

As for second names, people who live in a village are often named by the location of their house within the village. Atte Churche, Cherche or Chirche (i.e. at the church), atte Watere, atte Ponde, atte Medwe (meadow), atte Wode (the modern surname Atwood), atte Welle, atte Gate, atte Stile, atte More (moor), atte Laneende (lane end) and atte Fosse (ditch) are some examples. This system is also sometimes used in bigger towns as well: in London in the 1320s to 1350s, we find Thomas atte Rededore, who must have lived in a house with a red door, and Simon atte Holeweceler, literally 'hollow cellar', which presumably means 'empty' in this instance.[6] Two men in Sussex in the late 1200s and early 1300s are Roger Bithewalle ('by the wall') and Robert Biwestestrete ('by west street').[7] It is also common to be known by your place of origin, though this only works if you no longer live there; calling you 'John of Coventry' is unhelpful if you still live in Coventry, but much more useful if you move to Lincoln. The Franciscan friar William Ockham or Occam, after whom Occam's Razor is named, is born in *c.*1287 in the Surrey village of Ockham, and dies sixty years later in Munich.

Many other people are called by their profession, family names which often still exist in modern English, such as Baker, Carpenter, Fletcher (the person who attaches feathers to arrows), Cooper (person who makes barrels), Carter (person who drives a cart), Mercer (dealer in textiles, usually high-end ones), Chapman (itinerant pedlar), Saddler (person who makes, sells or repairs saddles), Latimer (interpreter, person who knows Latin) and Roper (rope-maker). Middle English is a gendered language, and men's job titles end with -er, e.g. carpenter, baker and brewer, while women's end with -ster or -stere. Some examples are brewstere (a female brewer), spinstere (a female spinner), webbestere (a female webbe, i.e. weaver), bakstere (a female baker), bredmongestere (a female bread-seller), frutestere (a female fruit-seller), gildestere (a female goldsmith), kempstere or cambestere (a woman who disentangles wool or flax with a comb), heklestere (a woman who uses a type of comb called a hatchel, *hekel* in Middle English, to separate flax fibres), nopstere (a woman who shears the nap of fabric), callestere (a woman who makes or sells headdresses), shepstere or shapstere (a seamstress), and rokstere (a woman who rocks the cradle of an infant). Some of these names still exist as modern English surnames: Brewster, Webster and Baxter, formerly bakstere. The word 'spinster', which originally had no negative connotations nor any implications of being unmarried, later, of course, changed its meaning completely.

If you move into a larger town from a rural village, you will be known by the name of your place of origin, or by your profession, or both. It is common for people to be known by two names, sometimes three or four. A man who dies in London in 1312 is called both Solomon Cotiller and Solomon Lauvare. Cotiller is his profession, spelt 'cutler' in modern English (i.e. someone who makes, sells or repairs cutlery), and Lauvare is where he comes from, one of the Essex villages now called High, Little and Magdalen Laver. Richard Goldbetere or 'gold-beater', one of the sheriffs of London just before the first pandemic of the Black Death in the mid-fourteenth century, is also known as Richard Basingstoke, his hometown in Hampshire. A resident of Leicester in the 1330s is called John Northrene, i.e. 'Northerner'.[8] Women usually adopt their husband's name when they marry, though by no means always, and some women who marry more than once keep the surname of a previous husband. In the 1340s, Joan Sautemareys ('saltmarsh') of Bath is named as the widow of both Benedict Stoke and John Freman; Sautemareys is either her maiden name or the name of her first husband.[9] Beatrice Hynde of Holborn, who dies in the 1330s, is the daughter of Robert and Alice Hynde, while her husband is John Coblyngton and her son is William Coblyngton.[10] This is a fairly rare example of a woman retaining her maiden name.

Some people, both men and women, use their father's given name as their second name. Amyel Honesdon comes from the Hertfordshire village of Hunsdon and has three daughters from his marriage to Maud Manhale (d. 1341): Margaret, Joan and Christine. Margaret dies young, while Joan and Christine, still only in their late teens or early twenties, die days apart in the plague year of 1349. Amyel works as a chandler, i.e. a candle-maker, then spelt *chaundeller*, and his daughters call themselves Joan Amyel and Christine Chaundeller.[11] James St Edmunds, who lives in London in the late thirteenth and early fourteenth centuries, is the son of Fulk St Edmunds, and sometimes appears on record as James Fulk. The other name by which he is known refers to the Suffolk town of Bury St Edmunds, where the family comes from. Denys of Cambridge ('Grauntebrigge') has a son named Robert (d. 1321) who becomes a goldsmith and calls himself Robert Denys, and John Hamo or Hamond, mayor of London in 1343/45, is the son of a man called Hamo.[12]

A man's last name can, like a woman's, change throughout his life. Some apprentices take, and retain for the rest of their lives, the name of the master tradesman or craftsman who instructs them. The fishmonger Hamo Chigwell (d. late 1332 or early 1333), who serves as mayor of London eight times in the 1310s and 1320s, is originally called Hamo Dene, and takes the name of his master, Richard Chigwell (d. 1307). A pardon granted in 1344 to the apprentice of another fishmonger in London, Robert Mas, reveals the three names by which the apprentice is known: Alban Frere, Alban Mas, and Robert Alban.[13]

Andrew Cros, yet another fishmonger who dies in 1354, is still called Andrew Modyngham in 1328 in the early years of his apprenticeship to fishmonger William Cros (d. 1342).[14] Men instructed by women also sometimes change their name to hers: Warin Page, apprentice of the butcher Maud Fattyng in the early 1300s, also appears on record as Warin Fattyng.[15]

Second names start to become fixed and hereditary in the later Middle Ages, though the process takes a good long while, and names still sometimes remain fluid. Around 1300, it is virtually certain that a man called Robert Baker works as a baker, though some decades later, this is not necessarily the case anymore, and he may be a carpenter or cooper or brewer who is the son or grandson of a man who worked as a baker. As with the sisters Joan Amyel and Christine Chaundeller, siblings do not always bear the same last name. John Gernon of Norfolk has a brother named William Blofield in the late 1200s, and in the early 1400s Thomas Couper works as a cooper and uses his profession as his name, while his brother is known as Robert Beddington, their native village in Surrey.[16] A man who uses several last names serves as mayor of Leicester from 1346 to 1349 and again in the early 1360s; he is variously known as John Hayward, John Cook, John Waynhous or Wainhouse, and John Receyveur (Receiver).[17] The Norfolk knight Sir John Reppes (d. 1373) has illegitimate sons called John Martyn and Gregory Scarlet, and presumably in this case, the men use their mothers' last names.[18]

Robert Chaucer or Chausier moves from Ipswich to London in the late 1200s or early 1300s. His last name has long been thought to mean someone who works as a shoemaker (think of the French word for 'shoes': *chaussures*), thought might instead mean a hosier, i.e. a person who makes hose or leggings. Robert is the son of Isabel Malyn and Andrew of Dennington – a village in Suffolk 20 miles from Ipswich – who is also often called Andrew Taverner because he moves from Dennington to Ipswich and runs a tavern there. Like the mayor of Leicester a few decades later, Robert Chaucer is known by several other aliases in his lifetime: Robert Malyn, Robert Malyn the chaucer,

Robert of Ipswich and Robert of Dennington.[19] Robert's son John, born in London around 1312, keeps the name Chaucer though earns a living as a vintner or wine merchant rather than a shoemaker, and John's son Geoffrey Chaucer, born also in London around 1342/43, enjoys a highly successful career as a poet (and works as a customs official as well). Geoffrey's granddaughter Alice Chaucer, born in *c.*1404, is a very great lady who becomes countess of Salisbury by her second marriage and duchess of Suffolk by her third, and is the mother-in-law of Edward IV and Richard III's sister Elizabeth of York, yet she too carries the profession of her Ipswich-born great-great-grandfather Robert as her last name.

The point is to identify you and differentiate you from others, and in the same way that a man in the twenty-first century might be addressed as Mr Jones or Sir or Robert or Rob or Robbie depending on the situation and how well he knows his conversation partner, and might be identified as 'Robert at number 42' or 'Jane's son Rob' or 'our new accountant Robert Jones', a man in a late medieval English town might be known as Johan of Coventry or Johan the Carpenter or Litel Johan or Jakinet or Johan Rothyng, apprentice of the master carpenter Robert Rothyng, in different situations. As well as the diminutive forms of given names, nicknames also exist. At the beginning of the 1300s, Henry Rede is known as *Rofot* or 'roe-foot', meaning one as swift-footed as a roe deer, Thomas Hertford is called *Naverathom* or 'never at home', and Robert Tillere is *Renaboute* or 'runabout'. Olive, a widow in London in the early 1320s, is called *Sorweles* or 'sorrow-less' as her second name. Although this sounds as though she did not mourn much for her late husband Robert (d. 1319), he too was called *Soroweles* or *Soreweles*. Another London resident of the same era, a man who works as a mercer, is Hamo Godchep. His last name means literally 'good bargain'.[20]

Residents of Nottingham in the early fourteenth century whose nicknames are used as their surnames are Elias Overandover, Hawise Crist a pes or 'Christ have peace', and Henry Lytilprud, literally 'little proud' in the sense of 'little worth'.[21] Two men in the northeast of

England in the late 1200s are Adam Aydrunken, 'always drunk', and John Unkutheman, literally 'uncouth man' but meaning 'stranger' in medieval English.[22] A man who lives in the rape of Arundel in Sussex in 1296 is Thomas Affrigthe or 'affright' (frightened), another Sussex man a few decades later is William Blaknekke or 'black neck', and a man who lives near the Buckinghamshire village of Milton Keynes in 1349, just before the first pandemic of the Black Death, is William Withtheberd, 'with the beard'.[23] Clarice Claterballok works as a prostitute in London around 1340, and her names sounds as though it might represent a speciality of clattering her clients' privates.[24] Startlingly, a record of 1219 refers to a woman as Gunoka Cunteles or 'cunt-less', in the 1240s we find John Fillecunt or 'fill cunt', and a century later there is a record of one Bele Wydecunthe, 'Isabel wide cunt'.[25]

A resident of Leicester in the early 1300s is John *Laules* or 'lawless', and a resident of London a few years later is John *Gidyheued* or 'Giddyhead'. A man in Staffordshire in the 1320s is called Thomas *Saunfayl* or 'without fail' (the first part of his name, *saun* or *saunz*, is the medieval French word for 'without', which is also often used in medieval English; *sans* in modern French). A Londoner called William Foucher is arrested in 1418 and imprisoned for a year for calling Nicholas Wotton (d. 1448), a former mayor of London, 'Nicholas *Wytteles*' or 'Witless'.[26] Ralph Hunte, a wheelwright of the early 1300s, is usually addressed as *Dawe*, rather unkindly given that this means a stupid person – unless the name is meant ironically because Ralph is very bright. Or perhaps, as Ralph's brother, who is also a wheelwright, is named Jack, the two are collectively known as 'Jackdaw'.[27]

Calling people, especially men, *grete*, i.e. 'great' or large and well-built, *litel* or little, and *longe* if they are tall, is common; Edward II has men called Litel Wille or 'Little Will' and Grete Hobbe or 'Big Rob' working in his household in the 1320s, and residents of London in the first half of the fourteenth century are named Littele Hobbe, Litelrobyn, Lyttle Jakke, and Longe Watte. A man accused of theft in Essex in the late 1200s is known as Little Jacke, *parvum Jacke* in the Latin original, and in all these cases, the surnames of the people in question are not recorded. In the 1390s, the evidently aged Agnes atte Wode of London is called Olde Annot, and some people are known as *Yonge*, 'young'. A woman who lives in Ware in Hertfordshire in the late 1200s is Proude Kytte or 'Proud Kit' (Kytte is a diminutive of the name Katherine).[28]

As noted above, apprentices often, though by no means always, adopt the last name of the master who teaches them their trade, and servants also sometimes take the name of their employer with the word 'servant' attached as well as their master's last name. Ralph Duboneye, whose given name is spelt 'Rauf' in his own lifetime, employs a man named Raufservant Duboneye, Henry Middulmore employs a carter whose name is William Henryscartere Middulmore, and Hugh Horshale has a servant named Alan Hughesservant Horshale. The word *knave*, meaning 'boy' or 'young man', is also used in the sense of a servant, and in the 1350s Amice and John Odyngseles employ Thomas Amisservant Odyngseles and William Jonesknave Odyngseles.[29]

As well as people, domesticated animals in the Middle Ages are often named too. A fifteenth-century list of over 1,000 names for various breeds of hunting dogs still exists, and includes Persyvale, Gaweyne, Absolon, Joskyn, Lumpe, Havegoodday, Mustarde, Holdefaste, Andymay, Sykamore, Stalkere, Gilmote, Ryngewode, Merymowthe, Honydewe, Garlik, Frankeleyne, Bragger, Nosewise, and Crapawde.[30] Horses are given names which for the most part consist of two elements: the colour of the horse's coat followed by either the place where it was born or purchased, or the name of the person who gave it to the owner. Examples are Dun Skelton, Sorrel Hunsdon (a chestnut horse born in Hunsdon, Hertfordshire), Grisel Kyng (a grey, given to Sir Hugh Audley by Edward II), Bayard Ros (a bay, given to Lady de Burgh by Lord Ros), Lyard Hobyn, which translates as 'dapple-grey pony', and Hobyn Ireland, a pony from Ireland.[31] Other horse colours and names include *ferant*, which means iron-grey, *morel*, which is black, and *bauzan* or *bawson*, which is piebald. If you think about it, this system makes sense in a world where most people are illiterate: they would not recognise a name that is written down but can easily see the horse's colour, and the stable hands looking after the horse will be the ones who purchased it or took possession of it from the giver, and therefore will be able to remember that 'this is the bay horse that came from Lord Ros'. Even Lady de Burgh's packhorses carry names which sound very grand to modern ears; one of them is Blauncherd Walsingham, i.e. a white horse from Walsingham in Norfolk.[32]

Finally, boats and ships are given names as well. These are often people's names, frequently women's: *Cecilie*, *Eleyne*, *Isabele*, *Jonete*, *Juliane*, *Katerine*, *Margarete*, *Marie*, *Mariote*, *Maudeleyne*. *James* is a very popular ship's name, as are *Cristofre* or Christopher and *Nicholas*. Edward II owns a ship in the 1320s which he names the *Alianore la Despensere* after his eldest niece Eleanor, Lady Despenser, and John Baddyng, a shipbuilder of Winchelsea, names a ship he has made the *Jonete Baddyng* after his wife or daughter. Other ship names include *Godyer* or *Godeyer* (goodyear), *Cristemesse* (Christmas), *Blithe* (joyful), *Plentee* (plenty), *Becoun* (beacon), *Seyntemariebot* ('Saint Mary boat'), *Seynte Croiz* (holy cross), *Swalewe* (swallow, the bird) *Faucoun* (falcon), *Trinitee* (trinity), *Charite* and *Welifare* (welfare).[33]

Chapter 4

Common Nightwalkers and Curfews

English towns in the late Middle Ages are enclosed by high stone walls and accessed via heavy wooden gates which are locked at night and reinforced with a metal chain. Medieval gateways are high and wide enough to allow loaded carts as well as groups of horsemen riding abreast to pass through easily. At each side of the main gateway stand much smaller, narrower gateways called wickets, intended for pedestrians. Leicester in the Middle Ages has four gates, as does York, and indeed all of York's four medieval gateways, called 'bars', still exist in the twenty-first century: Bootham Bar, Micklegate Bar, Monk Bar and Walmgate Bar. Leicester's West and South Gates are repaired in the 1320s and new locks, keys and hasps are made for them.[1] Southampton is another medieval town with gates to the north, south, east and west, called, with a certain lack of originality, Northgate, Suthgate, Estgate and Westgate. A fifth gate is called 'the gate of Neweton'. In 1360, a year when Edward III invades France, plans are put in place to guard the safety of Southampton in case the French launch a counter-invasion of England. All doors and windows which face the sea are walled up to a thickness of three feet or more, small postern gates in the wall are sealed up, a double ditch is made encircling the town, all the gardens outside the town walls are destroyed, and all the 'great gates' except the five mentioned are blocked up. The keeper of the town, Henry Peverel, tells the king that he has begun to have the apple trees and pear trees outside the walls cut down, and admits that Southampton resident John Clerk is one of many people who are 'grievously angry' about the destruction of their gardens. John Clerk has threatened to 'break the heads' of those responsible, and Adam Inwes, mayor of Southampton, has to intervene and calm him down.[2]

London has seven gates until the early fifteenth century: Ludgate, Newgate, Cripplegate, Aldgate, Aldersgate, and Bishopsgate, and an unnamed one at the south end of London Bridge. In the early 1400s, another, Moorgate, is opened, and in addition to the main city gates, there is a small postern gate near the Tower of London. Two serjeants stand at each gate during the daytime, keeping an eye on who enters the city.[3] A fragment of London's Roman and medieval city wall is still visible outside Tower Hill underground station. By the late 1300s, Newcastle-upon-Tyne has six fortified gates and a sizeable number of smaller postern gates; these include Pilgrim Street Gate (*Pilgrymstreteyate*), West Gate, Castle Gate (*Chastelyate*) and White Friars Gate (*Whitefrereyate*).[4] One of Bristol's gates, St John's Gate, is known as *Seintjohnesyate* in the late 1300s and early 1400s and still exists in the twenty-first century, and the Church of St John the Baptist or St John's on the Wall, built into the city walls of Bristol in the fourteenth century, also still exists.[5] The small Shropshire town of Ludlow has a surprisingly large number of gates: no fewer than seven from the thirteenth century onwards, including Broad Gate, Dinham Gate, Linney Gate and Corve Gate. Chester is the only English town whose medieval walls remain entirely intact in the twenty-first century, though much of York's medieval walls and part of Ludlow's, Shrewsbury's, Southampton's, and Carlisle's walls are among those that also survive. By the 1340s, the walls, three gates, bridges, stockades, and castle of Carlisle are in poor repair and will cost £500 to put right, a huge sum. The residents cannot afford it and are already busy guarding the city from Scottish raids (Carlisle stands close to the Scottish border). According to an inquisition, 'very many of them go away and live in Scotland and elsewhere'.[6]

As the resident of a medieval town, you will be subject to a curfew during the hours of darkness, and in theory will not be allowed to leave your home. Plenty of people do, of course, but it is officially prohibited. Any person found out and about on the streets after dark is called a 'nightwalker' (usually spelt *nyghtwalker* in Middle English) and assumed to be up to no good, especially if they fail to carry a light. They will be temporarily imprisoned.[7] In April 1382 in London, William Swalewe, Henry Clemme and John Medelond are arrested for 'wandering by night ... in a suspicious manner', and mainprised (i.e. bailed) under penalty of a massive £20 each. Almost a century later in 1467, Richard Colman of Nottingham, a weaver, is accused of being a nightwalker; in the Latin of the original document, he is called a *communis noctivagus*, literally 'common night wanderer'.[8]

In a world long before the invention of electricity, forbidding residents of a town to wander about at night makes sense, as malefactors do often use the long hours of darkness as cover for their activities. In the early 1400s, it is proclaimed in London that a lighted lantern must be hung 'outside every house in the high streets and lanes', albeit only on feast days or on special occasions. These are specified as being the period between Christmas and Epiphany (6 January), the night before the Nativity of St John the Baptist on 24 June – though the hours of daylight are so long at this time of year one wonders why anyone would need lanterns – and whenever parliament is held in London. Furthermore, taverners, brewers, hostelers, hucksters, cooks and pie-bakers and forbidden to keep their establishments open after 9.00pm on the eves of these festivals.[9] Otherwise, on every other night of the year, the darkness is total, and even in the middle of London, light pollution does not exist. Stargazing is – or it would be, if anyone in the late Middle Ages had a clue what they are looking at besides Mercury, Venus, Mars, Jupiter and Saturn – a much more viable pastime in England's main city than it will be a few centuries later. And even in the middle of London, there is almost total silence at night. You might occasionally hear voices and laughter as the nightwatchmen pass along your street, but anyone else who is out and about will not wish to draw attention to themselves and will be as furtively quiet as possible. Medieval London is darker and quieter than anyone who knows the city in the twenty-first century could possibly imagine.

The time of curfew varies according to the month of the year and is several hours later in the long light evenings of summer than in winter. In Leicester in October 1467, curfew is 9.00pm ('after ix of the belle').[10] In London, curfew ends when the bells of the church of St Martin le Grand ring for Prime at about 6.00am, and it is the bells of the same church which determine the start of curfew every evening. All the parish churches in London, and there are many dozens of them, will also ring their bells for the beginning and end of curfew as soon as they hear the bells of St Martin le Grand. Taverns are meant to close when taverners hear the evening bells, and though taverners are threatened with imprisonment if they do not, they sometimes keep their establishments open.[11] In Oxford, long after curfew has rung one night in May 1306, four men try to push their way into a tavern run in the house of one Henry Ocle, and demand to be served. They falsely claim to be nightwatchmen guarding the streets who are in need of a drink.[12] In 1418, the prior of the cathedral church of St Peter in Bath petitions Henry V on the grounds that it is 'the custom that neither the men of the city nor anyone else should ring any bells on any day before the prior and convent of the cathedral church have rung their bells, nor on any night after the prior and convent have rung their bells for curfew'. In defiance of this custom, the prior claims, the people of Bath are ringing the bells of the city for night-time curfew before the monks have done so, and are thereby interrupting the monks' religious services.[13]

As medieval towns are encircled by high walls, and as their gates are always locked at night, it is easy to find yourself shut out of your hometown when darkness falls and curfew begins. The concept of being locked out of an entire town seems unfathomably odd to a modern audience, and it helps to think of medieval towns as fortified castles writ large, with a mere handful of entry points that cannot be accessed during the hours of darkness. People can even be and sometimes are locked out of medieval London, which in the twenty-first century, when the city sprawls endlessly in every direction and it is hard to tell where it stops and the rest of the country begins, would be hilariously impossible. In July 1340, Gerard Armourer, John Lincoln, and John Keu threaten the *bedel* (beadle, an official appointed to keep order) of Aldgate ward because he refuses to open the gate and let them into

London in the middle of the night. They are arrested and put on trial as 'armed nightwalkers'.[14] A small number of men are entrusted with the keys to each town or city gate, and they will lock the massive doors and the heavy chain across them when they hear the bells ring for curfew.[15] The much smaller, narrower wickets may stay open a little longer than the wide main gate, so if you are a pedestrian hurrying back to your town before nightfall, you might just make it. Once the gates are locked, watchmen will take up their positions on top of the gates and on the town walls, and other watchmen will patrol the streets. When you hear church bells ringing early the next morning, curfew is lifted, the watchmen go home to sleep after their night shift, and you and everyone else can begin your day.

Some people who live near the gates of medieval towns seize the chance to make some extra money by inviting travellers who have missed curfew and find themselves locked out of a town to sleep in their home. This does not, however, always end well. Sometime between July 1323 and July 1324, Robert Kytewild, who lives just outside Leicester's north gate, allows a visiting stranger to spend a night in his house. Robert kills the man while he is asleep, perhaps intending to rob him, then, disturbingly, hides the body under his own bed. Neighbours discover the body, and Robert flees. His victim's identity remains forever a mystery, because, in a world where written forms of identification and photographs do not exist, there is no way of determining who he is or where he comes from.[16]

Whichever late medieval English town you visit, you will see countless churches, sometimes, it seems, on every corner. Your local parish church will be a major part of your life. As well as the Mass you will attend there regularly, funerals, weddings and baptisms take place there, and your local alderman or other representative will often hold meetings in the local parish church. The bells ring out the canonical hours, such as Prime, None and Vespers, which mark the rhythms of everyone's daily life.

After Edward I expels the entire Jewish population from England in 1290, everyone in the country is Catholic, at least nominally, though it is hard to tell if everyone truly believes or simply goes through the motions. Richard Rolle, born in Yorkshire in the early 1300s, attends Oxford University, but drops out before gaining his degree after he experiences a religious conversion and returns to his native Yorkshire to preach the word of God. He subsequently writes a great deal on religion and mysticism both in Latin and his native English.[17] The fact that such a thing as a religious conversion happens in the fourteenth century reveals that people's beliefs are not always necessarily heartfelt, even if they attend Mass regularly. In many cases, they may be merely superficial. In 1354, Henry of Grosmont, first duke of Lancaster and a kinsman of Edward III, admits that he hates getting out of bed early in the morning to hear Mass and prefers to lie in bed longer instead, and always tells himself that he will listen to it twice the next day instead.[18] It is all but impossible, however, not to partake in religious life on a regular basis, regardless of your personal feelings on the matter, and declarations of a lack of faith in God and the tenets of Christianity are all but unheard of. Beginning in the early 1400s, England begins to slide into a period of religious intolerance, and some people whose beliefs are deemed heretical or unorthodox are burned alive.

The number of religious houses in late medieval England is enormous. London alone has over 100 parish churches, and in and around the city stand the houses of the Dominican friars, the Franciscan friars, the Austin or Augustinian Friars (also called the Crutched Friars or Brothers of the Cross), and the Friars of the Penance of Jesus Christ, also called the Friars of the Sack, who settle outside Aldersgate in *c.*1257. Among others, there are priories at Bermondsey, Clerkenwell (the priory of St John of Jerusalem), Haliwell, Smithfield, Barking, Kilburn, Stratford-le-Bow (the priory of St Leonard), the priory of Holy Trinity near Aldgate, which is often called *Cricherche* or *Cristechirch*, i.e. Christchurch, and a house of Minoresses or Poor Clares, i.e. Franciscan nuns, near the Tower. Many people have a genuine vocation as a nun, monk, or friar, though members of the nobility often send their younger sons and daughters into the Church whether they have a true vocation or not. In the late fourteenth century, the archbishop of Canterbury is William Courtenay, son of the earl of Devon, nephew of the earl of Hereford, and a great-grandson of Edward I, aka Longshanks. Courtenay is succeeded on his death in 1396 by Thomas Arundel, son and brother of earls of Arundel, uncle-in-law of the first duke of Norfolk, and a descendant of Longshanks' father Henry III. Thomas Bourchier, archbishop of Canterbury from 1454 to 1486, is the brother of the earl of Essex, half-brother of the duke of Buckingham, and a great-grandson of Edward III.

Monks and nuns stay in their convents, and as a town dweller you will rarely if ever meet them unless you go to pray at their abbey or monastery, but friars go out into the world, preaching. You will often see the black robes of the Dominicans, also known as the Blackfriars or Friars Preacher, founded by Saint Dominic in 1216, as well as the Franciscans, also known as the Greyfriars or Friars Minor, founded by Saint Francis of Assisi in 1209, and the Carmelites, also known as the Whitefriars. Where Eldon Square shopping centre now stands in the middle of Newcastle-upon-Tyne is called High Friar Street in the twentieth century and *Freremenourchere* or Friars Minor Chare (a local word for a narrow lane) in the Middle Ages. An area of central London is still called Blackfriars after the Dominican priory which once stood there, and the story of Greyfriars Bobby, the dog who guarded his master's grave in the Greyfriars Kirk in Edinburgh, is famous. Seeing a tonsured friar declaiming on the streets is a common sight in medieval English towns, and they also travel overseas to preach. In 1313, an intrepid Franciscan friar named Guillerin Neville travels from England to Cathay (i.e. China), Georgia, the Empire of Trebizond (an area which covers what is now Anatolia in Türkiye and the Crimean Peninsula) and the Ilkhanate (a division of the Mongol Empire, now Iran, Azerbaijan, much of Türkiye and parts of other countries including Armenia, Iraq and Syria) 'to preach the word of Christ', as Edward II puts it.[19]

Chapter 5

At Whiche Hande Shall I Take My Way? Travelling

After spending several days taking in the sights and sounds of late medieval London, you decide to leave and travel elsewhere. You do not hurry, though, because when it takes days to get anywhere, there is rarely any rush. Edward I and his queen, Leonor of Castile, return to England in August 1289 after spending more than three years overseas, and their children are brought from Kings Langley in Hertfordshire to Dover to greet them. It takes a painfully slow two weeks to transport the royal children the distance of 100 miles.[1] Travelling the 200 miles from London to York can, depending on the season, the weather, the state of the roads, the mode of transport and how many possessions you are carrying, take anywhere from a few days to three weeks.

On the other hand, you might find it surprising to learn how remarkably fast news and gossip can travel in the late Middle Ages. The royal messengers who carry news of Edward I's death near Carlisle on 7 July 1307 take just four days to reach his son Edward II, staying in or close to London, travelling the 320 miles at 80 miles a day. They benefit from the long hours of daylight in early July, fresh horses all the way along the route, the old Roman road system that makes it relatively easy to travel between the north and the south, and, presumably, dry summer weather. Edward III arrests Roger Mortimer, earl of March, in Nottingham during the evening or night of Friday, 19 October 1330. Pope John XXII, 850 miles away in Avignon, hears of this on 3 November, fifteen days later. He waits until 7 November, when an English merchant who has just arrived in Avignon confirms the news and provides him with fresh details, before writing to King Edward on the matter.[2] The story of March's arrest thus travels close to 60 miles a day from the English Midlands to the south of France in autumn, incredibly fast given that it is passed on by word of mouth.

When momentous events occur, it can be frustrating to have to wait for someone to come and tell you what is going on, but as newspapers, television and radio will not exist for centuries, and as you are illiterate and unable to read the newsletters which already do exist, there is no other way. In the autumn of 1326, Edward II's wife Isabella of France brings an army of mercenaries to England to capture and execute her husband's loathed chamberlain and co-ruler Hugh Despenser the Younger, and ends up bringing about the abdication of her husband as well. The residents of Leicester are as eager as everyone else to follow these exciting and unprecedented political developments, and the mayor of Leicester, John Norton, sends two men to Bristol, where the queen and her followers are currently staying, to find out what is happening. He sends another man to Gloucester and Hereford in the belief that this is the part of the country where the king might be, and his information is accurate, given that Edward II passes through Gloucester on his way to South Wales.[3] News, rumours and gossip are carried by merchants, minstrels and pilgrims, among others, and contrary to popular modern belief, many medieval people do travel away from their village or town to trade, to go on pilgrimage, to visit family and friends, to see the royal court, to petition an influential person for help with a problem, and so on. People will travel a long way to see the king in person, or failing that, to air their grievances to someone associated with the royal court who might be able to pass on their petition to someone in authority. In the 1310s, John Pryg of Northampton rides to Lincoln, the best part of 100 miles away, to complain to the king that the mayor of Northampton, Henry Garlekmonger, has mistreated him and his wife.[4]

The most obvious method of medieval travel is, of course, walking. The journey from London to Dover, a distance of some 70 miles, is expected to take between three and five days depending on the walker's age and level of fitness.[5] Walking 20 to 30 miles a day is considered normal. There are no maps, or at least no maps that are even vaguely reliable and usable, but you can navigate by following a river or by making your way from the spire or steeple or flat-topped tower of one church, or occasionally cathedral, to the next. These are the tallest structures in the country – after its spire is completed in 1311, Lincoln Cathedral is the highest building in the world for almost two and a half centuries – and thus can easily be spotted rising above the landscape in the distance as you walk. Another way to navigate is simply to ask local people for directions: 'At whiche gate shall I goo out, and at whiche hande shall I take my way?' They will respond by saying something like, 'On the right hande. Whan ye come to a brigge, so goo ther over; ye shall fynde a lytill waye [little path] on the lyfte honde [left hand]. There shall ye see upon a chirche two hye steples. Fro thens shall ye have but four myle unto your logging [lodging].'[6]

Even when you reach the town to which you have been travelling for days or even weeks, it is difficult to find a particular building, as house numbers do not yet exist. To explain the exact location of someone's house requires a lengthy description of what lies to the north, south, east and west of it. In June 1312, for example, a vacant plot of land in London has to be described as lying west of a house that belongs to the king's cousin the earl of Richmond, east of houses that once belonged to Henry Waleys, a former mayor of London, and between the 'highway which extends from Ivylane to Eldedeneslane' and the north wall of the bishop of London's palace. This is a typically long-winded way of describing a section of what in the fourteenth century is called Paternosterstrete, later named College Hill, nowadays near Cannon Street station.[7]

Crossing rivers and streams as you travel through England can be difficult, and sometimes you will have to walk miles out of your way to find a bridge, or failing that, a ford. Even when you do find a bridge, you might have to exercise caution when using it, as many of them do not have rails or parapets or anything on the sides whatsoever. Many medieval bridges can be visualised more like humpbacked drawbridges than the bridges of later centuries with which you are familiar, and suspension bridges will not exist until hundreds of years after the Middle Ages. In January 1301, a young man named John Prodome drowns in the Nene near Peterborough in Cambridgeshire when his foot slips while he is crossing the river via a bridge, and he falls in. Almost a century later in 1396, a man called Roger, last name unknown, is crossing the Little Bridge over the River Cherwell in Oxford (in later centuries it will be called the Magdalen Bridge). He must squeeze past a horse being led in the opposite direction which is laden with a sack of wheat, and the sack bumps Roger off the side of the bridge and into the river. Although the person leading the horse and others who witness the incident jump into the water, pull Roger out and carry him into the nearest house, they are too late to save his life.[8] Bridges are often made of wood, though some are made of stone instead, and the bridge over the River Nene at Oundle in Northamptonshire has two (religious) crosses also made of stone in the early 1300s. As well as the many houses which line it, there is a public latrine on London Bridge, and a chapel dedicated to St Thomas Becket stands in the middle. An inventory is made of the 'books, vestments and other ornaments and goods' in the chapel in November 1350. These include three breviaries, two covered with white leather and one with red leather; two linen cloths for the altar; a silver cup for the Host; a silver vessel for incense; five candlesticks; relics in a chest with an iron lock, including a ring containing a tooth of St Richard Wych of Chichester (d. 1253); and an image of Thomas Becket.[9]

Despite the lack of physical maps, some people carry an accurate map of England, or at least some of it, in their heads, and know where places are located and how far they are apart. In 1325, the sheriff of London, John Causton, sends a man who is abjuring the realm (see Chapter 6 below) from London to Southampton and tells him where to spend each night on the way. During his journey of 80 miles, he will spend the first night in Cobham, the second in Farnham, and the third in Alresford before arriving in Southampton on the fourth day. All these places are almost exactly 20 miles apart, and Causton could not have planned the route better if he had had access to Google Maps. John Wheteley is given a route from London to Bristol when abjuring the realm in 1324. He will spend the first night in High Wycombe in Buckinghamshire, the second in Oxford, the third in Highworth in Wiltshire, and the fourth in Malmesbury, also in Wiltshire, before arriving in Bristol on the fifth day. London to Bristol is a journey that can now be driven in about three hours using the M4, and though the route which is assigned to Wheteley in 1324 takes him farther to the north than the route which the modern motorway takes, it is a well thought out one which involves walking between 20 and 35 miles a day.[10]

The second way to travel is by horse, and if you do not own one, you can hire a hackney horse (spelt *hakeneye hors*) from a *hakeneyman*. In the late 1200s, Godfrey Belstede hires a hackney from a man in his native village, Cheshunt in Hertfordshire, to ride to London, while William Despenser pays 12d to hire one for a few days in 1319 and Henry Dene pays 6d in 1339 for a hackney on which to ride from Ware in Hertfordshire to London. In 1265, it costs 1½ shillings (18d) to hire a horse to ride from Leicester to London and back, a round trip of 200 miles or a little more.[11] A century later in 1365, Thomas Bastard of Essex hires a piebald hackney horse from John Gace to ride from London to Canterbury and back. Thomas and his wife, who is an invalid and is the one riding the horse, are just past Gravesend, less than halfway through their journey to Canterbury, when the unfortunate horse dies. This is a result of illness, according to Thomas, or of the unfortunate animal being ridden too hard, according to its owner John Gace. John demands compensation from Thomas Bastard for the loss of his horse; Thomas counters that he has had to pay for another horse to ride from Gravesend to Canterbury then another one for the journey back to London, and claims that John Gace's horse was not fit for use.[12] Andrew Modyngham, later called Andrew Cros, a fishmonger's apprentice in London, hires a hackney horse to travel to the Sussex coast during the Christmas season of 1327 and spends a few days in and around Hastings and Winchelsea before returning home.[13]

If you wish to purchase a hackney horse rather than merely hire one for a few days, it will cost you between 20 shillings (£1) and 30 shillings, while a carthorse costs between 15 and 20 shillings.[14] The same problems of navigation arise when you are on horseback as they do when you travel by foot. In the autumn of 1326, John Gough, a servant of Lady de Burgh, gets lost at night while riding around East Anglia on the lady's business, and has to pay 3d for a guide to help him find his way and for a blacksmith to fit new horseshoes.[15] Saddles usually cost between about 18d and 30d, though when Edward II buys two with the harnesses and saddle-girths for his young great-nephews Huchon and John Despenser in 1322 and 1324, he pays a massive 160d each time.[16] In the late 1300s, Huchon and John's own great-nephew, Thomas Despenser, lord of Glamorgan, uses a saddle 'with red velvet studs with brass pineapples'.[17]

If you buy a horse to ride regularly, and have plenty of money, a palfrey, a jennet, or an ambler would be your best bet; they are trained to have a comfortable, ambling gait. A rouncy is another kind of small riding horse. If you are a knight who goes into battle or takes part in jousting tournaments, you will need to purchase a destrier, which is a highly-strung horse – usually a stallion – specially trained for war. They are ruinously expensive, in much the same way as buying a high-performance sports car will be a few centuries later. Or you might purchase a courser, which are slightly cheaper and are often used for hunting, though are also used to ride into battle on occasion. As well as the cost of buying a horse in the first place, you will, of course, have to feed it and look after it, and buy saddles, horseshoes and other equipment, all of which can prove very expensive. When the Scottish earl of Ross spends part of a day in Dunstable, Bedfordshire at the beginning of October 1303, hay for his horses costs 7d and bread for them 6d, and he pays the local blacksmith 6½d to shoe them. The next day in Northampton, he pays the same costs plus another 8d to mend his saddles. In Leicester in 1317, it costs 6s 9d to provide fodder for ten horses for two nights, 4s 7d to mend saddles and 1s 5d to shoe the horses, and five years later it costs between 10d and 12d a day for hay, 20d to 24d a day for oats, and 4d to 8d a day for bedding straw for the eight horses accompanying a teenage nobleman on a hunting trip. Later in the fourteenth century, a bushel (eight dry gallons) of oats for horses costs 6d.[18] Given that labourers earn 1½d or 2d a day and even highly experienced master craftsmen earn only 6d a day, to pay such amounts is beyond the reach of most. And another issue with horses is that their riders are forever tumbling from them and breaking a leg, arm or foot. Although many people recover and live for decades afterwards – often with a limp – it is common in late medieval England to die of gangrene after breaking a limb.[19]

For well-off ladies or elderly and infirm men, carriages or coaches pulled by five horses exist, though they are, despite the huge expense of buying and running them, extremely uncomfortable. There is no suspension, and you will feel every rut of the road as they jolt their way along the muddy tracks of medieval England. All you can do is buy plenty of cushions and resign yourself to a slow and bumpy journey. They do have windows so you can look out at the scenery if you like, or you might prefer to cover them with curtains. In her will of 1355, Lady de Burgh bequeaths her 'great coach with the equipment, curtains and cushions' to her daughter Lady Bardolf.[20] Thomas Despenser, lord of Glamorgan, owns a carriage which is pulled by five horses of different colours, though it is surely his wife, Edward III's granddaughter Constance of York, who uses it.[21]

Finally, you can travel by boat or ship along the rivers and coastline of medieval England and to the Continent, though crossing the Channel is not for the faint-hearted, and you are always at the mercy of the elements. Edward III sends his great-uncle Henry of Lancaster, earl of Lancaster and Leicester, as an envoy to the king of France in January 1331, in the dead of winter. Henry ends up having to spend twelve days in Dover before he can cross the Channel safely, while Philip VI waits in Paris for him to arrive.[22] In May 1325, it takes two men eleven days to sail from Portsmouth to Bordeaux.[23] Also in the 1320s, John and Agnes Hegham and their friend John Thorpe hire William Stedeman to take them along the Thames from London to

Kingston-upon-Thames in his *dongbot*. As this means 'dung-boat', it is hardly likely to have been the most fragrant mode of transport.[24] The English canal system does not exist yet, but you can sail along rivers, including the four so-called 'great rivers' of England: the Thames, Severn, Trent, and Ouse.

Many English people in the Middle Ages, by no means exclusively at the wealthier end of society, visit the great pilgrim site of Santiago de Compostela in northern Spain. John Ivot of Chigwell in Essex, in his late twenties, sets off for Santiago in October 1315, 19-year-old John Gamon of Chelsworth in Suffolk leaves in early February 1342, and Robert Westbech of Brabourne in Kent goes to both Santiago and the Holy Land in November 1340 and returns safely home in July 1342. Two friends from the Northamptonshire village of Hardwick, 25-year-old William Hunte and 23-year-old Richard Shephirde, set off for Santiago in February 1337, and when 35-year-old Andrew Plaitour of Aldbury in Hertfordshire returns to England from Santiago in July 1333, a large crowd of his neighbours walk several miles along the road towards St Albans to greet him on the final leg of his journey and accompany him home. In June 1353, a tragic event occurs when John Canty of Cowbridge and 'many other pilgrims' drown at Dunster, which lies on the Bristol Channel in North Somerset, as they are setting off on pilgrimage to Santiago.[25]

For those who do not wish or cannot afford to travel overseas – or who fear the perilous journey – the two most important places of pilgrimage in England are Our Lady of Walsingham in Norfolk, and Canterbury, where the shrine of St Thomas Becket is located. A few weeks after John, son of Robert Cracroft of Hogsthorpe in Lincolnshire, is born in March 1335, Robert goes on pilgrimage to Thomas Becket's shrine, 185 miles from his home, with two friends named Philip Thoresthorp and Eudo Billesby. Their stated reason is to fulfil a vow they made 'on account of danger in coming from assizes at Lincoln in thunder and lightning, from which they were in fear of death'.[26] In the late 1300s, Geoffrey Chaucer composes the *Canterbury Tales* about a group of pilgrims travelling from London to Canterbury to visit the shrine of the 'holy blissful martyr', Thomas Becket.

When the royal court comes to your town, you will know about it. It does indeed come to your town every so often, as, unlike in later centuries when the monarch spends most of the year in and around London, the medieval kings are constantly on the move and travel on a never-ending circuit through the south and Midlands of England, all year round. Only very occasionally do they visit the north – which is comparatively empty of people and remote – and usually only because they are on their way to wage war in Scotland. Otherwise, the royal court only rarely travels north of Nottingham or west of Bristol, and it is also rare that it spends more than a handful of days in one place.

The king has a household of a few hundred people, and if he is married, his queen has her own household of a couple of hundred people as well. As it is unthinkable for the king to travel alone, he is always accompanied by numerous earls, barons, and bishops, who all have their own sizeable retinues. All these people, and all the horses they are using to ride or to pull carts and carriages, will have to be accommodated somewhere and fed somehow. This is one important reason why the royal court hardly ever stays more than a handful of days in one location; the vast quantities of food these thousands of people and horses require means that the court's arrival is something akin to a plague of locusts descending on your locality. Your house might well be used as accommodation for some of the king's enormous retinue. His household marshals will requisition your house and will make a mark on the front of it with chalk, and will assign a group of people to sleep there. You have little, if any, say in the matter.[27] The king of England may stay wherever he wants, anywhere in the country.

When you travel around England for whatever reason, you will need to find somewhere to stay; one or several of the innumerable religious houses may be your best bet, though the accommodation will be very basic. Otherwise, there are hostels, which will provide stabling and food for your horse as well as you. You can check with your host if he or she provides food by asking 'Is there to ete [eat] here within?' Hostellers are allowed to make a profit of no more than 8d on a quarter of oats, and may charge no more than 2d for a day and night's worth of hay for your horse. Hostellers are called *hostelere* in fourteenth-century English or *haubergere* in medieval French (modern French *auberge*, 'hostel'), and their establishments are either called *hostellrys*, 'hostelries', or *herberwe*, also spelt *heberow*. One downside is that you may well have to share a room with strangers, though on the upside, your host or a servant of his will bring you hot water to wash your weary, dusty feet.[28]

If you have any valuable goods, hostellers will provide you with lockable chests or deposit boxes, called *trussyngcoffres* in medieval English, in which to place them for safe keeping. As well as providing a bed for a night or two, some hostels provide long-term accommodation. William Beaubek of Kent states in April 1345 that he has rented a room in an inn belonging to John Waltham for 1½d a week. He has a key to the room and believes it to be a secure place in which to keep his *trussyngcoffre* containing 10 marks in cash, gold and silver rings, silver ornaments and dishes, silk purses and girdles, and other valuables. While William is out, however, someone unlocks the door to his room with the garden door key and steals his box. The innkeeper John Waltham blames his brewer, Roger, as the only other person beside himself who had the key.[29] This interesting case shows that an inn has its own garden through a door that can be locked, and reveals that innkeepers are deemed liable for the theft of goods from rooms they let out and are held responsible for their guests' possessions. In 1380, Sir John Sapy stays in the hostel called the *Swerd in the Hope* on Fleet Street in London – which belonged to Hugh and Sarra Strubby a few decades earlier – and places the huge sum of £18 6s 8d in two *trussyngcoffres*. He accuses his host, Thomas Hostiller aka Thomas Taillour, of allowing the money to be stolen, though Thomas protests that it is four of Sir John's servants who have removed the cash from the chests. Just two years later, however, Sir Richard Waldegrave also accuses Thomas of stealing his goods and money while he and his servants are staying at the *Swerd*. The modus operandi is similar, though in Richard Waldegrave's case, the two *trussyngcoffres* which he has borrowed from Thomas Hostiller and where he has placed his seal and forty marks worth of jewellery are removed altogether from the inn.[30] Another London hostel is the *Sterre in the Hoope* or 'Star in the Hoop' (see Chapter 8 below for tavern and hostel names) on Bread Street, a few yards from St Paul's. Simon Chiksond runs it in the late 1360s, and several decades later, it is owned by John Starlyng, who bequeaths it to his brother in his will of 1399. His brother is also called John.[31]

Chapter 6

Faitours, Bocardo and the Thewe: Crime and Punishment

A common sight in medieval English towns is the pillory, a wooden contraption into which the head and hands of criminals are locked as punishment. The stocks, which secure the head and feet rather than the head and hands, are also sometimes used. In the centre of late medieval London there are at least two pillories, both located in places with a high footfall: Cheapside and Cornhill. The pillory in Chester stands on Bridge Street, one of the busiest streets in the city centre.[1] Pillories exist even in tiny communities; the Yorkshire town of Guisborough has one, which in 1405 displays the head of a knight who has died in rebellion against Henry IV. Officials in York, Scarborough, Helmsley and Richmond are ordered to display the heads of other dead rebels on their own pillories.[2] North Petherton in Somerset, which even in the twenty-first century has a population of under 7,000 and must have been tiny in the Middle Ages, has a pillory from the 1200s onwards, perhaps earlier.[3]

The usual sentence for anyone unfortunate enough to be subjected to this treatment is to be locked in the pillory for half an hour or one hour, occasionally two or even three hours if you are a repeat offender or unrepentant, or occasionally for an hour on two or more market days. The Middle English word for a judicial punishment is *juesse* or *iewisse*, as in 'the *juesse* of the pillory'. When sentenced, proclamation will be made that 'he shal stonde here on the pillorie thre[e] market dayes, eche day an hool hour' (each day a whole hour). In 1423 in London, Jhonet Cogenho is sentenced to the pillory with the words that she 'shal stond thys day an hour in thys open place to be seyn and knowen' (seen and known).[4] Market days are deliberately chosen because more people will be out and about in the streets doing their shopping; one of the aims of the punishment by pillory is to make the whole experience as public and as humiliating as possible.

If you have sold bad ale, you will be forced to quaff some of it, then the rest will be poured over your head as you are locked helplessly in the pillory, while onlookers hoot with derision and perhaps, if you are unlucky, throw things at you. This happens to the London vintner and taverner John Penrose in 1364 after he is found to have sold red wine that is 'unwholesome': 'the said John Penrose shall drink a draught of the same wine which he sold to the common people, and the remainder of such wine shall be poured on the head of the same John'. If you sell bad meat to your customers, it will be burnt beneath you as you stand there in humiliation and discomfort. In 1364, John Cockow sells a 'putrid rabbit' to John Hockele in London and is locked in the pillory with the rabbit burnt underneath him, and fourteen years later John Bakere of Ruislip in Middlesex sells John Burle a 'putrid partridge' and is sentenced to half an hour in the pillory, also with the bird burning beneath him.[5] When your torment is over – and an hour or two will feel like an eternity in such circumstances – your neck and wrists will be aching intolerably after holding them in a rigid position for so long. Then you will have to go home with your clothes and hair stinking of smoke and rotten meat and covered in whatever filth onlookers might have hurled at you, and perhaps your own vomit as well. It is not as though you can have a long hot shower and throw your clothes into the washing machine to get rid of the smell, either; it is going to linger for days, even weeks.

Selling rotten food or bad ale is not the only offence that will see you condemned to the pillory. In London in 1364, John Hakford is condemned to a harsh sentence: he will stand on the pillory for three hours on four separate occasions, barefoot and without hood or belt, with a whetstone hung from his neck marked with the words 'a false liar'. This is in addition to a year's incarceration in Newgate prison. John has wrongly accused one Richard Hay of telling him that he,

Richard, and 10,000 other men in London had formed an alliance to slay 'all the best people, and the great folks and officers of the said city'. At Richard Hay's trial for conspiracy to murder, it is found that John Hakford has lied and has defamed him, and John is duly punished while Richard is set free. A few years later, Stephen Scot is imprisoned in Newgate and condemned to an hour on the pillory for spreading a false report that the mayor of London has himself been imprisoned.[6] In 1264 in Leicester, Nicholas Chaloner is punished with the pillory for his rudeness to the mayor, Peter Blund. When he appears before Peter to pay a fine of 6d that he owes, Nicholas snaps, 'Do you want to drive me from Leicester? Do you need my 6d so much?', and 'with other words greatly abused and annoyed the mayor'. Peter responds that Nicholas should be excommunicated from God, and Nicholas replies 'Put your excommunication where you put your other goods'.[7]

John Sharryngworth, convicted of being an 'able-bodied vagabond' and a *faitour* (conman) who refuses to work and pretends to be an invalid, is put on the pillory in July 1355.[8] Richard Lynham of Somerset and John Warde of Yorkshire are condemned to the pillory for an hour on three days, Wednesday, Friday, and Saturday, 'for pretending to have suffered the loss of their tongues by robbers' in October 1382. This is done to support their false claim of being unable to work. Adam Ryebred of Spalding in Lincolnshire is another man who gets into trouble in 1381 for 'begging and pretending that he was unfit for work' when in fact he is 'strong and lusty, capable of labour and able to earn his food and clothing'. Adam is threatened with the pillory if he is ever caught begging again, because he is 'defrauding genuine beggars and poor people'.[9] Idleness and lazy people are despised in the late Middle Ages, in part because idleness is thought to be against scripture, and because in a world where everything is made with human hands, and life is relentlessly hard, everyone must pull their weight and do what must be done. People are enjoined to 'flee ydlenes, smal and grete' (flee idleness, small and great) because it is the source of all vices.[10] In 1349, Edward III's government forbids anyone to give alms to beggars who are physically able to work and could do so if they wished but prefer to be idle, so that 'they may be compelled to labour for their necessary living'.[11]

As well as the pillory, fifteenth-century Leicester is one of the many English towns that has a *cukstool* or cucking-stool, where men and women – though mostly the latter – convicted of being *scoldys* are punished. *Scoldys* or 'scolds' are people believed to be rowdy and abusive who disturb the peace, or who gossip incessantly; the phrase 'common scolds' sometimes appears in medieval documents as *communes garulatores* in Latin, implying a garrulous, chattering tongue.[12] A special pillory only for women called the *thewe* is built on Cornhill in London in *c*.1364, and is probably some form of chair or cucking-stool. Alice Salesbury, a beggar, is locked into it after kidnapping Margaret Oxwyke in 1373; she intended to force the child to beg with her to increase her takings. Alice Shether suffers the same penalty in 1375 after she is found to be a common scold who sows envy and discord and uses abusive words, and so does Isabella Lynchelade in 1391 after falsely accusing two men of stealing a bible.[13] A less harsh punishment instigated in London in 1364 for those who commit perjury or defamation is to stand on a high stool in the middle of the Guildhall, bareheaded. Anyone who commits the same offence twice is put on the pillory.[14] Defaming a person's good name and bearing false witness are taken very seriously in medieval England, and are always punished.

Between 1401 and 1439, the authorities in London go through a phase of clamping down on what they call 'acts provoking public immorality', and arrest people for committing adultery. They do not care if two unmarried people have sex, only if at least one of the people involved is married to someone else, or if they are a member of the Church who has taken vows of chastity. In November 1406, married woman Alice Gyboun is arrested for committing adultery with John Marchall, unmarried, and in August 1429, John Couper and Katherine Frensshe, both married to other people, are arrested and taken before the mayor and aldermen. In 1424, John Leche allows David Holland to 'lie naked in bed alone' with John's wife Joan, where they are caught by the local constable and beadle (who are evidently peeping through the windows of people's houses in the middle of the night). All three are sentenced to an hour on the pillory. A few years earlier in 1407, Richard Dod stands on the pillory for three hours, an unusually long time, after acting as a *bawd* – a procurer or pimp – between his wife Margaret and a chaplain named William Langford.[15] It is evident that men who allow their wives to have sex with other men are particularly despised and are harshly punished, and some women are punished for hiring out the young girls they employ for the purposes of prostitution. Elizabeth Moring is convicted in 1386 of being a 'common harlot and procuress' and of selling the sexual services of her female servants. Publicly, Elizabeth pretends to hire apprentices in the craft of embroidery, but instead forces the women to 'live a lewd life'. In November 1423, Alisoun Bostone is condemned to an hour in the pillory on three market days 'for having let to hire for immoral purposes her innocent young apprentice'.[16]

Another typical medieval punishment is to be dragged on the hurdle. In London in October 1282, while walking along Cheapside towards St Paul's, you hear trumpets and drums, and rush to see what is happening. Two minstrels dressed in bright clothes, one banging on a drum and the other blowing a trumpet, come into view. Behind them, another man is leading a small horse to which an assortment of wooden planks has been tied, and a fourth man is tied to the planks and is being dragged through the streets by the horse. The minstrels are there to draw as much attention to the victim, Robert Blake, as possible. Robert has been caught selling loaves of bread that do not weigh as much as they should, and he is slowly pulled through muck, horse manure, urine, and goodness knows what else. The procession begins and ends at his own home to ensure that his neighbours know exactly what he has done and why he is being punished, and also passes along Cheapside (then called Chepe), because it is the busiest street in medieval London.[17] The unfortunate Robert, covered head to toe in unspeakable filth, has to creep shamefacedly into his home when the ordeal is finally over and clean himself up as best as he can, and though the stench might linger for weeks, the embarrassment will surely last much longer.

Trumpeters also accompany the barefoot John Hakford from Newgate prison to the pillory on Cornhill or Cheapside on the four occasions when he is locked in the pillory in 1364, and do the same for Alisoun Bostone in 1423. Nor is Robert Blake the only baker who suffers the indignity of being dragged on the hurdle. In 1316, Godfrey Rede is found to be selling a penny loaf that is too light and is punished with the hurdle, and at the same time, Richard Lughteburghe (i.e. he comes from Loughborough in Leicestershire) is punished for the same reason. Adam Lyndeseye (originally from the area of Lindsey in Lincolnshire) is found to have baked *pain demaign* – the finest and most expensive type of white bread – that is 'of bad dough within, and good dough without', and is sentenced to the hurdle.[18]

Medieval justice is swift and harsh. The death penalty is frequently applied, and as there is no death row, the sentence will be carried out more or less immediately. In November 1300, William Sawiere stabs Christina Menstre to death in a rage after she rejects his advances in a London churchyard. He is hanged for her murder just six days later. Even this, however, is a relatively long delay compared to the fate of John Goldweye, who kills Peter Messeday in London in 1269 and is hanged for murder in Newgate prison the following day.[19] Unless you are a nobleman, who are usually executed by being beheaded with an axe or else are subjected to the horrific traitor's death of drawing, hanging and quartering, you will simply be hanged. Medieval hangings are not long-drop executions which break the neck and cause more or less instantaneous death, as they are in later centuries. Most probably, you will stand on a cart and will have the noose placed around your neck, then the horse drawing the cart will move away and you will be left dangling in the air with nothing under your feet. Or the rope around your neck will simply be thrown over the gallows and you will be hoisted up. There is either only a short drop or no drop at all, and you will be strangled to death. It can take a horrifyingly long time until you die. Men convicted of treason and given the traitor's death –

and it is only ever men who are convicted and executed for this in the Middle Ages – will have their head and the four quarters of their body displayed in public for years on end, almost always in five different places. Traitors' heads are usually spiked on London Bridge, and the four quarters of their bodies will often be taken to towns that are far apart, for example Bristol, Carlisle, York and Canterbury. To have your body cut into five pieces represents a punishment in the afterlife as well as in this world, as you will not have a whole body in which to stand up to face God on Judgement Day.

In a world where most people are poor and own very little, theft is viewed as a terrible crime, and you will be hanged for stealing goods with a value of just 12½d. Simon Berdesdale is hanged in London in 1346, for example, for stealing a woman's *surcote* (an overgarment) of *brounmedle* (brown medley, a type of dyed-in-the-wool cloth) worth 14d. If the amount is lower than 12½d, you will be imprisoned instead, and perhaps flogged for good measure, and additionally, you might be permanently banished from the town where you live.[20] The amount of 12½d is roughly a week's wages for an unskilled labourer, or just over two days' wages for a master craftsman. In the early 1320s, Richard Buckby steals a *tapet* (either a wall hanging or a coverlet) worth 7d from Thomas Lucas's house in Nottingham, and though he evades execution 'on account of the small value', he is ordered to leave Nottingham forever.[21]

People who commit crimes in London are sometimes ordered to leave their ward (of which there are twenty-four until the late fourteenth century, then twenty-five). Margaret Hontyngdone is banished from Bread Street ward in London on the grounds that she is 'a common strumpet and … harboured men of bad repute'. She is imprisoned in June 1311 after returning to the ward.[22] When beadles, i.e. officials responsible for public order, are sworn into office in London, part of their oath states that they will 'drive out' any robbers or prostitutes who settle in their ward.[23] To be banished from London in its entirety rather than simply one of its wards is reserved for very serious crimes or unrepentant criminals. Elizabeth Moring, who sells the sexual services of her female servants, is punished by an hour locked in the pillory followed by permanent exile from London in 1386.[24]

John Cheddele is imprisoned for a while and banished from Billingsgate ward in London in 1371 for 'being a common player of dice by night and a constant nightwalker to the nuisance of his neighbours'.[25] His offence is, however, nowhere near serious enough for him to be exiled from London altogether. Medieval people, who rise very early and work very hard, value their sleep and are unwilling to tolerate noise at night. In October 1381, three men are arrested in London for 'making a disturbance with *giternes*' (gitterns, a small stringed instrument with a round back) at 11.00pm. And half a century before John Cheddele is a night-time nuisance to his neighbours, fourteen men's disturbance of the peace at night has tragic consequences. William of Grimsby owns a shop in Broad Street ward in London, and during the night of 31 January 1322 is prevented from sleeping by the men's 'singing and shouting, as they often did at night' outside his shop. Furious at their refusal to let him and his neighbours sleep in peace, and goaded beyond endurance by their taunting him to come out of his shop, William runs outside with a *balstaf* (cudgel) and bludgeons one of them, Reynald Frestone, to death.[26]

Another typical punishment inflicted on criminals in the late Middle Ages is to lose an ear or a hand, and in your visit to a medieval town, you may see some people missing one or the other. Margery Dike is sentenced to the pillory in Leicester in 1263 for stealing wool worth 3d, and afterwards is ordered to leave the town for good. As she has already committed the same offence twice before and has already been banished from the town, but returns, she is condemned to a greater punishment as well: her ear is cut off (*ere cutte of* in medieval English). Margery is told that if she ever comes back to Leicester, she will be subjected to 'the other judgement that is not to be written', meaning the death penalty.[27] A fifteenth-century text states ominously that *Them that cutte purses, cutte men the eres of* or 'them that cut purses, cut men the ears off'. This is a reference to the fact that many people carry money in a purse hanging by a strap from their belt, and thieves or *cuttars of purses* simply slice through the strap to steal it.[28] Medieval kings sometimes issue notifications that a particular person has lost his or her ear or hand in an accident or while on military service, 'lest sinister suspicion arise' that they have been subjected to this mutilation because of a criminal act. Mariote of Carlisle, who stumbles in front of a cart in the early 1300s and has her right ear sliced off, is one, and another is John Sheperton, who loses his right hand while fighting in Scotland in the 1310s or early 1320s.[29]

You may see people dressed in a simple robe made of sackcloth, barefoot and bareheaded even if the ground is icy or covered in snow, trudging through a town clutching a wooden cross. They are people who have committed a felony for which they know they will receive the death penalty if convicted, and have taken another way out: abjuration of the realm, i.e. permanent voluntary exile from England, plus forfeiture of all their possessions. They are allowed to spend up to forty days in sanctuary in a church, abbey, or other religious house after committing their felony, and during this time must tell the local sheriff or coroner or one of their deputies of their wish to abjure the realm. Spending more than forty days in sanctuary is not permitted, and if anyone tries to stay longer than that, they will not be able to abjure the realm but instead will face trial – and most probably the death penalty – when they finally come out. After the forty days is over, if the person has not come out of sanctuary, nobody is permitted to give them food and drink or to communicate with them in any way, and anyone who does so will be declared an enemy of the king. While the criminal is in sanctuary, the local community will be expected to guard the church or abbey so that the criminal cannot escape. Failure to do so will result in a fine or other sanction.[30]

The sheriff or coroner will assign the abjurer a port from where to depart and will tell them the route they must take to get there and where they must spend each night during the journey. This will require walking about 15 to 30 miles a day, and they must spend no more than one night in any one place on the way, nor deviate from the route they have been given. Abjurers from London are usually sent to either Dover or Southampton, or, very occasionally, all the way over to Bristol. John atte Loke, son of Richard atte Crouche, comes from Canterbury, but moves to Winchcombe in Gloucestershire. In 1322, having fled to London, he confesses to having killed a man whose name he does not know in Winchcombe a few months earlier, and is sent to Dover to depart from England for good. His first night must be spent in Dartford, his second in Rochester and his third in Ospringe before arriving in Dover on the fourth day. Juliana Aunsel and her lover John Malton murder Edmund Brekles, a chaplain and another lover of Juliana, in London in June 1324. They both decide to abjure the realm and are sent to Dover. John is ordered to depart London for the port immediately, but Juliana is held back for a month, which is done in a deliberate attempt to prevent the couple from meeting up again. John is given four days to complete the 70-mile journey and Juliana five.[31] In Leicester in February 1307, a married couple named Richard and Isabel Pountfreyt kill a woman, Agnes Toprond. They abjure the realm, and, again to ensure that they do not travel abroad together, Richard is ordered to depart from Dover and Isabel from Portsmouth.[32]

People from the Midlands who abjure the realm are usually sent to either Bristol, Southampton, or Dover (Isabel Pountfreyt, sent to Portsmouth, is a rather rare exception because of the rather rare circumstance of a married couple committing murder together). John Plomer of Brixworth in Northamptonshire steals a mare worth five shillings from John Lucas in the summer of 1347, abjures the realm, and is ordered to depart from Bristol, about 120 miles away. The possessions which he, as an abjurer, is forced to forfeit are three piglets worth 8d, a foal worth 12d, and a soldering iron worth 3d. John Chesham of Barnwell in Northamptonshire confesses in July 1380 to having stabbed a chaplain named John Syreston to death. He is assigned the port of Dover, 150 miles away. In July 1367, David Walsheman (i.e. Welshman) steals a bay horse worth 16 shillings in Slawston in Leicestershire and flees 20 miles to Oundle in Northamptonshire, where he seeks sanctuary in St Peter's church and confesses his felony. David decides to abjure the realm and is assigned Southampton, 135 miles away.[33]

The Irishman Morice of Cork is imprisoned for an unspecified felony in Oxford in 1304 and manages to escape, but is soon captured again. He decides to abjure the realm and is assigned Dover as his port. Also in Oxford more than four decades later in 1346, Robert of Lincoln stabs a glover named John of Cornwall to death, flees to sanctuary in the church of St Martin and stays there for eleven days, then tells the coroner he wishes to abjure the realm. He is sent to Southampton.[34] Richard Lubbe from Eye in Suffolk steals a mare worth two shillings in Toseland, Huntingdonshire in March 1324, and tries to sell the animal in the market of Oundle in Northamptonshire, 30 miles away, but is recognised as a thief and flees to the chapel of St Thomas the Martyr (i.e. Thomas Becket) in Oundle. He agrees to abjure the realm from Bristol, which will require him to walk a good 130 miles. In July 1356, John Somer of Kent seeks refuge in the church of Ufford, a village in Suffolk, and admits to having stolen woollen and linen cloths worth 6s 8d a year earlier. He is imprisoned in Melton, two miles from Ufford, for this felony, and is assigned the port of Bawdsey, not far from Felixstowe.[35]

The reason that you are made to carry a wooden cross on your way to your assigned port is to signify to the public that you are an abjurer, though this will most probably be obvious anyway from the sackcloth you are wearing and the fact that you are barefoot. Technically nobody is allowed to harm an abjurer on their way to their assigned port, but if you have murdered a person and subsequently abjure the realm, their angry, distressed family and friends may well be lying in wait for you with weapons on your way to the port; this is part of the risk that you take, and few people will weep if an abjurer is killed before they leave England. If you do manage to reach your port safely, you must board the first ship whose crew will consent to take you overseas, and will have to try to make a life for yourself in France or Spain or the Low Countries or Ireland without any money, possessions, shoes or proper clothes.

If you decide to disobey, and think that it might be a good idea to build a new life for yourself in another part of England instead of departing for a foreign country, hoping that the authorities will not hear of it and come to find you, bear in mind that losing yourself in a medieval town is nowhere near as easy as you might think, even in crowded London. In the twenty-first century it is all but impossible to vanish and live off the grid without a bank card, driving licence or other ID, rental agreement, council tax and utility bills and so on, but as none of these things exist in the late Middle Ages, you might wonder how hard it can be to disappear. The answer is, very hard. As will be seen below in Chapter 16, apprentices who run away, even to the other end of the country, are frequently spotted and sent back. You may think that you are inconspicuous, but there are various things that will quickly mark you out as a stranger. One of these is your accent and way of speaking. The variant of Middle English spoken in London is enormously different to the way people speak in, say, York, to the point where they are almost separate languages. Your clothes, too, are perhaps of a different weave or different colour or style to those worn in the town to which you flee. When Andrew Modyngham, an apprentice fishmonger in London, visits Hastings and Winchelsea in Sussex at Christmas 1327 (see Chapter 5 above), a crowd of locals easily pick him out as a Londoner and, unfortunately for Andrew, beat him up.[36]

And people in medieval towns always belong somewhere, in a particular family or guild or household. Everyone has a place. If you arrive in a town where you have no place, where you do not belong and where no one knows your face and no one can vouch for you, you will be spotted and marked out very quickly. Medieval people often have an almost photographic memory for faces, and people who have only ever set eyes on you once might be able to identify you years later, perhaps to your detriment. In London in 1321, residents recognise a horseman who gallops recklessly along their street and almost knocks down a woman and her baby, and subsequently stabs a man named John Harwe to death in a rage after John shouts at him to ride more carefully, as a member of the earl of Arundel's retinue. They give his name, Thomas atte Chirche, to the coroner investigating John's murder. Twenty years later in 1341, the mayor of London, Andrew Aubrey, realises that a man who is trying to borrow money from him by pretending to work for the earl of Salisbury is an impostor and conman (a *faitour*, as Andrew would call him in fourteenth-century English). Looking at the man closely, it dawns on the mayor that he does not recognise him as a member of Salisbury's retinue.[37] Given that the earls of Arundel and Salisbury spend the vast majority of their time outside London, and given that they both have many dozens of servants, it is remarkable that city residents are able to recognise members of their large households by sight. Thomas atte Chirche is perhaps wearing the earl of Arundel's livery when he stabs John Harwe to death, but John's neighbours do not merely identify Thomas as a servant of the earl, they know his full name. Medieval people tend to have prodigious memories because they are, for the most part, illiterate and cannot write anything down to remind themselves. Likewise, in a world many hundreds of years before photography exists, people who cannot look at photos or newspaper articles to remind themselves what a person looks like often have, out of necessity, an astonishingly accurate memory for faces and names.

Only the king has the power to pardon an abjurer and bring him or her back to England, and if you are seen within the realm without a royal pardon, you will, if male, be declared an outlaw. Contrary to the rather heartwarming image of outlawry seen in numerous Robin Hood stories and films, being an outlaw is not a romantically stealthy life which involves becoming part of a brave and heroic community in a forest, stealing from the rich to help the poor, and taking part in exciting archery contests with your associates, but means that you do not exist legally and do not have the protection of the law. If someone decides to hurt you, nobody will intervene to help you, not even to save your life, and indeed, you may lawfully be killed on sight. A man who is outlawed is declared to have 'a wolf's head', meaning that he may be treated – and killed – as though he is not a human being but a dangerous and feared wild animal. John Ditchford is one of a group of men who rob and kill another man in Northamptonshire in 1322. He informs the local coroner that he wishes to abjure the realm, which is granted, but during his first day's walk to the coast, he abandons the king's highway on his way to his assigned port and flees towards a nearby wood. Unfortunately for John, he is spotted and pursued by a group of locals, and when he is caught, his pursuers decapitate him on the spot. By order of the coroner, they take his head to Northampton Castle as proof that an outlaw is dead. Women cannot be outlawed because they are not considered to have legal rights or to be 'in law' in the way that men are, and if you not in the law, you cannot be out of the law either. They can, however, be 'waived' or excluded from the protection of the law, which in practice amounts to the same thing.[38]

If you commit a felony for which you are neither executed nor exiled but imprisoned, you have every right to be apprehensive about the ordeal you will have to endure. Medieval prison are hellholes, and there are lots of them; every town will have at least one, and larger towns have several. Leicester, for example, has two prisons until 1309, one in the castle and the other in the High Street. From 1309 it has a third prison as well, the county gaol, which accepts prisoners from Leicestershire and Warwickshire. The county gaol was previously located in Warwick, but in August 1309 the newly built one in Leicester is ready and secure, and all the prisoners are transferred there from Warwick.[39]

Your guards have no obligation to feed you, and you risk dying of starvation unless you have the wherewithal to pay them for food, or unless you have friends or family who will bring it to you regularly. Three men convicted of theft, William Brich, Thomas atte Grene and Adam May, are allowed to starve to death in Newgate prison, London in 1322.[40] In 1322 and 1323, at least ten prisoners die of hunger and thirst in Northampton Castle, and at least another seven die of the cold. One of these seventeen prisoners is William Cook, who stole a colt and dies of 'hunger, thirst and privation' on 1 August 1322, and another is Robert Rushton, a clerk convicted of false accounting, who dies of the same causes on 20 March 1323. Another prisoner in Northampton Castle, John Swan, who has committed burglary in the cellar of one Eustace Burneby in Watford (a village in Northamptonshire, not the Hertfordshire town of the same name), dies of 'hunger and the flux', meaning dysentery. A few decades later in 1378, Thomas Skynnere of Burford in Oxfordshire dies of 'a disease called the flux of blood, of which disease he sickened for three weeks' while incarcerated in the prison of Oxford Castle.[41] As well as having to pay the guards for your food if you have nobody on the outside to bring you some, you will have to pay them 1d per night for a bed with blankets and sheets unless you bring your own, or unless some kind and charitable person provides you with one. Otherwise, you will have to sleep on a bare stone floor.[42] As well as the awful discomfort, having no blanket over you on a freezing winter night will leave you vulnerable to sickening and dying of the cold, as happens to at least seven men in Northampton in 1322/23.

Numerous medieval people compassionately leave bequests to 'poor prisoners' in their wills, though whether the prisoners ever actually benefit from their generosity is another matter.[43] One of the prisons in medieval London is Ludgate, and in 1388 a former prisoner complains about the keeper, John Bodesham, and his deputy, William Rounde. The two men have received alms sent by kindly people for the prisoners but have distributed it instead among the warders and their own servants. The 'common alms-box' is meant to be opened in the presence of all the prisoners, but instead, Bodesham and Rounde have opened it in Bodesham's own private chamber and have given some of the money therein to three or four favoured prisoners to give out to their fellows as they wish. The furious prisoners have 'raised a great clamour' against this injustice, and their complaint makes clear that two prisoners are allowed to go outside the prison daily to beg for alms from passersby.[44]

To be dependent on prison guards for your very existence is bad enough, and to make things even worse, some of them are brutal and corrupt. A former prisoner of Newgate in London, probably the largest and most notorious gaol in medieval England, complains in 1314 that although he 'ought not to have been placed in the depths of the gaol as a felon or thief', he was placed in a cell 'with notorious felons and thieves and horribly laden with iron fetters', thanks to the malice of one of the guards. Twenty years later, Edward III states that the Newgate guards 'have been guilty of oppressions and extortions' by putting men incarcerated for minor offences in the same cells as 'notorious felons', by committing torture, and by taking bribes and ransoms from prisoners.[45] In June 1370 there is a reference to 'a dreadful prison called *Julianesboure* in Newgate'. *Julianesboure* means 'Juliane's Bower', and the place seems to be a particularly notorious section of Newgate, already a particularly notorious jail itself. John Bambourgh, a clerk, complains that he has been imprisoned in Juliane's Bower for eleven weeks 'without any legal process'. For five weeks of his sentence, he is held in fetters, tortured, and 'made sport of', or so he claims, though an investigation finds that he has been rightfully imprisoned after using 'many insulting expressions' against Edward III's late queen Philippa of Hainault (d. August 1369) and has not suffered torture or abuse.[46]

In 1386, Joan Payn is imprisoned in Ludgate, and claims after her release that the keeper of the prison induced other prisoners – whether men or women or both is unclear – to 'beat her in her bed and elsewhere so continually and so horribly that her life scarce endured'. Transferred to Newgate, Joan's ordeal sadly continues. She is driven there almost naked and confined to a cell which is so awful that she endures 'horrible and outrageous hardship', though thankfully does live to tell the tale.[47] Two brothers from Woodstock in Oxfordshire, Edmund and Robert Tailor, die just three days apart in May 1342 while incarcerated in Oxford Castle. This seems suspicious, yet the two inquests which are held to investigate the issue both say that Edmund died a natural death of an unspecified disease from which he had long suffered, and that Robert 'was sick with diverse diseases' and also died a natural death. In both cases, it is found, whether correctly or not, that the brothers 'endured no undue injury or oppression from the warden of the prison'.[48]

As well as the risk of dying of hunger, thirst, cold, general privation and the miseries caused by cruel and corrupt warders, another horror is that gaol fever, or typhus as it is known in later centuries, is widespread in medieval English prisons. Perhaps rather remarkably, however, it is recognised that being kept in a dark, dank place twenty-four hours a day can cause illness, and some prisoners in Newgate – the more privileged ones at least – are allowed to go 'every day at convenient times' to the chapel and to 'two spacious and well-lit chambers' on either side of it if they are male. Female prisoners can go periodically to a large chamber on the south side of the jail.[49] Men and women are housed separately in medieval prisons. In 1406, the mayor and aldermen of London deal with a complaint that the female prisoners in Newgate are uncomfortably detained in a very small cell. When the women need to use the privy, they must pass through a much larger cell where men are held, 'to their great shame and hurt'. The solution is to build a new stone tower just to the south of the prison solely for women, with its own facilities. A series of ordinances regarding the treatment of prisoners in Newgate, issued a few years later in early 1431, makes apparent that women now have their own chamber there, which is much larger than the old one. Water is brought to Newgate from the hospital of St Bartholomew via an underground leaden pipe and is provided for free, and the prisoners are allowed to purchase ale if they wish. They can also buy coal for cold nights in their cells at a cost of ½d for a full heaped peck, 1d for half a bushel, and 2d for a bushel.[50] At least the Newgate prisoners are given the option, unlike the unfortunates imprisoned in Northampton Castle who are allowed to die of the cold or of thirst.

In the late Middle Ages, prison is often known sarcastically as *Bocardo*, because in scholarly logic, a *bocardo* is a logical argument from which one cannot escape. In fact, plenty of people do break out of prison. In 1325, no fewer than ten people escape from Newgate one night, and only five are recaptured by the prison warders, assisted by local residents. Ten years earlier, the prison is said to have 'certain chambers which are in a ruinous state' and which might make it easy for prisoners to escape, and this prediction is proved correct.[51] John Richedale is imprisoned in Ipswich gaol in late 1357 after stealing a heifer but escapes mere weeks later.[52] By the early 1350s, the gaol in Aylesbury in Buckinghamshire has become 'ruinous' and 'unfit for the custody of prisoners' to the extent that five of them manage to escape on Monday, 21 October 1353. They are Richard of Essex, Thomas Marche, William Porser or Purcere of Beaconsfield, William Blaket, and William Moldesone or

Moldesson of Cublington, seven miles from Aylesbury, who killed a man named Richard North in Cublington on 12 July 1353. The deputy keeper of the gaol, Richard Bermynton, is, perhaps rather unfairly given the inadequacy of the prison buildings, held responsible for the escape of the five prisoners. Evidently distrustful of the notion that he might be treated fairly and justly, Richard flees, and all his goods are seized and confiscated. After taking advice from fourteen masons and carpenters, the sheriff of Buckinghamshire orders Aylesbury gaol to be entirely rebuilt.[53] In 1306, the town gaol of Oxford is also in urgent need of repair. Richard Lindraper, a cook, is imprisoned there on an upper floor with other prisoners, and one night rises from his bed to relieve himself. Unfortunately, the floorboards turn out to be unsafe, and Richard falls through them and dies instantly. The coroner records that 'his skull was utterly broken behind even to the brain'.[54]

Chapter 7

Tallow Candles and Penny Loaves: Sleeping, Washing and Eating

Medieval people generally go to bed early and rise early, and to stay up late at night or to eat a meal late at night is considered injurious to health. To rise by 6.00am at the latest is considered 'holy, healthy and wealthy', and to sleep too long is believed to dull your wits and make you more prone to disease and pain. During the night, in the total darkness of a world without electric light, you might decide to have a candle in your chamber.[1] Be very careful, however, if a lighted candle is fixed to the wall, as candles falling onto a bed, soft furnishings or straw during the night cause many serious fires. In London in 1337, Maud Cambestere and, tragically, her 1-month-old daughter Margery succumb to flames and smoke caused by a candle which Maud leaves attached to a wall as they sleep, and which falls onto a pile of straw. Fifteen years earlier, also in London, Robert of Kent and his son William die during a conflagration in their house also caused by a candle falling from the wall of their solar as they sleep. Robert's wife Maud and their other son John manage to escape. The 2-year-old child of Richard Shyrese, whose name is either John or Joan, dies in Cottesbrooke, Northamptonshire in the late 1410s after a lit candle falls onto the infant's cradle, and in Oxford in August 1298, 20-week-old Roger Trivaler and his mother Alice are overcome by smoke and 'the greatness of the fire' after Alice leaves a candle alight in her shop one night.[2]

In Oxford in October 1341, William Daundeseghe dies in the kitchen of his landlord William Mersh's house. He sleeps in the kitchen, and one night, forgets to blow out the candle he has fixed to the wall above him, and goes to sleep. The candle falls on him, and he is horribly burnt and dies the next day of his injuries, though his friends carry him upstairs after discovering what has happened and do what they can for him. The same thing occurs to Symon Plommer a few decades later, also in Oxford, after he leaves a candle on the wall above his bed and goes to sleep. As is very often the case, Symon's bed is made of straw, which burns fiercely and quickly and gives him no chance to escape the fire.[3] Hot coals from fires left burning overnight are also dangerous, and Robert French dies in bed in his father Simon French's house in West Smithfield, Middlesex a few days after Christmas in 1365 after a burning coal falls out of the fire onto his bed. A similar thing happens to William Bierde in Salisbury in early November 1381: he leaves a fire burning near his bed, and though he is not asleep or lying in bed at the time, he dies of smoke inhalation when he tries to put out the fire.[4] In all these cases, the candle in question will be made of tallow, not expensive wax. Tallow comes as *moltetalew*, i.e. rendered tallow, and *roughtalew*, literally 'rough tallow' or unrendered. A pound of tallow to make candles will cost no more than 2d per pound, and if you buy it in bulk, it costs 22 shillings for a wey (256 pounds) of *moltetalew* or 18 shillings for a wey of rough tallow. A tallow candle made for you by a chandler costs just a penny, whereas a single wax candle can cost as much as 60d.[5]

You will probably sleep in a pallet-bed or truckle bed, perhaps in the hall of your residence with lots of other people, as the idea that everyone should have their own bedroom has not reached medieval England. As is the case with Symon Plommer in Oxford in the late 1380s, you may sleep in the kitchen, or anywhere else where you can find some floor space. A typical pallet-bed has a counterpane, cushions and mattress (*materas* or *materace* in Middle English) which is stuffed with loose straw and hung on a framework. Higher-ranking people will have a featherbed with a canopy, curtains round it, cushions, bolsters, and a coverlet.[6] In the 1360s, Mary Seint Leir of London owns a 'red bed embroidered with leopards' heads', and in 1379 a fishmonger called John of Croydon leaves a bed 'worked with dolphins' to his wife

Elen. Among the items which the duke of Lancaster bequeaths to his son and heir at the end of the 1390s are a 'great bed of red and white checked camaca [a type of expensive silk cloth] embroidered with a gold tree and a turtledove sitting on the tree' and a 'great bed of cloth-of-gold, the field partly worked with gold trees, and next to each tree a black alaunt [a breed of dog, now extinct] tied to the same tree'.[7] As privacy while sleeping is considered unimportant, high-ranking people will usually have attendants sleeping in the room with them, or at the very least just outside the door. Dogs and cats are usually not allowed in bedchambers at night and are shooed out at sleeping time, though there are exceptions; Henry IV (r. 1399–1413) – who inherits the great beds with a turtledove and alaunts from his father the duke of Lancaster – allows his dog to sleep on his bed.[8]

It is not necessarily the case that everyone in the Middle Ages sleeps naked, as modern people often think; some people surely do, but as in later centuries, it is a matter of personal preference. In 1292, Edward I's teenaged son-in-law Jan of Brabant leaves his nightshirt (*tunicam nocturnam*) in Berwick-upon-Tweed by accident. He sends a servant all the way back to fetch it, at a cost of 9d to hire the hackney horse which carries the servant. As well as a nightshirt, some medieval men wear a cap in bed on cold nights.[9] On the other hand, Isabel Carleton of Ely in Cambridgeshire is asleep naked one night in 1324 when a group of men break into her house and drag her out of bed. Just a few months later in Dunchurch, Warwickshire, Margery Dunheved is also pulled naked from her bed in the middle of the night by a group of men – and one woman – who have come to kill her husband John in revenge for his murder of another man.[10]

Once out of bed in the early morning, you will cross yourself on your chest and your forehead, ask for God's help for the new day, wash your hands and face from a pitcher of water, comb your hair, dress yourself, and go to Mass. With any luck, you will have been able to keep your clothes warm in winter by keeping them close to a fire overnight. Many people have a pole (*perche* in medieval English) affixed to a wall on which to hang their clothes while they are in bed.[11] Modern people often assume that their medieval forebears must have been filthy and smelly all the time. In fact, cleaning your face, your hands and under your nails, especially after getting out of bed and before eating, is emphasised, as is the general importance of looking clean and neat, with clothes and shoes that are well cared for, sponged, and brushed, and a 'well kempt' head with washed, combed hair. Children are enjoined to 'keep thy clothes fair and clean/Let no foul filth on them be seen'.[12] Washing clothes is a job that is almost invariably performed by women in the late Middle Ages, and the job title of those who do so professionally is *lavendere*, the Middle English word for 'laundress'.

It is extremely difficult to have a full sit-down bath, as this requires a huge amount of time and effort, unless you are one of the medieval kings of England, who have hot and cold running taps in several of their palaces. For everyone else, you must fill numerous buckets of water from a well or a stream, make a large fire to heat all the water, fill a tub with the water, then empty it all again later. This is so time-consuming and effortful that few people bother, though the lack of baths and showers certainly does not mean, however, that you cannot wash yourself regularly from a jug or pitcher. The water will be cold, perhaps even lightly iced over in winter, unless you have a metal implement which you can heat up in a fire, then use it to warm the water. If you are married to or related to a blacksmith, or have one as a neighbour, you might be able to persuade him to heat an iron rod for you in the fire in his workshop.[13] If you grow roses in your garden or have a few pence to spare to buy some – in the late Middle Ages, roses come in simple 'red' or 'white' varieties – you can use the petals to make rosewater, which is pleasantly scented, for washing yourself.[14]

In the warmer months, you might also choose to bathe in a nearby stream or river, though this requires caution; some people drown while doing so. In Kingsthorpe near Northampton in 1353, a young adult named Thomas Spicer goes to bathe in the local river, and drowns; his father Peter finds him.[15] In June 1322, Robert Leyre drowns at the *Fisshwarf* (Fishwharf) in London while he is bathing in the Thames. His body is found the next day. The same thing happens to another young man, Thomas Pountager, three years later when he goes to bathe in the Thames one Friday in August at dusk. In July 1343, John Coc of Somerset drowns in the Isis in Oxford while bathing. On this occasion, the danger inherent in John's decision to bathe alone in the fast-flowing river, without a companion to help him or to raise the alarm, is specifically noted. Almost 100 years later, on a hot day in early July 1438, John Walton, an Augustinian canon of the priory of St Frideswide in Oxford, is making hay in the meadow called *Frisewithmede* with his fellows. He goes to bathe and refresh himself in the nearby brook, which has a *lokpole* or 'lock pool', and drowns there.[16]

Medieval people generally feel that it is a good thing to hear Mass as often as possible, and especially first thing in the morning. After Mass you might choose to break your fast, though as breakfast is not a big or important meal in the Middle Ages, this will be merely a light snack of perhaps bread and cheese. The main meal of the day is eaten around 10.00am, and most of the time you will eat pottage consisting of several kinds of vegetable and perhaps some small quantity of meat. Many people crumble pieces of bread into their pottage, but if you are sharing your dish with another person at table, do not do this. Trenchers, thick slices of bread that are about four days old and are squared off with a knife, are often used as plates.[17] Throughout the Middle Ages you can always buy a loaf of the cheapest bread for a farthing, i.e. ¼d, and it is called a *ferthinglof* in Middle English. Cheap bread is often known as *horsbred* or 'horse bread', and is of low quality but edible. White bread is more expensive than brown, and bakers and baksters (female bakers) must specialise in making either white bread or brown bread but are not allowed to bake both. Types of white bread are *pain demaign* or *paindemaigne*, the most expensive kind (and known as *manchet* by the fifteenth century), *wastel*, the second-best kind, *pouf*, *coket* or *cocket*, and *symnell* or *simnel*, later the name of a kind of fruitcake. Bakers of *pouf*, a light, white bread, are called *freynsshbakers* or 'French bakers'. *Tourte* is rough brown bread, and a *penilof* or a *penitourte* is a large loaf of *tourte* which costs a penny (you can also buy a *halpenilof* or half-penny loaf). In 1375, a loaf of *whete-bred* or wheat bread costs

½d, and for the same price you can buy a loaf of *maslin*, which is a mixture of wheat and rye or barley.[18]

Should you prefer to bake your own bread, you can buy corn in a sack from a *cornmongere*, a corn-seller, then take it to the miller, who is an important figure in any medieval town. The Middle English word for the place where he works is variously *mille*, *milne*, *melne* or *mulle*. You give him your corn to be ground into flour, and it will be carefully weighed first. Once the job is completed, the miller must give the same weight back to you in flour, minus a small amount he will take as his fee. After you have prepared and proved your dough, you can bake it in the oven of a local professional baker or bakster, for which he or she will charge you a small sum. Bakers and baksters often hire a person to operate their oven, and these people are called *furners*; this job title derives from the medieval French word for 'oven', *fourn* or *forne*. As always in medieval English towns, it is wise to exercise caution and to be alert for people doing their best to trick you. In London in 1327, eight bakers and two baksters come up with an ingenious method of stealing their customers' dough. When their neighbours bring their dough to be baked in their professional ovens, the bakers and baksters place the dough on a table called a *moldingborde* (moulding-board). Unbeknownst to their customers, they have all made a small hole in the table and have an accomplice sitting beneath it, who 'bit by bit craftily withdrew some of the dough aforesaid ... falsely, wickedly, and maliciously'. The customers are unlikely to notice, as the amount of dough stolen from each of them is small, but over time, the bakers and baksters build up a sizeable quantity of it. All ten of them are committed to Newgate prison and subsequently locked in the pillory with some of the stolen dough hung around their necks until Vespers (the sunset bell) is rung at St Paul's. This particular con is taken so seriously by the city authorities that they have it proclaimed that anyone else found to have done the same thing in future will be locked in the pillory for an entire day, a remarkably long time given that the usual sentence is an hour or two, and banished from London forever.[19]

The cost of food is comparatively much higher in the Middle Ages than it will be in the twenty-first century, and takes a much higher percentage of people's income than is the case now. In the mid-1310s, a long period of incessant rain means that harvests fail catastrophically two years in a row across England, and in some places three. This leads to the Great Famine of 1315 to 1317, and the price of food rises enormously as a result of the severe shortages. In early 1316, the English parliament attempts to fix the prices of certain victuals so that people can afford to eat: eggs should cost no more than 1d for two dozen (1d for twenty in London), a live fat chicken 1½d, a live fat cow 12s, a fat sheep no more than 14d if shorn, and four pigeons (three in London) 1d. In Newport Pagnell a few years earlier in 1303, a hundred eggs cost 4½d, while in York that same year, four geese cost 14d while an unspecified amount of mutton costs 7d. In Leicester in 1307, four chickens cost 4d and two capons 5d.[20] In London in 1363, the 'best rabbit' costs 4d, a *fesaunt* or pheasant 2d, a suckling pig 8d, a roast goose 7d, a leg of pork 3d, and a *perdriche* or partridge 5d. In 1378 also in London, ten eggs cost 1d, double the price they were in 1316, three roast pigeons cost 2½d, also much more than sixty years earlier, and a roast capon 6d. If you give your own capon to a professional cook, he will charge you 1½d to prepare it for you, and will charge 2d to prepare a goose.[21]

An English cookbook is produced in the late 1300s and is called *The Forme of Cury*. This means 'the method of cookery' and has nothing to do with Indian food; likewise, the street name which still exists in modern Cambridge, Petty Cury, means the area of the town where cooks and bakers congregate in the late Middle Ages. The recipes in *The Forme of Cury* include *Blank Dessorre*, a dish with almonds and wine, *Caboches in Potage*, a rather fancy-sounding name for cabbage soup, and *Egurdouce*, essentially meat in a sweet and sour sauce. Another cookbook which dates to roughly the same era is known in Latin as *Utilis Coquinario* or 'useful for the kitchen', and includes such delights as *Pyany*, a poultry dish garnished with peonies, *Heppee*, rose-hip broth, and *Primerole*, primrose-flavoured pottage.[22] These cookbooks reveal that in the late Middle Ages, heavy use is made of spices and that the colour and appearance of food is also deemed important. Contrary to an oft-repeated modern belief, spices are not used to disguise the smell and flavour of rotten meat; medieval people are not stupid enough to eat rotten meat unless they are truly desperate, and use spices for the same reason that modern people do, because they enjoy the enhanced flavour.

The people who import and sell spices are called pepperers, while 'spicer' is often used as another word for an apothecary. Later in the Middle Ages, the people who sell spices wholesale are sometimes called *grossours* or grocers, and they will have many painted boxes full of their confections available for purchase.[23] As are all those who sell food and drink to the public, pepperers are subject to strict regulations. In 1316, an ordinance of the guild of pepperers states that they must not put new spices in with old ones or mix items of different prices, and must not moisten any items such as ginger, alum, cloves or saffron to increase their weight when selling them. A few decades later in 1394, a Gloucestershire merchant called Thomas Keys, who works in Stow-on-the-Wold (then called 'Stowe Seint Edward'), is ripped off by a merchant of London, William Whitman. William gives him *setuwale*, later known as valerian, which has gone rotten and is unfit for consumption, instead of the much more expensive 'good powdered ginger' for which Thomas has paid, and gives him 'tansy seed of no value whatsoever' in place of *wormsed* (wormseed or *Artemesia santonica* is still used in modern times for its excellent antiviral properties).[24]

Garlic (*garlek* or *gharlyk*) is very commonly used, and a sauce made from garlic is called *ganselyn*. Black pepper (*broun pepre*, literally 'brown pepper') and peppercorns, ginger, galingale, cumin (*comyne*), cloves (*geloffres*), parsley (*persely*), sage, fennel, white and brown sugar, and anise are other commonly used herbs and spices. Another is *graynes of paradys* or Grains of Paradise, which comes from West Africa and is related to cardamon and black pepper. In the 1320s, saffron costs 4d an ounce, and sugar costs 3½d per quarter. The Middle English word *dighten* or *dyghten* means to prepare food, and in cookery books you will read instructions such as 'Dyght the venyson with broun pepre'.[25]

Because food is expensive and often scarce – medieval England is a place where malnutrition and starvation are not uncommon – strict regulations are enforced on those who produce and sell it. The authorities of medieval towns are keen to ensure that people do not waste their hard-earned money on food that has gone off or on food that weighs less than it should, and, as noted in Chapter 6 above, bakers, butchers and other food-sellers who try to deceive their customers are punished harshly. Suspicion as to the source of the meat you buy will serve you well. In 1348, John Gylessone, who comes from Norfolk and moves to London, admits that he 'found a certain dead sow, thrown out near the ditch without Aldgate', flayed it, and sold its meat in various places across the city. He is punished with the pillory.[26] There is a widespread belief that 'bad air' is hazardous to health, and killing, skinning and burying animals is often forbidden within towns because it is believed to corrupt the air and endanger residents.[27]

In Leicester in 1279, butchers are not allowed to put the same meat out for sale for more than three days, and in London in the thirteenth and fourteenth centuries, butchers may not cut meat for sale after the bells of St Paul's ring for None (mid-afternoon), and any meat they have already cut has to be sold by Vespers or sunset. Selling meat by candlelight is strictly forbidden and you will be punished if you are found to have done so, because the assumption is that if you are trying to sell meat in inadequate light, you are intentionally trying to deceive your customers and the meat is probably bad.[28] The mayor of Nottingham, John Plumptre, holds a great assembly in October 1395 at which he invites residents to air their concerns and complaints, though perhaps comes to regret his decision to do so, as there turn out to be many. One of them is that 'all the cooks of Nottingham' sell meat and fish that are either not prepared properly, or have been kept too long, or have been reheated (*recalefactas* in the Latin original of this written document) and are therefore 'harmful to the human body' (*nocivas corpori humano*).[29]

Middle English words for food are often the same as the English words many centuries later: *brede* or *bred* or *breed*, *chese*, and *butter*, for example. The word *mete*, however, means food in general, not just meat, which is *flessh*. Dairy products are called *white mete*. People in late medieval English towns eat cheese made both in England and in the Champagne region of France, and consume eggs from hens, geese and ducks. The people who sell meat in the modern sense are called *flesshewere*s or *flesshmongeres*, and the part of the town where they work and run their shops is called the *shameles* or *flesshshameles* or *flesshammes*, a word which survives in the modern street name Shambles in York. The part of a medieval town where you can buy chicken, pullets and capons – not turkeys, which will not arrive in England until the sixteenth century – is called the *Pultrie* or Poultry, which also still survives as the name of a street in modern-day central London.

Medieval people eat lots of birds that modern people generally do not, including woodcocks, nightingales, sparrows, plovers, pigeons, doves, turtledoves, larks, peacocks, storks and swans. On the other hand, eating the meat of birds of prey, horses, mares, colts, bulls, mules, wolves, foxes, cats and dogs is frowned upon. For some strange reason, the meat of a bear (*bere* in Middle English) is considered good to eat, and although bears became extinct in Britain well before the Middle Ages, they still exist in Germany in the fourteenth century: the German emperor, Ludwig of Bavaria, dies in 1347 while hunting bears near Munich.[30] So although it might seem unlikely that a medieval English person could possibly have experience of eating bear-meat, it is certainly not impossible. The medieval Church forbids the eating of meat on certain days and at certain times of the year, and on these days, fish is usually eaten instead. At the great food market called the Stocks in London, meat and fish are sold on different days, called flesh-days and fish-days. Alongside the Stocks, the only other places where selling meat and fish is allowed in late medieval London are Bridge Street, Old Fish Street ('Eldefisshestrete'), and 'the Weststrete of the butchers in the parish of Saint Nicholas'.[31]

Pottage, a broth with a base of peas or beans, is very popular, as is frumenty or *furment*, a pottage made partly with wheat. The *fatte of a swyne* is used to make *siewet* (suet), which is also used in pottages.

Growell or gruel, despite the Victorian workhouse connotations which the word has to a modern audience, already exists in the late Middle Ages, and is a pottage thickened with oatmeal. Another alternative is *browet* or *browettys*, a spiced broth made with whatever powdered spices you can get hold of.[32] Street food is popular in medieval towns: you can, for example, buy pasties filled with capon or rabbit (rabbits are called *conyes* or coneys in medieval England), apples from a cart, or, rather less appealingly to modern tastes, eels from a bucket. In 1388 in London, it is ordained that *birlesters* (peddlers of fish) who have oysters, mussels and salted fish to sell must 'always be moving about … from street to street' rather than selling them from a stall or a shop.[33] Pies are also very popular as street food. In 1373, four male cooks of London are appointed to 'exercise supervision over the men of their trade and the *pybakers*' (pie-bakers), and will 'prevent the sale of unhealthy food and the charging of unreasonable prices'.[34]

In 1322, when the teenage nobleman Hugh 'Huchon' Despenser goes on a three-month hunting trip with a group of lower-born companions, the food they consume includes suckling pig, young pigeons, chickens and young chickens, pheasant at a cost of 8d each, a rabbit on two occasions at a cost of 4d and 5½d, eggs, onions, half a gallon of vinegar, 'white grease', fennel, galingale powder, unspecified 'sauce', freshwater fish, butter, milk, almonds and rice. Almonds (*almandes*) and rice (*ris*) are often bought and used together, always with double the quantity of almonds to that of rice. Probably, *Blawmanger*, literally 'white food' in medieval French, is prepared with these ingredients; it is a hugely popular dish consisting of rice, almonds, almond milk, chicken and white grease. Saffron, which costs a pricy 4d per ounce, is purchased several times during the trip, though almost certainly only to flavour the food of young Huchon Despenser, a great-grandson of King Edward I Longshanks, rather than the food of his companions of vastly lower rank.[35]

Even in late medieval towns, and surprisingly even in London, many people have fruit trees in their gardens. If you have no space or no inclination to grow your own, those who sell fruit as a profession are called *fruters* or *fruterers* if male and *frutesteres* if female, and you can buy apples, pears, figs, quinces, cherries, plums, medlars, sloes, strawberries, mulberries (*morberies*) and peaches (*pesshes*) from them. The earliest known varieties of English apples are pearmains, cultivated from *c.*1200 onwards, and costards, first recorded in the late 1200s. Some people walk around the streets selling costard apples from a cart or a tray and are called costers. If you are buying in bulk, a hundred apples cost a shilling, and a hundred pears cost two shillings.[36] When Edward II spends a few days in Leicester in early July 1317, he is given strawberries and cream, 560 years before the annual tennis tournament at Wimbledon – which famously serves them, and at the same time of year – is founded. This is amusingly written in the records of the borough of Leicester as *crem et streberiis*, which reveals that the clerk who compiles this entry does not know the correct Latin words for these items and pretends that the English words are in fact Latin (the Middle English word for 'strawberries' is almost exactly the same as the modern word, *strawberies*; the real Latin word would be *fraga*).[37] They must have been tiny wild strawberries and cream from the top of the milk. Evidently a fan of *white mete* or dairy, Edward II, surprisingly, buys four cows in 1326 to provide 'milk for the king's mouth'; it is very rare for medieval adults to drink milk.[38]

The 'gardeners of the earls, barons, bishops, and of the citizens' of London petition the mayor, John Hamond, in August 1345. They wish to continue selling the garden produce of their employers in the same place where they have always sold it, in front of the Church of St Austin, at the side of the gate in St Paul's churchyard. Hamond and the aldermen, however, decide that this fruit and vegetable market was a 'nuisance to the priests who are singing Matins and Mass' in St Austin's and to clerks and laymen passing by 'in prayers and orisons'. Residents have also complained about the 'scurrility, clamour and nuisance' of the gardeners' market, and they are therefore ordered to move to the space between the south gate of St Austin's churchyard and the garden wall of the Blackfriars' convent.[39] Vegetables often eaten in medieval England include onions, white and red cabbages (*caboches* or *coul/cool*), beans, peas (*pesen*), leeks (*poret* or *porreette*), spinach (*spynache*), beets, and lettuce (*letews*), and green vegetables are collectively known as *wortes*.[40]

Less healthily, you can indulge a sweet tooth in late medieval England if you happen to have one, though nothing like to the same extent as in modern times given that sugar is rare and expensive, though of course you can sweeten things with honey as well. Marchpane, an early version of marzipan, is made with ground almonds, sugar and rosewater. *Wafres* or wafers made from sheep's milk and sweetened are very popular, as are *eyrekakis*, cakes made from eggs, and *rastons*, a type of sweet bread also made with eggs and eaten hot with butter.[41] In 1325, Edward II gives his pregnant niece Lady Despenser two gallons of honey to make *sucre de plate*, apparently a kind of icing sugar.[42] The honey costs two shillings. Dried and sweetened fruits such as raisins and dates are much consumed, as are figs (*fyggis*).

Contrary to the popular image of medieval people gnawing on bones then throwing them to large hounds prowling around the dining hall, table manners are extremely important in the late Middle Ages. A fifteenth-century text whose aim is to instruct young people how to behave properly states that they must wash their hands and nails before eating, cut their bread with a knife rather than break it with their hands, eat their pottage quietly and not leave the spoon in the dish when they are finished, clean their knife on some bread and certainly not on the tablecloth, not lean or place their elbows on the table and to be careful not to spill things on the tablecloth, not to pick their nose, teeth or nails at table, and to wipe their mouth clean with a cloth every time they have drunk from a cup. They are strictly instructed not to pick up food with their hands or bring a knife to their mouth, to cut their meat daintily rather than hacking at it, and to clean themselves and their utensils once they have finished. Gobbling your food, eating with your mouth open, talking with your mouth full, and blowing on your food to cool it are all frowned upon, as is allowing cats and dogs in the dining area. A medieval proverb states that 'Good manners always make good men', or as William Wykeham puts it when he founds Winchester College in 1379, 'Manners makyth man'.[43] Forks are usually said to

Broad Gate in Ludlow, Shropshire, a thirteenth-century gateway.

Photos by author unless stated otherwise.

Where Dinham Gate, demolished in the late 1700s, once stood in Ludlow.

Part of the town walls of Ludlow, built in the thirteenth century.

Lendal Tower, York, built *c.*1300 as part of the city defences.

Monk Bar, York, built around the early 1300s, with the wickets for pedestrians on either side.

Bootham Bar, another of the four medieval gateways into York.

Town Walls Tower, Shrewsbury, a fourteenth-century watchtower that once formed part of the town's defences.

The Olde Black Bear Inn in Tewkesbury, claimed to be the oldest in Gloucestershire, founded in 1308.

St Mary's Water Gate, Shrewsbury, sometimes also known as Traitor's Gate since the Civil War. Built in the thirteenth century, it provided access to the town from the River Severn.

Ludford Bridge over the River Teme in Ludlow, built in the early fifteenth century.

A packhorse bridge over the River Clun in the village of Clun, Shropshire, built around 1450. (*Mike Finn on Flickr*)

The Talbot in Southwark, which stood on the site of the Tabard Inn. The Tabard was founded in the early 1300s and made famous a few decades later in the *Canterbury Tales*. (*Public domain*)

The fourteenth-century Saint John's Gate and the church of Saint John on the Wall, Bristol, in 1818. (*Public domain*)

Saint John's Gate and Saint John on the Wall in the twenty-first century. (*Tim Green on Flickr*)

The Shambles in York, a narrow medieval street that was once the location of the butchers' shops in the city.

LITTLE SHAMB
Little Shambles Jewellers
W. HAMOND
YORK
THE ORIGINAL WHITBY JET SHOP
8

A late medieval packhorse bridge at Allerford in Somerset. (*Dave Morton on Flickr*)

Westminster Hall in 1809. (*Public domain*)

The Palace of Westminster and Westminster Abbey in the sixteenth century. (*Public domain*)

have come into use in England in the seventeenth century, though in 1312 Edward II owns 'three silver forks for eating pears' (*trois furchesces dargent pur mangier poires*).[44] And medieval people's teeth, though they may be worn from eating coarse grain, are better than you might think, given that sugar is a rare treat. The thirteenth-century physician Gilbertus Anglicus ('Gilbert the Englishman') suggests drying your teeth with a linen cloth after eating to ensure that food does not stick to them and rot them. Picking your teeth after eating, with a fingernail or your knife, should not be done; instead, use a toothpick.[45]

Chapter 8

Water, Wine and Ale: Drink and Taverns

Your choice of beverages is extremely limited: you will not find orange juice, fizzy drinks, milkshakes, or coffee, which will not arrive in England until the 1600s. This is also the case for tea, that apparently quintessentially English beverage. Your main choices are essentially water, wine, or ale, and it is not the case that no one in the Middle Ages drinks water, as some people a few centuries later assume. A fifteenth-century text states that *watre drynke the bestes*, 'water is the best to drink'.[1] In central London, the Great Conduit provides water for residents from the River Tyburn, several miles away, via underground pipes, and in July 1345 Edward III states that its purpose is for 'rich and middling persons' to have fresh water to prepare food and for the poor to have something to drink.[2] Those who consume a great deal of it must pay, such as fishmongers who use water for washing their produce and brewers who make ale with it, but it is free for everyone else. You can take vessels to the Conduit for filling, then carry them home. The vessels will generally be earthenware.[3] Londoners who do not live close to the Great Conduit can use the Thames instead whenever they need water – though as a lot of filth is dumped in it, this requires considerable caution – or one of the smaller rivers that flow through London. This is also the case for residents of other towns: you can go to the local river or stream and fill your vessels.

Medieval engineering and water supplies are more sophisticated than you might think. Saint Augustine's Abbey in Bristol (later Bristol Cathedral) has an 'underground leaden conduit' at Clifton, a mile and a half away, in the 1300s. In 1327, the Franciscan friars of Southampton begin to make an underground conduit from a well called 'Colewell' in the village of Shirley 'as far as *Houndewellecrouche*, and thence by

King Street to their dwelling-house'. This is a total distance of about 2½ miles, an impressive feat that is, however, dwarfed by the ambitious building programme of the Dominican friars of Boston in Lincolnshire that same year. They begin to construct a subterranean conduit to their house in Bolingbroke, 15 miles away.[4]

Wells are extremely common, and in Nottingham, the 'common well' is repaired in 1396 at a cost of 7s 7d, which includes 12d for two cartloads of stone for paving it.[5] They can, however, be dangerous; children, and on occasion adults, drown in them. The number of young children who drown in wells or in ponds is horribly high. At the end of the 1320s, 2-year-old John Dylly drowns in the well in his father Thomas's garden in Thurning, Northamptonshire, and the following year in Titchmarsh also in Northamptonshire, a little girl named Miriell, also 2 years old, drowns in the well belonging to her parents Elye and Maud Fishere.[6] Henry Scot falls into a well in Bread Street ward in London while drawing water and drowns. Whenever this happens, the well in question is covered or blocked up and is no longer allowed to be used.[7] In Oxford in June 1344, Maud Gareford draws water from a well belonging to a neighbour, John Swanebourne, but slips and falls in. Although she manages to clamber out with the help of a ladder, in going home she falls down and dies in the street. The jurors investigating the matter claim that the cause of death is that 'she fell in the well', though they do not explain how. John Swanebourne is ordered to fill up the well and threatened with a fine of 20 shillings if he fails to do so. Two men die at the bottom of a well in Oxford in July 1389: a weaver named Reynald Heliboth goes down a well to fetch the bucket (*bokette*) which had fallen in, and 'utterly suffocated from want of air'. Another man, Thomas Sclattere, 'perceiving that he was a long while in the well', tries to help him, but supposedly also suffocates at the bottom of the well.[8]

Almost everyone drinks ale, i.e. beer without hops; it is a mildly alcoholic fermented beverage made with water and barley and flavoured with various herbs. You can always buy a gallon (3.8 litres) of ale for a penny, while higher-quality ale costs 1½d per gallon, which rises to 2d late in the fourteenth century. If you do not wish to consume an entire gallon of ale, you can also buy it by the *potel* (half a gallon, 2 quarts, or 1.9 litres) or by the quart. In some parts of medieval England, a *quarte* is also called a *stope*. Ideally, ale is not drunk until it is five days old, though it will start to go off not too long after that and should be consumed while it is still reasonably fresh.[9] If you feel unwell, you will be given *caudell*, a hot drink of spiced ale or wine, and another drink is *boulie* or *boulye*, made with water, *leavyn* (leaven, a raising agent) and *wurte* (wort).[10] In the summer of 1326, England experiences a terribly hot few months and a widespread drought. Two chroniclers say that the level of the River Thames falls so low that it is overwhelmed by the sea, and that many people complain about the ale made from the salty river water, which tastes foul.[11] Just under half a century later, the summer of 1375 is also an extremely hot and dry one, and in London on 20 July, the mayor orders that there should be a large cask (*kowve* is the word he uses) full of water outside every house 'during the present and intensely hot and dry season'.[12] This is mostly in case fires break out, but also in case any residents out and about in the streets are struggling with the heat and need to slake their thirst.

An early mention of beer (*bere*, *beere* or *byre*), as opposed to ale, occurs in 1372, though it is considered inferior to ale at this early date and for a few decades more.[13] When Henry V's army besieges the French city of Rouen in 1418, some brewers of London provide large amounts of ale and beer for the soldiers' refreshment. For the ale, they receive £300 for 200 tuns, but for the beer, only £200 for 300 tuns.[14] This assumed inferiority is, in part, nationalistic: ale is deemed English, while beer comes from the part of continental Europe which late medieval England calls Alemayne, i.e. Germany and the Low Countries, and thus is foreign. A fifteenth-century text talks of '*ale of Englond, byre of Alemayne*'. In 1436, Henry VI's government issues a proclamation that beer is in fact a 'wholesome drink, especially in summertime' and that those from Holland and Zealand who brew it in England can continue to do so. English brewers have been making 'malevolent attempts' to claim that this imported product, crafted by foreigners, is 'poisonous and not fit to drink, and caused drunkenness'. Those who make beer are called *berebruers*, 'beer-brewers'.[15]

In much the same way that bakers must specialise in making either brown or white bread but not both, taverners are allowed to sell either *Renys* (Rhenish, i.e. white) wine or Gascon (*rede wyn*, red wine) but not both. It is not even permitted to keep both kinds of wine in the same cellar. Rhenish wine costs a maximum of 8d a gallon in the early fourteenth century and 10d in the last decades of the century, and Gascon wine a maximum of 4d, later 6d, a gallon. There are also dessert wines and spiced wines for sale, such as Oseye from Spain, Crek or Cret (from Crete), Vernage or Vernache (from Tuscany), Ypocras or Hippocras, Ryvere, Muscadel, Malveysin, and Romeneye. These must cost no more than 6d a gallon.[16] Anyone found to be selling wine that has gone bad will see it poured away in the street by people employed by the authorities to check it, and repeat offenders will be sentenced to the pillory after being forced to drink some of it, as noted in Chapter 6 above.[17] The English climate is changing; around the year 1300, the Medieval Warm Period gives way to the start of the centuries-long Little Ice Age, which reaches its coldest temperatures around the middle of the seventeenth century. The south of England has a flourishing wine industry in the thirteenth century when its climate is still very warm, and even as late as 1359, the Gloucestershire town of Tewkesbury still has vineyards.[18] *Mede* or mead, an alcoholic drink made of honey, is also often drunk, as is *syther* or cider.

To drink wine or ale to excess and to be drunk is frowned upon, but of course often happens anyway.[19] Late medieval England has no particular taboos around women drinking alcohol or being drunk, and generally they are not judged more harshly for doing so than men are.[20] Brewing ale is a job often done by women in late medieval England, and a woman who does so is called a *brewstere* or a *brewyfe* ('brew-wife'). Nor is there any prohibition on women owning and running taverns, and female tavern-keepers are called *tappesteres* while ale-sellers are called *alekonners*.[21] Female taverners of the fourteenth century in London include Alice atte Laneende, Agnes Ballard, Katherine Oveseye and Sarra Strubby of Fleet Street, and in 1341 Simon of Canterbury leaves his tavern to his wife Isabel for life, after which it will pass to their daughter, Alice. Katherine Cook runs a tavern in London in the early 1370s, renting it from its owner, Stephen Godwyne. She enjoys her job so much that when her three-year lease is up in 1374, she refuses to surrender the tavern to Stephen's putative new tenant, John Pioun. Stephen tells John that he should 'talk nicely' to Katherine to induce her to give up the tavern to him, but to no avail (an interesting reminder that although women are not legally equal to men in medieval England, they do not necessarily feel any obligation to obey men or to do what men want them to do).[22] In Nottingham in the 1370s, some women who work as *brewsteres* are Isabel Southwell, Cecily Bradmere, Margaret Wilford, Agnes Deynteth and Alice Bereman, and a female tavern-keeper is Elisote Tapester, whose establishment is located 'in a lane'.[23] A tavern called the *Bell* in fifteenth-century Leicester is run by the *tappestere* Amia Vylers, while another Leicester tavern of the same era is called the *Gorge* or George.[24]

Throughout the late Middle Ages, taverns are often run out of people's homes. At an uncertain date in the thirteenth century, Rose Bokland keeps a tavern at her home in Plymouth; there is a tavern in the grange of William the local miller in Stanway, Essex in 1277; and in the 1290s Walter Eyton runs one in his home near the east gate of Chester. A century later at the end of the 1300s, Rose Asshe runs a tavern in her home near St John's Gate in Bristol.[25] Henry Hales meets his friend William Lemman at a tavern in Rockbeare, Devon one October evening in 1265, though Henry is only 15. They probably do not stay out too late: in London in September 1410 and again in June 1413, taverns are forbidden to stay open past 9.00pm.[26] In London in 1309, there are, according to the St Paul's annalist, 354 taverns.[27] Assuming a city population of 80,000, this equates to one tavern for every 225 people, or if there are 100,000 residents of the city, one for every 282 people.

Taverns often provide bread as well as ale and wine, and one in London in the early 1300s sells half-penny loaves to customers.[28] In the early 1300s, Thomas of Lancaster, earl of Lancaster and Leicester, a nephew of Edward I Longshanks, holds a feast at the tavern run by Henry Mercer in Leicester, and on another occasion the earl's household eat at a tavern in the town belonging to Simon of the Buttery. Sir John Chandos, a knight of the earl's household, consumes bread and five quarts of wine at a Leicester tavern run by Stephen Giffard, at a cost of 8½d.[29] Taverns are also places where people met their friends to play games and drink to excess, sometimes – as in later centuries as well – to unpleasant effect. In Canterbury in 1268, a group of twenty-two young men who include several sets of brothers, called 'wilful and quarrelsome youths', spend 'night and day' in their local tavern, and 'played and drank there and quarrelled on the way home'. Not all tavern visits and games end in quarrels and fighting, of course. Friends called Henry Bateman and William Gamelingey play *penyperche* (see Chapter 13 below) in the tavern run by another friend, John Mareschal, at his home in Eaton, Bedfordshire in June 1300. One Monday evening just before Christmas 1323, Stephen Lenne plays at 'tables', i.e. a board game such as chequers, for money with Arcus Rikelinge of Brabant (in modern-day Belgium) in a tavern run by William Staneforde in London.[30]

As few people would be able to read a tavern's name written on its sign, a pictorial image is used instead, and is often a wooden carving hung within a hoop. Taverns, therefore, are often called things like *Bere* [bear] *in the Hoop*, *Aungell* [angel] *in the Hoop*, *Swanne in the Hoope*, *Fesaunte* [pheasant] *on the Hope*, *Lyon* [lion] *in the Hoope*, *Cok in the Houpe*, *Swerd* [sword] *in the Hope*, *Mayden in the Hoope* and *Sterre* [star] *in the Hoope*, and the carving will represent a bear, an angel, and so on. Some towns ordain that no tavern should have a stake which extends more than 7 feet into the street, with a penalty of 40d imposed for longer ones. As well as the tavern's pictorial name, some of them have branches and vines hung outside to make it clear to all that they provide wine.[31] In the 1300s, taverns in London which do not have a 'hoop' name include *Drinkewaterestaverne* or Drinkwater's Tavern, owned and run at the north end of London Bridge by Thomas Drinkewatere,

Chirchegatetaverne or Churchgate Tavern, run by William Chirchegate, *Paulestaverne* (Paul's Tavern), the Tumbling Bear (*ubi le Bere tombeth*, 'where the bear tumbles'), the *Catfethele* (Cat and Fiddle), and the *Lioun atte Dore* (lion at the door). In the 1400s, there are the *Mone* (moon), the *Sonne* (sun), the *Boreshede* (boar's head), the *Flourdelys* (fleur-de-lis), the *Sarsynhede* or *Saresinshed* (Saracen's head) and the *Cardinalshatte* (cardinal's hat).[32] On the other side of the Thames in Southwark stands the Tabard, founded in the early 1300s and made famous a few decades later in Geoffrey Chaucer's *Canterbury Tales*; it is the inn where his characters meet and set off on pilgrimage to the shrine of St Thomas Becket in Canterbury. Another Southwark inn is the White Hart, first mentioned in the early 1400s but almost certainly dating to Richard II's reign (1377–1399), as the white hart was his symbol. Some medieval inns still exist in the twenty-first century, such as Ye Old Trip to Jerusalem, Ye Old Salutation Inn and the Bell Inn in Nottingham, the Olde Black Bear in Tewkesbury, Gloucestershire, and the New Inn in Pembridge, Herefordshire.

Chapter 9

Surcotes and Scrimpyn: Clothes

As you walk around a medieval town, what will the people around you be wearing? To a great extent, that depends on which decade you visit, because, as in later centuries, fashions change and evolve, and what is trendy in the 1270s will be deemed uncool and frumpy by the 1320s. One thing you will notice is that everyone covers their head, men as well as women; men wear hats, caps, coifs or the hoods of their cloaks pulled over their heads, and women wear headdresses, veils, coifs or cauls. Caul is spelt *calle*, and the people who make and sell such items are *calleres* if male and *callesteres* if female. The medieval word for a close-fitting cap or coif is *huve* or *houwe*, and the people who make and sell them are *hurers*. Hats are often made of felt or of beaver skin.[1]

One important thing you will notice immediately is that people wear very different clothes depending on their rank and status. The first sumptuary laws in England are passed in 1363 – though informally are in place long before that – and dictate what materials everyone is allowed to wear, and even how much embroidery they are allowed to have on their clothes. Only members of the nobility are allowed to wear gold jewellery, for example, and people who work on the land may only wear rough russet cloth of poor quality that is either white, black or grey and costs 11d to 14d an ell (45 inches), with a belt made of rope. Cloth worn by the wealthy will be many times more costly and will be much softer and more colourful. You can buy cloth by the ell from a draper or a mercer, and the latter tends to sell fabrics of a higher quality. You will either have to make all your garments yourself or pay someone to do it; either a *sower* (person who sews), a *taillour* (tailor) or a *shepstere* (seamstress or dressmaker). Those who specialise in dying clothes are dyers, and the *paintures* or pigments which they use include azure, verdigris (*grene of Spayne* or 'green of Spain'), vermilion (*vermeyllon*) and bright yellow.[2]

People wear *mantellis* or cloaks (often called *heukes* or *hewkes* if they have a hood); *frockes*, also called *surcotes* or supertunics, which is an overgarment either without sleeves or with sleeves that are shorter than the sleeves of the undergarment; *cotes* or tunics; and *hosen* or leggings. Men will wear shirts, belts, *doblettes* (doublets, a tight-fitting garment that covers the body from the neck to the hips or thighs), *paltoks* or *courtepies* (short jackets), and *cotes hardies*, a close-fitting surcoat often with a hood. This latter garment is also often worn by women over a kirtle or gown and undergown. Women also wear a simple shift under their gowns.[3] In late 1325, Edward II buys very pricy black and vermilion medley cloth to make elbow-length cloaks for a group of carpenters working for him, and at around the same time pays 30 shillings for eighteen ells of 'clear blue English cloth' to make *cotes hardies* for the wives of five of his servants.[4] In 1362, a man's robe made either of *say* (a woollen cloth like serge) or *sendal* (a type of light silk) costs 18d, and one made of *bokeram* (a type of linen or cotton cloth) costs 14d; a *cote* with a hood costs 10d; a woman's gown containing both *say* and *sendal* costs 30d; and a pair of sleeves costs 4d.[5] In Leicester at the end of the 1200s, a woman's supertunic or *surcote* of blue fabric costs 4s, and another one, worn by the wife of a tanner and trimmed with squirrel fur, costs 8s.[6]

The phrase 'a robe of/with three (or four or five) garments' is often found in medieval documents, and means a complete set of clothes, an entire matching outfit. A robe of three garments might consist of a *cote*, *surcote* and *mantel*, and one of four garments made for a man would be a *cote*, *surcote*, *mantel* and shirt. Throughout the fourteenth century in England, women wear sideless gowns with another gown underneath in a contrasting colour. The cut-out at each side of the gown is either square or oval depending on what is fashionable at the time, and as the century progresses, the side-less part of the gown becomes larger and larger until eventually there is just a strip of fabric at the front. Buttons become common in England and elsewhere in Europe in the thirteenth and fourteenth centuries, and tightly buttoned sleeves on women's garments become fashionable. The glorious effigy of Blanche Mortimer, Lady Grandisson (d. 1347) in the church of St Bartholomew, Much Marcle, Herefordshire, shows her wearing a tight-fitting garment with a long row of small buttons from wrist to elbow. Pockets in clothes do not, for the most part, exist, and people use purses to carry money and small items instead, which are attached to their belt with a strap.

In the colder months of the year, you will need to wear some kind of fur to keep warm. As a modern person, you may shudder in revulsion at the thought of wearing the skins of dead animals about your person, but you have little choice unless you want to freeze in winter. The most expensive kinds are miniver (white or light grey fur made from the winter coat of the squirrel) and ermine (the white fur of the winter coat of stoats). Cheaper kinds include budge or sheepskin, *stradlynge* (fur of the squirrel between Michaelmas and winter), *roskyn* (fur of the squirrel in summer), *stranglin* (fur of the squirrel around Michaelmas, 29 September), *polan* (fur of the black squirrel), and *gris* or *grisevere*, 'grey fur'. A particularly poor-quality and cheap fur is *scrimpyn*. Fur is often known as *greywerke* and furriers as *greywerkers* in Middle English, and a fur-lined or fur-trimmed cloak is called a *pilche*, i.e. pelisse.[7] In her will of 1376, Margery Broun leaves 'a mantel of a colour called *violette*' which has a hood and is furred with *gris*.[8] Beaver skin is also often used as fur, and in December 1324, John 'Jankyn' Harsik of Norfolk pays 24d for six pieces of otter-skin to make himself a jerkin.[9] You will pay about 2d for a basic pair of gloves or mittens to keep your hands warm in winter, and for those with a higher income, leather from a stag or a hart is used to make gloves. If you cannot afford that, leather made from dog or sheep skin is the alternative.[10]

Noblewomen and noblemen, and wealthy merchants, sometimes bequeath some of their clothes to their servants when they make a will. Clothes are, of course, all stitched by hand and made individually, and are far too precious just to throw away simply because they have become rather worn or because their wearer is dead. This is the medieval equivalent of donating 'pre-loved' clothes which you no longer wear to a charity shop or a dress agency. In her will of September 1355 – though she does not die until November 1360 – Elizabeth, Lady de Burgh leaves five 'robes with the garments' to five of her ladies in waiting, and lists the five from second best to sixth best; the best set is not specifically mentioned, and it may be that Elizabeth wishes to be buried in them. Her attendant Elizabeth Torel is given the second best set, Agnes Southam is given three garments of the third best – a *cote* (tunic), *surcote* (overtunic) and *mantel* (cloak) – and Alison Wodeham receives the sixth best set (*ma sisme meillurs robe*). A few decades later in 1392, the Spanish duchess of York, Isabel of Castile, bequeaths numerous items to relatives, friends and servants. These include her best gown and her best *mantel* furred with miniver, which she leaves to her attendant Marie Saint Hilaire, while three other gowns furred with miniver are left to three other female attendants.[11] Miniver is extremely expensive, so these are very generous bequests. As most medieval people are desperately poor, clothes must be made to last for as long as possible, and the Middle English word for mending a garment is *stoppe*, used in the sense of filling in or stopping up holes that have appeared in the fabric.

People cover their heads all year round. The working men depicted in the Luttrell Psalter, made in the 1330s or thereabouts, wear coifs or hoods pulled over their heads, and the long peak of the hood falls past their shoulders. Edward II in the 1320s owns a black hat lined with red velvet and decorated with butterflies made of pearls and a white hat lined with green velvet and decorated with gold trefoils. When his wife Isabella of France moves to England in early 1308, her trousseau includes two gold circlets and three hats adorned with rubies and emeralds, and Isabella's daughter-in-law Philippa of Hainault wears 'a hood made of brown scarlet studded with 154 stars of pearls and trimmed with gold'.[12] Two noblewomen depicted eating at a table in the Luttrell Psalter wear their hair pinned in coils at each side, with a narrow band of material around their head holding in place a diaphanous veil, which falls down their backs. Their hair is visible, not bundled away under a thick, heavy headdress.

The effigy of Elizabeth, Lady Despenser, who dies in 1359 and is buried in Tewkesbury Abbey in Gloucestershire, depicts her in a square headdress which is surely the height of contemporary fashion. Both the Luttrell Psalter and the effigy of Blanche, Lady Grandisson in Much Marcle show that fourteenth-century noblewomen often cover their neck, chin and the sides of their faces with a wimple, and in Leicester at the end of the 1200s, a wimple and coif cost 4d.[13] When 17-year-old Costanza of Castile arrives in England in 1371, her new husband John of Gaunt, duke of Lancaster, purchases almost 500 pearls to make a 'fret', i.e. a headdress of interlaced wire decorated with jewels, for her. Two years later, the duke buys two fillets, headbands also made of interlaced wire, for his daughters, 13-year-old Philippa and 10-year-old Elizabeth. Each has three balas rubies and twenty-eight pearls.[14] The effigy of John's mother Philippa of Hainault, Edward III's wife and queen, in Westminster Abbey wears a reticulated headdress, where the hair is encased on either side of the head in bags made of gold or silver thread. As the fourteenth century passes into the fifteenth, women's headdresses become larger and more elaborate. Beatriz of Portugal, countess of Arundel and Huntingdon (*c*.1380/82–1439), is depicted on her effigy wearing a horned headdress of astonishing width and height, with material draped over the two points and her hair gathered in large coils at each side of her head and encased in jewelled hairnets. Headdresses called hennins, in the shape of a cone and often remarkably high, also become popular, while another popular horned style of the fifteenth century is the bourrelet or escoffion, made from a thick padded roll of material. Men's hats also become much heavier and more elaborate in the fifteenth century, and often consist of a yards-long piece of cloth wrapped around the head in different styles.

Medieval women almost always have very long hair. The trend for much of the fourteenth century is for men to have long hair as well, shoulder-length or longer, parted in the middle and falling either side of their face. The effigy of Edward III, who dies in 1377, depicts him with wavy hair past his shoulders that is even longer than the curly long hair worn by his father Edward II. Edward III is, however, 64 years old when he dies, and it seems that his flowing locks are a fashion of his youth which have, by the time of his death, gone hopelessly out of style. His grandsons Richard II (d. 1400) and Henry IV (d. 1413), both of whom are 10 years old when Edward dies in 1377, are shown with much shorter hair. Portraits of Henry IV's four sons, Henry V (d. 1422) and the dukes of Clarence, Bedford and Gloucester, depict them with hair so short that it looks, peculiarly, as though they are wearing caps; their hair is cut halfway up the backs of their heads. The effigy in St Mary's church in Warwick of Richard Beauchamp, earl of Warwick (1382–1439), shows him with extremely short but delightfully curly hair. Whether a man wears a beard and/or a moustache is generally a matter of personal taste, rather than a fashion issue; some men are clean-shaven, others are not.

Living in England, you will, of course, need to deal with frequent rain, and surprisingly, umbrellas are not in use until after the Middle Ages; your cloak will have to protect you from wet weather instead. In Hamstead near Birmingham, it is raining hard when the brothers Richard and Stephen Honesworth come out of their local tavern, which is located in the home of Geoffrey the miller of Hamstead, around sunset on Sunday, 4 July 1288. Stephen is wearing only a light summer tunic, and asks his sister-in-law Juliane to shield him from the worst of the rain with her cloak.[15] Finally, spectacles have a longer history than you might imagine; the first known pair of glasses is made by a monk in Italy in the thirteenth century. Walter Stapledon, bishop of Exeter, founds Exeter College at the University of Oxford in 1314 and is murdered in London in the autumn of 1326 during the chaos that accompanies the end of Edward II's reign. An inventory of the bishop's possessions made shortly after his death includes *unum spectaculum cum duplici oculo*, literally 'one spectacle with a double eye' or rather with two lenses, valued at 2 shillings. This is the first recorded pair of glasses in England.[16]

Chapter 10

Eme, Mome and Cousyns Germain: Family Relations

Your father and mother – particularly your father – have more control over your life even when you are an adult than will be the case in England a few centuries later. In the fourteenth and fifteenth centuries, children and young people are taught to 'worship' their parents and 'serve them with all thy might'. It is considered respectful and appropriate to treat your parents with great reverence, and if you have not seen them for a while, kneel and ask them for their blessings on you. For their part, parents are encouraged to punish their children harshly when it is necessary: *chastyse them with the rodde*.[1]

Confusingly, your mother, your stepmother and your mother-in-law are, especially in the earlier part of the late Middle Ages, all addressed and referred to as your mother (*moder* or *modre* in Middle English). The same goes for your father (*fader* or *fadre*), though later, the words *stepfadre* and *stepmodre* develop. Your grandparents can be called either *godsire* ('good sire') and *goddame* ('good dame') or *belfadre* and *beldame*, and in medieval French the words are *tayon* (m) and *taye* (f). The medieval word for 'uncle' is *eme*, while 'aunt' is more or less the same as in modern English, *aunte*, though the word *mome* also exists. The words for 'brothers and sisters' are often spelt in the same way as in modern English, or otherwise *brethern* and *sustres*. Your first cousins – the children of your parents' siblings – are *cousyns/cosens germains*, 'cousins german', and your cousins by marriage are called *cosens alyed*.[2]

Medieval wills can be deeply confusing: when the will-maker refers to her daughter, does she actually mean her daughter, or is she referring to her granddaughter? Elizabeth de Burgh's will of 1355 is a case in point; she talks about her 'daughter' the countess of Ulster, who is in fact her granddaughter, the daughter of Elizabeth's late son, William de Burgh. Agnes and Isabel Bardolf, named in the will as Elizabeth's 'young daughters', are also really her granddaughters, the daughters of her youngest child Lady Bardolf (Elizabeth de Burgh is 60 years old in 1355 and has been widowed for more than three decades, so cannot have young children of her own). The 1409 will of Elizabeth, Lady Despenser, is another example of this confusion. It mentions her 'daughter' Philippa, who is in fact her granddaughter, the daughter of Lady Despenser's daughter Margaret, Lady Ferrers. In 1399, Edward III's son John of Gaunt, duke of Lancaster, leaves gold cups to two of his many grandchildren, Henry (b. 1386) and John (b. 1389), the future King Henry V and the duke of Bedford. Gaunt refers to both boys as 'my beloved son [*mon tresame filtz*]', though clarifies their identities by also calling them 'son of my dearest son the duke of Hereford' (i.e. the future King Henry IV, often known as Henry of Bolingbroke).[3]

As reliable contraception will not exist for a few more centuries, medieval families are often large, though the mortality rate among children is horrific. King Edward I Longshanks fathers at least seventeen children from his two marriages, and his grandson Edward III has twelve legitimate children and at least three illegitimate ones. Longshanks is, however, survived by only six of those seventeen or more children, four from his first marriage to Queen Leonor and two from his second to Queen Marguerite. Edward's grandson Edward III outlives eight of his and Queen Philippa's dozen children. To have eight, ten or twelve children is relatively common; William Hedrisham, for example, a London victim of the plague in 1349, has seven brothers and two sisters, and near Canterbury in Kent, John Northwode (d. in or not long before 1319) has nine sons and an unspecified number of daughters.[4] The Church prohibits sex during Lent, Advent, on feast days and other occasions, but many people pay little if any heed, and no less a person than Edward III is conceived during Lent in 1312. Contrary to popular modern belief, it is not the case that every medieval person marries and has children at a very young age, and townspeople almost always marry in their mid to late teens or twenties. In almost all cases when at least one person in a couple marries before s/he (more often she) reaches adolescence, there will be a gap of a few years before pregnancy.

Very young mothers, though nowhere near as common as modern people believe them to be, do exist: Margaret Beaufort, the most famous example, gives birth to her only child, Henry Tudor aka King Henry VII, in January 1457 at the age of 13 and 8 months. Joan Montacute is another girl who falls pregnant at a very young age. She is born in Bungay, Suffolk on 2 February 1349, and is already pregnant by her husband William Ufford, who is almost 25 years old, on 14 February 1363, just days after her 14th birthday.[5] The child does not survive, however. Some boys in the late Middle Ages also become fathers at a very young age. When Henry Kelkefeld, son and heir of Pernel and Conan Kelkefeld, is born in Yorkshire in September 1278, their neighbours gossip that Conan is 'of such tender age' when his wife Pernel is pregnant that it is 'commonly said he could not have begotten a child', and after their son Henry's birth, there is 'much talk about it' in the neighbourhood.[6] Conan's age is not stated, but it sounds as though he is perhaps 12 or 13 when Pernel bears their child. Another young medieval father is William Planke. He is born in Curry Mallet, Somerset on 2 October 1325, and Katherine, the eldest of his and his wife Elizabeth Hillary's three daughters, is born in Bescot, Staffordshire on 6 January 1341. William is thus only 15 years and 3 months old when he becomes a father. Katherine is baptised in nearby Walsall on the day of her birth, and two of the men present in the church during her baptism recall a few years later how they see her carried back home amid 'singing and a great concourse of people praising God for her birth'. Fourteenth-century England is a place where people sing and dance with joy when children, including female children, are born.[7]

For women to give birth when they are past 40 is not particularly uncommon, and a woman's period of childbearing is often long. Leonor of Castile, queen of England, is born in *c.*November 1241 and gives birth to her youngest child, Edward II aka Edward of Caernarfon, in

April 1284. Edward III marries his queen, Philippa of Hainault, in January 1328 when he is 15 and she is shortly to turn 14. Philippa gives birth to their eldest child in June 1330 when she is 16 and bears their youngest in January 1355, a quarter of a century later. Much further down the social scale, Katherine Escote is the third and youngest daughter of Eugenia and Adam Bukesgate (d. 1333) and is born on *c.*2 February 1312. She marries Giles Escote and gives birth to their son William in West Tytherley, Hampshire on 26 May 1353, when she is 41 years old.[8]

If you live in the late Middle Ages for long enough, you might decide to find a life partner. At the higher end of society, marriages have little or nothing to do with the personal feelings of the people involved. Rank is of the utmost importance; the king of England marries the king of France's daughter, the earl of Warwick marries the earl of Surrey's sister, Sir Andrew marries Sir Humphrey's daughter, and so on. So-called 'disparagement', arranging someone's marriage to a person of lower rank, is forbidden, and not only for members of the elite. Walter Wolf, a minor landowner from Barnstaple in Devon, dies in the summer of 1352, leaving a baby son, Richard. A few years later in the early 1360s, the prior of Pilton Abbey near Barnstaple arranges a marriage for 10-year-old Richard. The bride is the prior's 12-year-old illegitimate daughter Denise, whom – despite his vow of chastity – he fathered while a monk at Malmesbury Abbey in Wiltshire. As Denise is below Richard Wolf in rank, their marriage is considered to disparage him, which is contrary to the Statute of Merton of 1236. Edward III takes a keen interest in the matter, and sends men to take custody of Richard until it is decided what should be done about the marriage.[9]

The medieval Church insists that those to whom you are related by marriage are every bit as much your family, and therefore every bit as off-limits sexually, as your own blood relatives are. To have a sexual relationship with, say, your late husband's uncle will be deemed as incestuous as having a relationship with your own uncle, and you may be punished by excommunication. You will have to be very careful when choosing a spouse, because marrying a relative of a person with whom you have previously been intimate, even down to your putative spouse's third cousins (the people with whom s/he shares a set of great-great-grandparents), will be considered incest and your marriage will not be valid until such time as the pope issues a dispensation for consanguinity. Even acting as a child's godparent creates a binding tie between families. If you have a goddaughter, and wish one day to marry her mother after her father dies, this will also require a dispensation from the pope. Although it is certainly not unheard of, it is uncommon in the Middle Ages to marry your first cousin, even among royalty. The notorious interbreeding in royal families comes later, and reaches its peak, or perhaps its nadir, between the sixteenth and eighteenth centuries.

If you are a boy or young man under the age of 21, your father or male guardian owns the rights to your marriage and will arrange it for you, and the same applies if you are a girl or woman of any age; your marriage is, or at least it should be legally, controlled by your father, brother or other close male relative. In the spring of 1352, Thomas Staple of Southwark offers his 20-year-old ward John Amory of Leicestershire (b. November 1331) a choice between two brides: Alice Cleet of Berkshire or Isabel St Albans of Surrey. John 'utterly refused both, and of his own accord' marries Eleanor Baryngton instead. An inquiry ordered by Edward III finds that Thomas Staple has lost £200 from John's marriage, and John is ordered to pay Thomas this amount.[10] Marriages at the higher end of society are somewhat akin to mergers between two large companies and are a long way from being a private matter between a couple. Noble people of the late Middle Ages tend to be open about wishing to marry in order to gain a benefit of some kind either for themselves or for their families or both. This benefit will usually be the acquisition of land or money or influential in-laws, or all of them.

If you marry someone who brings you none of these, your contemporaries will regard you uncomprehendingly and scornfully. A prime example is Thomas of Brotherton, earl of Norfolk, born in 1300 as the elder son of Edward I Longshanks and his second wife Marguerite of France. Thomas is the son of a king of England and grandson of a king of France, and in 1320/21, his half-brother Edward II attempts to arrange a marriage for him to Violante, daughter of the king of Aragón in Spain. Given that both Thomas and Violante are the children of kings, this is a highly suitable choice, but when the planned alliance falls through – Violante decides to become a nun – Thomas weds Alice Hales, daughter of the coroner of Norfolk, instead. This is a mismatch that is utterly baffling to his fellow royals and nobles. Almost a century and a half later, Edward IV's marriage to Elizabeth Grey née Woodville, a widow considerably beneath him in rank, also raises many eyebrows. The cheerful admission of the earl of Westmorland's brother Sir John Neville in 1446 that he wishes to marry the dowager duchess of Somerset because of her rich dower lands makes far more sense in the late medieval context.[11] At the lower end of society, marriages are also, at least to a certain extent, arranged, and medieval people, as in all societies, marry those with whom they are most likely to come into contact and those who have a similar background to themselves.

You will usually have much more freedom regarding any second or third marriage you make, and while you must marry to please your family the first time, you are far more likely to be allowed to marry to please yourself the second time. Second, third and even fourth marriages are extremely common, for both men and women, and late medieval England has no cultural expectation that widows must mourn their only husband for the rest of their lives and never re-marry. Elizabeth Arundel is born in the mid or late 1360s as the daughter of the earl of Arundel, and marries the earl of Salisbury's son and heir as her first husband. After he is killed jousting when Elizabeth is still in her teens, she marries the earl of Nottingham, Thomas Mowbray, who later becomes the duke of Norfolk as well. After she is widowed again in 1399 in her thirties, Elizabeth marries one of her late husband's squires, Robert Goushill, in what is clearly a love-match given that she is an earl's daughter and a duchess while he is not even a knight. Widowed for a third time in 1403 when Robert is stabbed to death and robbed by one of his own servants while lying wounded after the battle of Shrewsbury, Elizabeth later marries a fourth husband, Sir Gerard Usflete or Ufflete, and outlives him too. Much lower down the social scale, Rohese Convers loses her husband Robert, a goldsmith of London, shortly before 27 July 1310, and marries her second husband David Cottesbroke very soon afterwards, before 29 August 1310. She marries her third, Nicholas Stratstede, before June 1321.[12]

Women in medieval England tend to disappear from written record when they marry, and will need the permission of their husbands to make a will or undertake legal action. Usually, an Englishwoman who marries a man who owns lands and property and dies before her has the legal right to hold one-third of his lands as dower for the rest of her life. In London, the custom is different: a widow takes 'a third part if there were children, and one half if there were no children'.[13] A man who marries a woman who owns lands has the right to keep all her lands for the rest of his life even if she dies many years before him, but only if they have at least one child together; otherwise, he has no right to any of his wife's lands after her death. The child must live long enough to take a breath, and stillbirths do not count. This custom is known as the 'courtesy of England'. Widows' entitlement to a third (or a half in London) of their late husbands' estate, however, holds in all circumstances, regardless of whether they have children or not, whether she remarries or not, whether she has any lands or wealth of her own, and regardless of how many years she outlives her husband.

If you are invited to a wedding, it will take place at the door of a church or in the porch; as Geoffrey Chaucer's Wife of Bath says, 'housbondes at chirche dore I have had fyve'. The bride and groom will be dressed in the best finery they can afford. In 1241, the child-couple John Giffard and Aubrey Camville both wear green robes when they marry in the church of Cookhill Priory in Worcestershire, and in September 1410, 25-year-old Matthew Honorre of Odell in Bedfordshire has himself a silver belt 'studded with bells' made for his wedding.[14] Weddings are often celebrated by playing football or another type of ballgame. During a wedding procession in Yorkshire in 1268, a local resident asks one of the guests for a ball, 'which it is the custom to give'.[15]

Although intimate relationships outside marriage are frowned upon by the Church and society at large, they happen regularly, and illegitimacy is extraordinarily common. Thomas Werlingworth, born in London in or not long before September 1337, loses his parents Nicholas and Joan in the first massive pandemic of the Black Death in 1349. Tragically, the two guardians subsequently appointed to take care of the 12-year-old boy, a married couple named John and Joan Bret, also die shortly afterwards. Thomas, however, survives both the plague and the loss of his carers and becomes a successful, well-off goldsmith who runs a tavern as well. He has a long-term relationship with a lover, Christine Ippegrave, which results in three sons, John, Thomas and William, born in the late 1350s and early 1360s. Even though Christine also comes from a family of goldsmiths and would seem to be a suitable wife for Thomas, the couple never marry, for reasons that are unclear. In March 1364, Thomas Werlingworth becomes seriously ill, and dies in May 1365, aged just 27. He leaves the house he has inherited from his parents and everything in it to his partner Christine for the rest of her life, and also gives their three young sons £5 each and leaves them in Christine's custody. This is a kindness both to her and to the boys, as in the fourteenth century it is not always a given that a mother will be appointed as her children's guardian, especially when they are born outside marriage.[16]

Another long-term couple who never marry, and indeed would not be able to do so even if they wished to, are Master Richard of Gloucester and Katherine of St Albans. Richard is a lawyer and the parson of Stevenage in Hertfordshire, but despite the vow of chastity he has taken as a member of the Church, he has two sons with Katherine: John, born in 1317, and Nicholas, born in 1319. In his will of 1328, Richard leaves his house and custody of the two boys to Katherine, and they are openly acknowledged as his sons by the authorities and use his name.[17] Richard and Katherine's contemporary, John Ashford, a woolmonger who dies in 1329, fathers six illegitimate children, two sons and four daughters, with two women, Joan Stodleye and Lettice Bilham. John leaves generous bequests to both women and all six of his children.[18] Your lover can be called your *leman* (or *lemman* or *lemmon*) or your *lief* (or *lef* or *lyef*), and both words can be used by men and women about a man or a woman. *Lief* has the meaning of a darling, beloved person, while *leman* has more of a sexual connotation.

Chapter 11

Midovernone and Right Grete Gramercy: Time and Talking to People

You will be aware of the passing of years and will know how old you are, at least approximately, though your birthday is of little or no importance to you. Far more significant is your name-day, the feast of the saint whose name you bear. English people are accustomed to thinking in regnal years rather than calendar years, a system which requires a knowledge of the exact dates on which the present king and his predecessors came to the throne. Edward I's reign begins on 20 November 1272, and his regnal year thus runs from 20 November to 19 November every year, the first from 20 November 1272 to 19 November 1273, the second from 20 November 1273 to 19 November 1274, and so on. The 19th of November 1295 is in Edward's twenty-third regnal year; when you wake up the next morning, it is now his twenty-fourth regnal year. Edward dies on 7 July 1307 during his thirty-fifth regnal year, so his son and successor Edward II's reign begins on 8 July 1307, and his own regnal year runs from 8 July to 7 July. In January 1327, halfway through the twentieth year of his reign, Edward II is forced to abdicate his throne to his teenage son Edward III, whose regnal year runs from 25 January to 24 January.

You are also accustomed to reckoning the date by using saints' days and feast days, so you will not think of a particular date as, say, '27 August 1301' but as 'the Sunday before the Beheading of St John the Baptist in the twenty-ninth year of the reign of King Edward, son of King Henry' (i.e. Edward I, son of Henry III). Edward III is born on what we would call Monday, 13 November 1312, but he and his contemporaries think of it as the Monday after the feast of St Martin in the Winter in the sixth year of his father Edward II's reign, which runs from 8 July 1312 to 7 July 1313. Edward III's brother John of Eltham is born on the feast of the Assumption in their father's tenth regnal year, i.e. on 15 August 1316. Edward III dies on the Sunday before the Nativity of St John the Baptist in his fifty-first regnal year, or 21 June 1377, and is succeeded by his grandson Richard II, whose reign begins on 22 June 1377 and whose regnal year thus runs from 22 June to 21 June. Richard is forced to abdicate his throne to his cousin Henry IV, and the last day of his reign falls on the feast day of St Michael in Richard's twenty-third regnal year, i.e. 29 September 1399. The system does not have the virtue of brevity, but as this is how medieval English people calculate dates you must get used to it, and be able to figure out that 'the feast of the Annunciation, 47 Edward III' means 25 March 1373, and 'Wednesday before St Luke the Evangelist, 9 Henry V' means 15 October 1421.

Some late medieval administrative or financial systems, while still using the present king's regnal year in place of the calendar year, utilise an important Christian festival to mark the start of their accounting period. The mayor of Leicester's accounts, for example, begin every year on 29 September, the feast of St Michael or Michaelmas, and the mayor of London's period of office begins annually on the feast of St Simon and St Jude, 28 October. Medieval popes, meanwhile, still use the old Roman system of Ides, Kalends and Nones. The Ides of March, famous to anyone who has heard of Julius Caesar, fall on 15 March, and if you have cause to receive a letter from the pope, it will be dated something like 'the 17th day before the Kalends of September'. An oddity of medieval date-keeping is the tendency to use formulations such as 'the octaves of the Purification' or 'the quinzaine of Easter'. 'Octaves' is eight days after a particular feast day, including the day itself, so this means a week after the feast day. The feast of the Purification, also called Candlemas, falls on 2 February, and therefore its 'octaves' gives you a date of 9 February. The 'quinzaine' means the same thing except two weeks, not one, so the quinzaine of Easter means the Sunday that falls two weeks after Easter Sunday. And another oddity of English medieval calendars is that the new year is generally deemed to begin on 25 March, the feast of the Annunciation of the Virgin Mary, also known as 'Lady Day'. (The 1st of January is usually known as the feast of the Circumcision.) If you have ever wondered why the modern UK tax year begins on 6 April, a date that seems utterly random, the first part of the answer is that it originally began on 25 March. The second reason is that in 1752, we switched from the Gregorian to the Julian calendar and lost eleven days, so the tax year now began on 5 April. In 1800, which was not a leap year in the Gregorian calendar but would have been in the Julian, another day was added to make 6 April the start of the tax year.

You will be woken around 5.00am or 6.00am by the bells of your local church ringing either for Lauds at dawn or for Prime a little later. Terce or the third hour is 9.00am, midday is Sext or the sixth hour, Nones is the ninth hour or 3.00pm, or simply mid-afternoon generally, and Vespers is sunset. Mid-afternoon is also called *midovernone* in Middle English. The canonical hours are how most people mark time (although hour candles exist, they are mostly used in religious houses and not by the general population). The French expression *entre chien et loup*, 'between dog and wolf', often rendered in Latin as *inter canem et lupem*, is used in late medieval England to describe the time around dawn or dusk, i.e. when it is still mostly dark or is getting dark and it is impossible to differentiate visually between a dog and a wolf.[1]

Richard of Wallingford, born in *c.*1292 as the son of a blacksmith, studies for many years at Oxford and becomes abbot of St Albans in 1327, and shortly afterwards writes a treatise called *Tractatus horologii astronomici*. In it, Richard describes an astronomical clock, and starts to build one which chimes the hours and shows the movements of the sun and stars. Twenty years later, Edward III has himself a mechanical clock made at Windsor Castle, his birthplace and one of his favourite residences. In 1377, the year of Edward's death, it needs a new bell, and on this occasion is called a *clokke* in English (as opposed to Latin or French), one of the earliest recorded uses of the word in our language.[2] Another example occurs the previous year, on 19 May 1376, when a proclamation is made in London that 'no taverner keep his hostel open after the tenth hour has been sounded by the bell called the *clocke*'. In the late fourteenth and fifteenth centuries, the words *clocke* and *belle* are often used interchangeably, and the ringing of the bell which announces early in the morning that it is time for work is called either the *clocke for to goo to werke* or the *belle of werkemen*.[3]

As noted above, few people care about their own birthday or their exact date of birth, and they have no real reason to do so. One exception is the handful of English people who are born into the landowning class and are tenants in chief, that is, they hold land directly from the king. Strict rules apply to such people, and one of them is if that they die when their heir is still underage, the king himself becomes the heir's legal guardian, and the dead tenant in chief's lands are taken into the king's hand. When the heir comes of age – 21 for men, 14 for girls/women if they are already married, or 16 if not – they must prove that they are indeed now of age and are old enough to take possession of the lands that once belonged to their late parent (or grandparent or uncle, etc.). A jury of a dozen or so men – always and only men, never women – is summoned to the heir's birthplace to confirm his or her date of birth, and the jurors give the reason why they remember the date. This is almost the sole occasion in the late Middle Ages when anyone's date of birth is precisely recorded, the only exceptions being births in the royal family and the births of high-ranking noblemen and noblewomen, which are sometimes recorded in chronicles, annals, missals and psalters kept at religious houses. The annals of Wigmore Abbey in Herefordshire, for example, record the birthdates of some members of the important Mortimer family, earls of March and lords of Wigmore. Parish registers which record baptisms, and thus provide approximate dates of birth, do not exist in the Middle Ages; they first appear in the 1530s.

Proofs of age are often illuminating and entertaining. In Higford near Shifnal, Shropshire in December 1308, for example, 60-year-old Hugh Bolledon remembers that Margaret Harle née Brompton was born in Higford on 27 October 1292 because he 'had a son who fled from his house with a greyhound to Huggeford [Higford] on the said day and did not return for two days'.[4] William Haye of Gloucester remembers in August 1305 that John, son of his neighbours Robert and Maud Stallinge, was born on 8 November 1283 because Robert and Maud held a great feast to celebrate John's birth, 'but did not invite him, at which he was angry'.[5] At Beatrix Hauley's proof of age in Louth, Lincolnshire in April 1400, two jurors recall her birth on 22 February 1384 because they and numerous others saw their neighbour Simon Wryght 'caught by a gust of the north wind and blown to the ground' as he was building his new house. Simon broke 'two bones in his right side' but otherwise survived the fall.[6]

As well as becoming familiar with the methods of timekeeping in medieval England, you must abide by the social conventions of the era. When you are out and about in public, it is important to greet everyone you pass with a courteous salutation, perhaps a simple *God morwe* or 'Good morning', or alternatively 'God you save', 'Sire, God you keep', 'God give you good day' or 'Dame, good day give you our lord'. You learnt the rule when very young that as a child, you must greet your parents and the rest of your family every morning with the utmost formality and courtesy, and that when you pass people in the street you must greet them politely too, and doff your cap or hat if you are male. If you stop to talk to someone, it is polite to ask them 'how is it with you?'. You should also enquire politely about their family and ask your conversation partner to pass on your greetings to them: 'Greet me the lady of your house', for example, or 'God gyve her gode happe' (good luck or good fortune). Women are usually addressed as Lady or Dame if older and married or *damoyselle* or *damishel* (young lady) if they are younger, while men can be addressed as Sire if they are of high rank, or as *felawe* (fellow) or *frende* (friend) otherwise. The words 'sire' and 'dame' are also used to refer politely to other people's parents, as in 'Wer es ty sire?' or 'Where is your father?'. *Mome* or 'aunt' is another cordial way to address older women, and the word can either be used alone or in front of the woman's given name, as in Mome Johane. When departing, you should bid the person farewell by saying 'Goo ye to god' (Go you to God), 'To god mote ye be commaunded' (might you be commanded), 'God you have in his holy kepyng', 'God te blis' (God bless you) or 'to God I you commaunde. I take leve of you'.[7]

Medieval England is a strictly hierarchical society, and you must not behave as you would in the twenty-first century, as though almost all men and women you meet are your equals. When you encounter someone of higher rank, it is vital to treat them with respect and deference. If you meet a lord or even, perhaps, the king, you must kneel to him with the right knee all the way to the ground – kneeling on both knees is reserved for God – and remove your cap, hat or hood if you are a man. You do not need to scrape and cringe, however; keep your head up when entering the room where the lord is sitting, maintain a cheery countenance, and say 'God speed' or 'God be here!' to all who are present. Unlike later centuries, when it is forbidden to look directly at the sovereign or make eye contact with him or her, in late medieval times you must look the king, lords, and everyone else in the face while you are talking to them. Wait for a person of higher rank to address you first, stand perfectly still while he or she speaks to you while looking them in the eye, then make obeisance before you answer. Do not turn your back on anyone of higher rank, as far as this is possible. When talking to them, adding 'yf it plese you' will always go down well, as will saying 'right grete gramercy of your courtoys wordes' or 'very many thanks for your courteous words'. People of high rank are, in turn, enjoined to be polite and mild in speech to those beneath them, and not to talk to them insultingly. Although of course many people will fail to obey this injunction, they will be aware that they are indeed breaking a social convention by doing so (as modern people are also aware that they are doing something wrong if they speak rudely to a shop assistant or a server in a restaurant). *Godlynes*, literally 'goodliness' though meaning kindliness or graciousness, is an important social virtue, while *vylonye* or *vilainie* means rudeness or discourtesy and is strongly frowned upon.[8]

Despite this, some medieval knights live on a hair trigger and will react very badly if you do not give them their rightful due, deeming this a dire insult. As they have been highly trained in violence and warfare since childhood, and always carry weapons, this will not end well for you. Sir Roger Swynnerton (*c*.1281–1338) kills Henry Salt in Stafford in the early 1300s because of Salt's 'insulting language' towards him, and a few years later Roger's brother Sir Richard Swynnerton beats Thomas of Warwick almost to death in the middle of Newcastle-under-Lyme market after he decides that Thomas has insulted Roger.[9] And knights are not the only men who are quick to take offence and quick to react with aggression. Late medieval England is a place with a high homicide rate and a considerable amount of violence, and as most men are armed, even minor squabbles can result in someone's death. In September 1323, Jonette Staunton goes out for a walk near Newark in Nottinghamshire with a chaplain named Hugh Whassyngbourn and another man, Henry Mustiers. They encounter three brothers, one of whom, Robert Sireston, is attracted to Jonette, and tries to embrace her. Her two companions, furious, call for help, and three other men answer the call and tell Robert and his brothers Nicholas and Thomas to back off. As the two groups stand shouting abuse at each other, Hugh Whassyngbourn, the chaplain, decides that it is a good idea to attack Robert Sireston with a pitchfork. He wounds him, whereupon Robert draws a knife and stabs Hugh to death.[10] In the same year in Leicester, John Dodeman comes out of a tavern one evening and aggressively accuses Ralph Cokinbred of looking at him and his companion 'with an evil eye'. Ralph tries to placate John and tells him that he wishes him and his friend no harm, and merely wants to go home in peace, but John attacks him with his knife.[11]

You are likely to find yourself in trouble, even hauled up in court, if you are anything less than entirely respectful to public officials (and see also Chapter 6). This happens to Beatrice Langbourne in London in 1364 after she is caught throwing rubbish into the street by her local alderman, Simon Worstede. Beatrice reacts to Simon's reprimand by calling him 'a false thief and an old, crooked yokel', and is arrested and placed in the custody of the two city sheriffs. Ralph Atteswych also appears in court in London in 1376 when he is accused of using 'insulting and opprobrious words' and 'unseemly words' to William Neuport, one of the two sheriffs. A few years later, Simon Driffield is bound over to keep the peace after he insults a man who comes to his door collecting a tax 'on carts and horses, to raise money for cleansing the streets'.[12] Thomas Flete appears before the mayor of London's court in August 1307 after mocking the mayor, John Blount, and the two dozen city aldermen by neighing like a horse whenever they ride past him.[13] Do not make the mistake of assuming that officials have a sense of humour and will appreciate, or even just ignore, your silliness; they stand very much on their dignity. Physically assaulting a public official is likely to see you executed. In 1340, Thomas Haunsard grabs Andrew Aubrey, mayor of London, by the throat while the mayor is attempting to placate a group of people involved in an altercation. Thomas is publicly beheaded in the middle of Cheapside four weeks later.[14]

Serving those of higher rank is considered honourable, not demeaning. The English noble elite rush to perform seemingly menial tasks at the banquet which follows the coronation of 10-year-old Richard II in July 1377. The earl of March, for example, holds the young king's crown above his head as it is too heavy for him to wear comfortably while he eats, the earl of Warwick dispenses the bread, the duke of Lancaster carves Richard's meat, and the earl of Oxford provides the king's water, 'taking the basins and towels'.[15] At the age of about 7 or 8, sons of the nobility are sent to live in other great households, where they will learn how to serve at table and how to comport themselves while doing so. One of the many things taught to them is they should not touch meat with their right hand. Although this is a result of most people being right-handed and carving meat with the right while they hold it with the left, over time it becomes seen as improper to touch meat with your right hand at all. The boys must also learn order of precedence and where to seat people in the dining hall. The mayor of London, for example, is the highest mayor in the land and is equal in rank to the three chief justices of the realm, the Speaker of Parliament, a baron of the exchequer, and a mitred abbot. Lords of royal blood who are poor take precedence over lords of non-royal blood who are rich, and a lady of royal blood maintains her rank even if she marries a man whose status is lower than hers.[16]

Although the English elite for much of the later Middle Ages speak French, and the Church uses Latin, you yourself, like the vast majority of people in England, speak only English. In stark contrast to the prestigious global language that it becomes a few centuries later, English in the Middle Ages has no status at all, and is spoken only in England, the south-east of Scotland and in the part of South Wales known as the Englishry. When English people meet French people, it is taken for granted that the English people, or at least some of them, will have to speak French, but there is no expectation whatsoever that French people, or indeed any other nationality, should learn English. On various occasions in the thirteenth century, French writers compose parodies of the ungrammatical and inaccurate French they believe to be spoken by the English: *Fabliau des Deux Anglois*, *Chartre de la Pais aus Englois* in 1264, and an untitled parody of the Treaty of Montreuil between France and England in 1299. As well as their inept verb conjugations, and case and gender disagreement, malapropisms abound: the English confuse *coer* (heart) with *cul* (anus), and *navire* (boat) with *naviau* (turnip).[17] Hilarity ensues. The English are presented as figures of fun and as primitive country bumpkins who speak a peasant language and struggle with a more sophisticated one. As late as the end of the fourteenth century, Geoffrey Chaucer (*c.*1342–1400) pokes gentle fun at the character of the prioress in his *Canterbury Tales*, who is of noble birth and speaks French but only 'after the school of Stratford-atte-Bowe' rather than Parisian French, i.e. an inferior variant. One wonders how the French people who mock the bad French spoken in England would cope with the niceties of English, but the idea that they might learn a word or two of such a lowly language surely never even occurs to them. Charles, duke of Orléans, captive in England for a quarter of a century after being taken prisoner at the battle of Agincourt in 1415, is one of the very few French people in the Middle Ages who learns any English, and this is only from strict necessity.

For all its poor status, however, English evolves rapidly, and by 1450 is almost unrecognisable from the language of 1250, let alone 1150. There are numerous dialects which are so different from each other that to the modern eye they almost appear to be different languages. Geoffrey Chaucer writes in the London dialect, and can, with some difficulty, be read more than 600 years later. By contrast, the poems *Pearl* and *Gawain and the Green Knight* are written around the same time in north-west England, yet look almost unrecognisable to modern readers as English. William Caxton (d. *c.*1491), a merchant who brings the printing press to England, tells the story of a group of sailors who travel a few miles along the coast of southeast England. When they go ashore, they encounter a woman whose dialect is so different to theirs that she cannot understand them and assumes they must be talking French, presumably because this is the only foreign language she has ever heard of. One of the men asks her for *eggys* or eggs, but she does not understand, as for her, the word for 'eggs' is *eyren* (the similarity to the modern Dutch word, *eieren*, and the modern German word, *Eier*, is obvious). Be aware, therefore, that people may look at you with blank incomprehension even if you are completely fluent in a particular variant of Middle English, and may assume that you are speaking a different language altogether.

At times, the use of the French language in English documents achieves an unintended hilarity. Henry, Lord Beaumont (*c.*1280–1340) is French by birth and ancestry but spends most of his life in England, moving there in or before 1290 when he is still a child. When his kinsman Edward II gives him the lordship of the Isle of Man in 1310, some of the English barons complain rather xenophobically that it should be given instead to 'some good Englishman'. This is, however, written in French, *askun bon homme Engleys.*[18] If you reach a certain level of wealth and sophistication, you will be expected to know some French. William Melton, archbishop of York from 1317 to 1340, comes from a humble background in Yorkshire but sends letters in French. Petitions are also written in French or sometimes in Latin, and the same goes for wills. Richard II's older half-brother Thomas Holland, earl of Kent, makes his will in English in 1397, a very early example of such. English is first used in the law courts in 1362 when an act known as the Statute of Pleading in English is passed by parliament. Again ironically, this act is recorded in French, and states that 'all pleas which shall be pleaded in any courts whatsoever … shall be pleaded, defended, answered, debated and judged in the English language' (*en la lange engleise*).[19] As the fourteenth century progresses, English appears more and more as a written language and begins to be used more and more by the higher nobility. In the 1390s, the archbishop of Canterbury, William Courtenay (*c.*1342–96), addresses parliament in English, which is an interesting development as he is a nobleman by birth. The earl of Arundel also addresses parliament in English in the 1390s, as does Henry IV when taking the throne from his cousin Richard II in 1399.

Chapter 12

Tisik, Apostomes and Quinsy: Health

If you break your arm or leg and the broken bone pierces the skin, there is a reasonable chance that you will die of gangrene a few weeks or months later. Maud Coffeur of London is drunk shortly before Christmas 1276 as she makes her way home, stumbles and falls to the ground, and breaks her right arm. For two months, she lives 'in a languishing state' and dies in mid-February 1277. Seven-year-old Robert Saint Botolph (i.e. the family comes from Boston in Lincolnshire) breaks his leg in May 1322 when a piece of timber falls on him while he is playing in the street with friends; he dies two months later. On the other hand, Robert Holte of Colchester trips over some casks and breaks an arm in 1347, and is still alive more than twenty years later. Ditto William Bretby, who falls from his horse and breaks his left arm while riding to the market in Penrith, Cumberland in 1390, and lives for many years afterwards. William Hopegras, who lives just outside Hungerford, close to the border of Berkshire and Wiltshire, and is about 45 or 47 years old, falls from his horse 'in a stony lane' on his way to a baptism in Ramsbury in April 1388, and breaks his shin. William lives for another thirty years or more after this incident, though does complain of the pain he has suffered ever since.[1]

Being drunk, as Maud Coffeur is when she falls over and breaks her arm, is very risky: in Leicester in November 1298, Geoffrey Curlevach gets up 'mad and raving and drunk' in the middle of the night, walks to the River Soar outside the north gate, falls in, and drowns.[2] In London two years later, Henry Curteis falls down some steps while very drunk, hits his head hard and dies, and one evening in August 1339, the goldsmith John Markeby is 'drunk and leaping about' in his home in London with his daughter Alice and his servant Robert, when he manages to stab himself in the thigh with his own knife.[3]

The 'falling sickness' (*morbus caducus* in Latin), which modern people call epilepsy, is often given as a cause of death in coroners' reports. John Sadeler, found dead in Oxford in July 1394, is said to have been 'taken with the falling sickness and suddenly fell to the ground and died'.[4] Another long-term sufferer of 'falling sickness' is Emma atte Grove of Guildford in Surrey, a beggar. Emma dies in the Tower of London in February 1337; while carrying a large earthen pot full of water, she falls headfirst into the Tower ditch. In July 1383, Margery Saddler of Devizes in Wiltshire dies while she is crossing a water-filled ditch called *Denningsditch*; she is 'suddenly stricken with the falling sickness' and drowns. Jaundice is called *jaundyse*; dysentery is the *blody flyxe* or 'bloody flux'; and malaria, endemic in the low-lying, marshy areas of eastern England, is called the tertian fever or quatrain fever (*fever quartayn* and *tercian*), and sometimes *ague*. Another disease, known as *tisik* or *tesyke* in the late Middle Ages and in later centuries as *phthisis*, is pulmonary tuberculosis or a similar progressive wasting disease.[5] Master Lodowyk Arecia works as a physician in London in the 1340s, and sells a medicine called *allumine de tysik* which he claims to be a remedy for *tisik*.[6]

A *quinsy* means an inflammation or swelling of the throat.[7] Richard St Albans dies around midday on 7 June 1301 in his workplace, a stable in London. While 'grievously suffering from a *quinsy*', Richard 'fell down and suddenly died of that malady'. The jurors who investigate his death note that his neck and throat 'appeared large and swollen'. On 3 April 1339 around Vespers, John Lynche is walking along the high street of East Smithfield in London 'when by reason of a *quinsy* from which he had long suffered, he fell to the ground and died'.[8] William Hampme suffers from 'a certain malady in his leg called a *festre*' for three years at the start of the 1300s, and one evening slowly bleeds to death. A *festre* means a fistula, ulcer or festering wound.[9]

A fifteenth-century text says that a surgeon (*surgyan*) can heal wounds (*woundes*), sores, *apostomes* (swellings, abscesses or inflammations) and *mormales* (ulcers or abscesses with a dry scab) with *oynementis* and *plastres* (ointments and plasters or poultices). *Apostomes* are also sometimes called *postemes*, *postumes* or *imposthumes*, while bladder stones are called *gravelle* or 'gravel', and *brekynge* is the word for a rupture of some kind. Gout is called by the same name that it is in later centuries, *goute*, and *dropesye* (dropsy) refers to what in the twenty-first century is called oedema. A doctor or physician is called a *maistre of phisike*, and he will examine your urine to diagnose your ailment; he is able to tell his patients *wherof they be seke*, 'whereof they be sick' and why they have a *heed ache*, *toth ache*, *payne of the eyen* or *payne of the eres* (headache, toothache, eye or ear pain). He will also examine your chest (*breste*) and, perhaps surprisingly, women's *pappes* or breasts, if you have pain in these areas.[10] Late medieval England has, or believes that it has, an antidote to the bite of 'venomous beasts' (*bestes venemous*) such as snakes, lizards and scorpions. The word for 'antidote', in both medieval English and French, is *triacle*, which survives in modern English, rather peculiarly, as 'treacle'.[11]

If you fall ill or have an accident, you can go to your nearest apothecary or spicer as a first port of call. An unnamed apothecary in London in July 1322 sells *drogeries* which include 'Apostle's ointment', which is an antiseptic; *saunguys draconis* or 'dragon's blood', a resin for healing wounds; 'God's grace', which is another ointment; calamine, ragwort, fenugreek, linseed, frankincense and myrrh; and what he calls 'white' and 'dark' ointments.[12] In London, the apothecaries congregate in four places: Cheapside, Sopereslane (now Queen Street), the Ropery, and Bucklersbury.[13] Many apothecaries are skilful and will genuinely be able to help you; some are not. In 1351, the mayor, aldermen and sheriffs of London ask surgeons named Master Paschal, Master Adam Poletrie and Master David Westmerland to examine a 'certain enormous and horrible hurt' – which is typical fourteenth-century medical language – that has appeared on the right side of Thomas Shene's jaw and that John Spicer has attempted to treat. The surgeons state that 'if he had been expert in his craft' and if he had asked for aid and counsel, he might have cured the injury, but 'through want of skill' John has probably made the unfortunate Thomas's injury incurable.[14]

Not all surgeons and physicians are competent, either, and you do need to watch out for charlatans. Roger Clerk 'pretend[s] to be an expert in medicine' in 1384, and gives Joan atte Hacche, who suffers from an unspecified illness, a leaf torn out of a manuscript wrapped in a piece of cloth of gold as a cure. He is convicted of being a charlatan and sentenced to the pillory with the torn leaf and, of all things, a urinal hanging around his neck.[15] In June 1320, the London surgeon John of Cornhill goes to the Fleet Street home of Alice Stockyngge, and promises to cure her 'infirmity of the feet' within two weeks, on payment of half a mark (80d). He applies 'diverse medicaments against the said infirmity', but unfortunately, not only do they fail to work, Alice is 'unable to put her feet to the ground and her malady became completely incurable' six days later. She takes John to the court of the two sheriffs of London.[16] In February 1377, one Richard Cheyndut is imprisoned in London for failing to cure Walter Hull of 'a malady in his left leg, whereby, owing to his lack of care and knowledge, the patient was in danger of losing his leg, as testified by John Donhed, John Garlikhuth and Nicholas the Surgeon, three surgeons who had viewed the leg'.[17] Alice Stockingge's case reveals that, as well as the legal comeback patients have if medical carers fail in their duty, physicians and surgeons will make house calls if their patients are unable to go to them.

The Middle Ages is an era when physicians will often attempt to cure you with bloodletting and will attach leeches to you. In July 1324, the goldsmith Nicholas Walsh is attacked in the Tower of London by a man wielding a sword and is carried about 800 yards to the house of Robert le Leche to be 'medically treated' for his head injury. Robert's name means 'the leech'. Bloodletting carries its own risks: in 1278, William Paumere falls down dead in Cheapside, London after excessive bloodletting the previous day.[18] There is, however, not a great deal else anyone in the late Middle Ages can do for your head injury, unless you are extremely lucky. Adam Hikesman of Northumberland, aged about

24, is standing outside a stable in March 1368 when a sudden gust of wind loosens a beam and it falls on him, and 'broke his head almost to the brain'. Two weeks later, Adam visits his local leech in Warkworth 'to have his head cured', and rather astonishingly, this works; Adam is still alive in the 1380s. Near Cheltenham in August 1357, John atte Halle, who is in his early forties or thereabouts, attends a baptism. During it, for reasons which John fails to explain, the chaplain performing the ceremony, Geoffrey Whyte, 'struck him with a stick and broke his head'. Thankfully, John is still alive to recall this event eighteen years later, and has evidently received some kind of effective treatment.[19]

In and around Bedford in October 1271, two men are attacked, one with an axe wound to the top of the head that 'extended through the skull to the brain, so that the blood and brains flowed forth'. He dies soon afterwards. The other is John Brettville, who is attacked by Simon Cainhoe; Simon strikes him 'wickedly and feloniously with a certain sword of iron and steel on the top of the head on the left side between the parting of the hair and the ear; he thus inflicted upon him a big wound which was five inches long, three inches wide, and which extended downward as far as the brain, so that thirteen pieces of bone were extracted from the wound'. Furthermore, Simon cuts the little and ring fingers on John's left hand, then strikes him numerous times with the flat of his sword on the right side of John's head. Rather astonishingly, John survives this brutal and vicious attack and accuses Simon of assault before the county court of Bedfordshire.[20] People who suffer head injuries and who live not too far from London tend to go there to seek medical treatment. In April 1325, Thomas Hodesdone quarrels with his friend Thomas Brid in their native Hoddesdon, Hertfordshire, and Brid hits him on the top of his head with a weapon and inflicts a wound 'penetrating to the brain'. Thomas's friends take him to London for treatment, presumably on a cart – it seems most unlikely that he is able to walk or ride 20 miles with such a serious head injury – but he dies there six days later.[21]

Cases of sudden or unexpected deaths are investigated by the local coroner and a sizeable number of jurors aiding him, though as it is all but guaranteed that none of them will have any medical knowledge or training whatsoever, some of their findings can seem surprising. In Bedford in June 1272, a man accidentally shoots an arrow into a pregnant woman's right eye, and she dies fifteen days later. A group of jurors are adamant that the cause of death is 'illness due to pregnancy' rather than the terrible head wound she has suffered.[22] In London twenty-nine years later, Robert Brewere is drunk one Sunday evening in June and picks a fight with an acquaintance named Robert Amyas (who is French and lives in London for many years). This results in Robert Amyas hitting Robert Brewere repeatedly with an oak stick. Rather than trying to make his way home, the inebriated and badly bruised Brewere spends the night lying by a tree in a churchyard. When he reports for work the following morning at the home of his master, fishmonger Henry Poteman, Henry reprimands him for leaving his house without permission, gives him his wages, and orders him to leave. Robert dies in the home of a friend three days later. Despite noting that Robert Brewere's body is bruised all over, the jurors who investigate his death declare that he 'was not nearer death nor farther from life by reason of the beating, but died from the illness he contracted from spending the night in the street'. They fail to explain which lethal illness would be contracted by spending a night outside in summer.[23]

Also in 1301, two brothers named Nicholas and Richard Mandevill are playing some kind of game with stones in their home in Northamptonshire, and one of the stones thrown by Richard hits Nicholas's head. On the third night after, as Nicholas lies asleep, he suffers an attack of paralysis (*morbus paraliticus*), and dies a few days afterwards. The jurors investigating his death insist that he 'did not die of the blow, but of the said illness' (i.e. the paralysis), evidently not making a connection between the two events. As, however, Richard flees into sanctuary in fear after his brother Nicholas's death, it seems that he at least believes that he inadvertently killed Nicholas with the stone.[24] On 31 December 1309 near Kettering in Northamptonshire, Thomas Clerk is watching a wrestling competition when he gets into an argument with some other spectators which results in one of them shooting an arrow into his stomach. Thomas dies in his own home not long afterwards. According to the jurors, he has fully recovered from the wound and dies from the 'flux', not from being shot in the stomach.[25]

In the year 1376, near the end of Edward III's long reign, the barber-surgeons of London ask the king's permission to issue a series of regulations for their guild. These are needed because some barbers practising in the city are 'inexperienced in the art of surgery' but take 'many sick and maimed persons' under their care, and end up making them worse off than they were before. These barbers come from *uppelande* ('upland', meaning the rest of the country outside London) and 'intermeddle with barbery, surgery and the cure of maladies, while they know not how to do such things, nor ever were instructed in such craft, to the great damage' of London residents. If you are in London and require surgery, be very apprehensive about what might happen. Almost forty years later in 1415, in Henry V's reign, the situation has not improved, and it is intimated to the mayor and aldermen, 'not without alarm', that 'some barbers … inexperienced in the art of surgery', are nevertheless practising. In 1423, several members of the 'Faculty of Physic' decide to form a 'joint college for the better education and control of the physicians and surgeons practising in the city'. They include Thomas Morstede and John Harowe, two of the masters of the craft of surgery in London, and Master Gilbert Kymer, who calls himself a doctor of 'medicyns' and is the physician to the infant king Henry VI's uncle Humphrey, duke of Gloucester. Master Thomas Southwell, a *bachiler* (bachelor) of medicine, and Master John Suntbreshete, a *comensour* (someone who holds a higher university degree) in medicine, are the two surveyors of the Faculty of Physic in London at this time.[26]

Sometimes it is impossible for your modern descendants to determine what medieval descriptions of illness and death mean, and coroners' reports can be almost impossibly vague. In June 1340, the investigation into Henry Callere's death determines that 'after the hour of curfew, the said Henry was going upstairs alone when he fell down and died'. When a sailor named Henry Ambelcowe dies suddenly and unexpectedly near the Tower of London in August 1278, the jurors declare, not entirely helpfully, that he 'was suddenly struck by death'.[27] Sometime in the first year of Henry V's reign, which runs from March 1413 to March 1414, a resident of Northampton called William, last name not recorded, 'died of weakness and fell to the ground'. This is the entire explanation.[28] Robert Balsham of London dies in his home in the middle of the night on 10 February 1301, and the jurors state that he had been 'afflicted with a grievous infirmity' for three weeks, rose from his bed, lay on the floor, and 'immediately died'. The infirmity is left unexplained.[29] In March 1326, John Dene, one of the ushers of Edward II's chamber, is said to be 'very ill in one side' of his body, and is still ill and recuperating at home in Canterbury more than two months later.[30] 'Ill in one side' seems as though it could mean anything from a stroke to appendicitis to kidney stones. Bedfordshire resident Simon Langhoe is about to milk a cow in July 1271 when he is 'stricken with a disease called *mau del flaunke*' and dies immediately.[31] This means an illness of the side of his body, and typically is not further explained. Another example of a condition not clarified is the *French Chronicle of London*'s statement that in 1308 'there was a great malady of the eyes, whereby many persons lost their sight' in London.[32]

Some English people of the late Middle Ages die of starvation or of a disease exacerbated by malnutrition, and prisoners who have no access to food are allowed to die; see Chapter 6 above. As medieval England is a place where the majority live hand to mouth, whenever harvests fail or are poor it is all but inevitable that some people will die of hunger or as a result of malnutrition. In May 1253, an 'unknown beggar' is found dead from hunger in a London street, for example, and at the start of the 1260s, Alexander Caby starves to death also in London.[33] In 1257, harvests fail across England, and much of the kingdom stares starvation in the face that winter. King Henry III's brother Richard of Cornwall, who has recently been elected King of the Romans – which essentially means the king of Germany and Holy Roman Emperor-elect – compassionately sends fifty ships full of grain to England from his new kingdom, which has had much better harvests.[34] No one, however, can help England during the Great Famine of 1315 to 1317; the endless months of rain which destroys crops affects the whole of Northern Europe. As well as the risk of starving, other medieval English people die of cold, and one of them is Walter of Warwick, who perishes in Oxford during the night of 27/28 January 1346. He has no home and no shelter, and dies in the middle of Catte Street. On 30 January 1269, a woman is found dead in a ditch near Bedford, and it is determined that she 'died of exposure to cold'. Her name and identity remain a mystery.[35] As temperature scales will not be invented for another few hundred years, it is impossible to know just how cold it must have been to kill Walter and the unknown woman, but in January, it is likely to have fallen well below zero degrees.

Life expectancy in late medieval English towns is, however, higher than modern people generally think. It is certainly not the case, despite the common assumption to the contrary, that medieval people get married and become parents in their early teens then die of old age at 30. The infant mortality rate is, however, terribly high, which drags down the average age, and it goes without saying that numerous diseases and injuries which are treatable centuries later often kill people in the late Middle Ages. Many young (and not so young) men are killed in war, and many young (and not so young) women die of some pregnancy- or childbirth-related issue. This also helps to pull down the average life expectancy. If, however, you survive these things, you have a good chance of living to a decent age, and not only at the more privileged end of society. Simon Simeon, steward of the earls of Lancaster, is born before 1310 and dies in 1386 or 1387; the thrice-married Margaret Hydon from Devon is born before 1278 and dies in 1357, when her heirs are her 38-year-old grandson and her great-granddaughters; William Causton, a merchant working in London, is old enough to have qualified as a master of his trade and to act as someone's executor in 1306, and lives until 1354; and Alice Warle of London gives birth to one of her five children in 1317, so is unlikely to have been born much after 1300 and was perhaps born well before that, and dies in 1361. In fourteenth-century London, nobody over the age of 70 is allowed to serve on juries or assizes, a rule that would hardly need to exist if virtually nobody reaches such an age.[36]

By far the deadliest disease of the Middle Ages is the Black Death, usually assumed to have been bubonic plague, which first reaches England during the dismal wet summer of 1348 and rages through the country until the early autumn of 1349. It kills perhaps as much as a third of the entire population in little more than fourteen months, though some parts of the country, most notably Yorkshire, suffer disproportionately and lose as much as 60 per cent of their residents. Even if you are lucky enough to survive this first horrendous pandemic, the Black Death – known as pestilence, 'the mortality' or 'the great mortality' to those who experience it – returns to England in force in the early 1360s, the late 1360s, and the mid-1370s. In other years, too, small numbers of English people die of it. And in 1485, the year of Henry Tudor's victory over Richard III at the battle of Bosworth, a virulent and terrifying disease called the sweating sickness or simply 'the sweat' reaches England, and returns periodically in horrible outbreaks until 1551, when it departs English shores never to return. Even with the medical knowledge of the twenty-first century, the sweating sickness remains mysterious and has yet to be conclusively identified.

Chapter 13

Foteball and Penypryk: Having Fun (1)

In the Middle Ages, as in later centuries, lots of people enjoy physical exercise, being outdoors, and getting fresh air, and they appreciate the benefits and pleasures of team games. Some modern sports have a surprisingly long history. Edward II orders Nicholas Farndone, mayor of London, to ban football (soccer) in 1314, complaining about the 'great noise' caused by 'rumpuses over large footballs'.[1] More than half a century later in 1373, eight men are arrested for carrying weapons and intending to cause a disturbance of the peace and assault 'under colour of playing with a football'.[2] Medieval weddings are often celebrated by playing *foteball* or another type of ballgame. In 1409, Henry IV forbids 'the levying of money for the games called *foteball* and *cokthresshyng* on occasion of marriages' (*cokthresshyng* or 'cock-thrashing' is the pastime, unfortunate to modern sensibilities, of throwing sticks or lashing at tethered birds while wearing a blindfold).[3]

In Odell, Bedfordshire, William Ballard and John Cook collide during a game of football in September 1410, and John's shin is broken. This is, in fact, an ill-fated match: on his way to Odell to play it, an overly eager John Haukyn jumps over a stream, misjudges it, and also breaks his shin.[4] In April 1266, two men in Yorkshire, Alan Hayward and Walter Wyndhul, play a ballgame of some kind with friends, apparently football, which involves 'running together, trying [to see] which could get the ball first'. Afterwards they go to a tavern to drink ale. Fourteen years later in Newcastle-upon-Tyne, a large group of men run around 'playing at ball'.[5] While staying at Langdon Abbey in Kent in September 1325, Edward II gives a shilling each to twenty-two men – which implies two teams of eleven players – who play a ballgame for his entertainment. Nine months later at Saltwood

Castle also in Kent, Edward himself goes out into the park with some of his servants to 'play at ball'.[6]

The wording 'playing at ball' (*iewer a pelot* in medieval French, *ludens ad pilum* or *ad pilum ludendo* in medieval Latin) often appears in medieval documents. Although the nature of the ballgame in question is rarely specified, in the spring of 1277 in Lincolnshire, a group of boys play a game that sounds like hockey or lacrosse. Two of them are Robert Provost, aged 12, and Geoffrey Pestur, aged 10, and 'both their sticks [*baculis*] hit the ball at the same time'.[7] *Creaget*, which probably means cricket or at least some very early version of it, is found in 1299: 'playing at *creaget* and other sports' at Newenden in Kent. *Criquet*, the first certain reference to cricket, appears in 1478.[8] *Jeu de paume*, literally 'palm game', is an early form of tennis known in France by the early 1300s, and is enjoyed by Louis X (reigned 1314–16), brother-in-law of Edward II of England and uncle of Edward III. The English authorities forbid the playing of tennis by servants and labourers in 1388 and again in 1410.[9] Tennis (*tenes*) and bowls (*bowlys*) appear in a Leicester document of 1467, and in Nottingham in the same year, five men are accused of playing 'an unlawful and prohibited game called *tenys*, unlawfully'.[10]

Games where the winner comes closest to the jack or to a mark of some kind by throwing or shooting are popular. In London in early January 1280, John Burton, William Cordwaner and other neighbours shoot 'with crossbows at a mark fixed in a target'. A group of boys under 9 years old in Yorkshire throw sticks at a mark made on a wall in 1285, and the following year some other boys in Cambridgeshire shoot at marks with bows and arrows.[11] In Leicester in 1467, this is called *pykkyng with arowes*, and other games are *penypryk* or *penyperche*, where pieces of iron are thrown at a stick which has a penny coin placed on it, and *coytyng with horsshon*, i.e. quoits with horseshoes, or throwing the metal shoes from a distance so they land over or near a spike set in the ground.[12] In 1344 in the village of Yardley Hastings near Northampton, John Wylk kills his friend John Neubonde in a rage following an argument over a game of *penyprikke* which they are playing at the home of another friend, Roger Eston.[13] Another game which involves throwing 'tiles' of some kind results in the death of John Fuatard in 1276, while playing it with his friend John Clerk in Southwark. Clerk accidentally strikes Fuatard on the head with a tile, and he dies a few days later.[14] *Palet*, which involves throwing discs onto a board from a distance and trying to get closest to the jack, is recorded in 1324.[15]

In 1363 and again in 1365, Edward III orders that 'every able-bodied man' should practise archery on feast days rather than 'dishonest and unthrifty or idle games' such as football and handball. A proclamation is made in London in May 1414 forbidding the playing of football, *dyces* (dice games), *coytes* (quoits), *kailes* (skittles), throwing stones, and 'other such fruitless games'. Young men are ordered to practise archery instead, on pain of six days' imprisonment. As this proclamation is made less than eighteen months before Henry V's great victory over a French army at the battle of Agincourt, it does make sense.[16] The fields called The Elms outside the city walls of London are often used for archery practice and sport.[17] A hazardous hobby is the shooting of pigeons and other birds perched on churches or houses with stonebows, a catapult for shooting stones, and arbalests, a kind of crossbow. This is often prohibited by authorities because the missiles wound passersby and break windows. Two men in London in 1376 shoot 'with bolts and arrows' at pigeons perched on houses, 'whereby, but for God's abundant grace, men, women and children might have been killed or seriously wounded'.[18] One Robert Duke is arrested in September 1374 for 'shooting arrows by night at the inhabitants of Fleet Street, to the terror of the city'.[19]

Choppecherye or chop-cherry, a game where you try to catch a cherry hanging from a thread with your teeth, is recorded in the late 1300s.[20] Playing-cards arrive in Europe in the 1360s or 1370s, having been invented in China a few centuries earlier, and chess is known in medieval England, as are other board games. In 1264, Juliana Cordwaner plays chess with her friend David of Bristol in her London home, with her husband Richard and a few other friends watching.[21] *Quek* or *queek*, i.e.

chequers, is mentioned in March 1301 when Joce of Cornwall plays it with his friend Thomas of Bristol in the London home of another friend, Alice of Waltham, one Monday evening. Some people cheat by using a false *quek-bord*, but anyone who plays with false dice or a false board is accused of *joukerie* or cheating. They are sentenced to an hour locked in the pillory either with the dice hanging round their neck or with the *quek-bord* burning beneath them. Stephen Lalleford, a 'common gamester' who has cheated William Brounyng out of the huge sum of £17 – tens of thousands in modern terms – by cheating at dice and chequers is imprisoned in 1375.[22] Later in the Middle Ages, the game becomes known as *cheker* or *schekker*, or *cheker in the myre*.[23] Fox and geese, an asymmetrical board game with one fox and thirteen geese, or two foxes and fifteen or more geese, is known in medieval England and many other countries, and another popular game, *shovegrote*, is now known as 'shove ha'penny'.

A game played with coins is cross and pile, the medieval equivalent of heads or tails, and dice games are also hugely popular. They are often played in taverns, and some people are accused of using 'false dice' in order to cheat.[24] *Hasard* or 'hazard' is a popular game, and so is *rafle*, 'raffle'. The simple objective of raffle is to roll three dice with the same number; the rules of hazard, played with two dice, are far more complicated. Another game is knucklebones, called *Piggesfot* or 'pig's foot' in the Middle Ages, which involves tossing and catching small animal bones. Henry Pykard, Wauter Waldeshef and Roger Fynch, big fans of it, are arrested in 1339 for leading their apprentices into gambling habits.[25]

Chapter 14

Wrastleng, Mommyng and Romanse: Having Fun (2)

To celebrate a wedding held in Romney, Kent in 1257, a crowd gather to watch a group of men tilting at the quintain, and jousting tournaments are perennially popular entertainment.[1] Edward III holds one on Cheapside in the middle of London in the early autumn of 1331, though tragedy strikes when some of the stands collapse and injure spectators. Jousts are dangerous; in 1286, the son and heir of the earl of Surrey is killed while jousting, as is the 17-year-old earl of Pembroke a century later in 1389. Tournaments are often banned for months or years on end as they provide a convenient excuse for large groups of armed men to assemble, and are thus deemed risky. In November 1305, Edward I forbids a jousting tournament due to be held in Oxford the following autumn for another reason: that 'the quiet of the scholars studying in that town may be disturbed'.[2] In a much sillier vein, in 1351 his grandson Edward III forbids a popular prank where people rush up behind others and pull the hoods off their heads.[3]

Swimming for pleasure is vanishingly rare in the late Middle Ages, and few people know how to swim at all, as evidenced by the large number of people who drown when they fall into rivers or even just into slow-running streams (see Chapter 7 above). Fishing is, perhaps surprisingly, practised by two kings of fourteenth-century England, Edward II and his son Edward III. The elder Edward – who, most unusually, also enjoys swimming in rivers – borrows a boat from a local fisherman called Henry on the Medway in Tonbridge, Kent in the summer of 1324 and goes out alone on the river to fish. A few months later, he goes onto the lake at Beaulieu Abbey in Hampshire in a boat with a local fisherman called Jack Bere and several unnamed others. His account makes clear that the king participates in fishing (*il ala pescher*) rather than merely watching the others do it. His son the younger King Edward acquires a splendid fishing rod in 1344.[4] For just about everyone else who goes fishing in the fourteenth and fifteenth centuries, it is a job and a means of earning a living, not a pastime, and is one performed by numerous women as well as men. In the 1320s, for example, there are references to the fisherwomen of Lambeth and the fisherwomen of Kennington, both close to London. In the same era, Alice atte Churche and Isabel Fisher both also earn a living by fishing in the Thames and its tributaries.[5]

Wrestling is a common pastime in the late Middle Ages, and on 4 September 1261, a wrestling contest takes place in Bermondsey between a large group of men from London and men from the Cluniac priory of Bermondsey. A few decades later on 31 December 1309, 'a game called *wrastleng* … which attracted many people' takes place just outside Kettering in Northamptonshire.[6] In 1411, however, it is forbidden within the boundaries of St Paul's in London and any other open places in the city.[7] Fencing is also forbidden in late medieval London. Master Roger Skirmisour (his name means 'fencer', though survives in modern English as 'skirmisher') is imprisoned in March 1311 for keeping a fencing-school for men somewhere in London. He is accused of enticing the sons of 'respectable persons' to attend, 'so as to waste and spend the property of their fathers and mothers on bad practices; the result being that they themselves became bad men.' In London, no one is allowed to keep a fencing-school, and anyone who opens one will be imprisoned for forty days.[8] And in July 1366, William Toucestre is arrested for 'preparing to fight a duel outside the city' of London.[9] Duels are not yet common in the late Middle Ages, though in the early 1350s no less a person than the king of France is forced to intervene to prevent one taking place between the English duke of Lancaster and the German duke of Brunswick.[10]

Christmas festivities in the fourteenth and fifteenth centuries often involve wearing masks (sometimes called 'false faces') and false beards, and *mommyng*, i.e. a performance, play or pageant in mask and costume. In 1418, the mayor of London proclaims that at the coming Christmas, nobody in the city should 'walk by nyght in eny manere mommyng, pleyes, enterludes, or eny other disgisynges with eny feynyd berdis, peyntid visers, diffourmyd or colourid visages' (walk by night in any manner mumming, plays or interludes, or any other disguises with any feigned beards, painted visors, deformed or coloured faces). The assumption is that anyone deliberately concealing their identity might be up to no good.[11]

As in modern times, people in the late Middle Ages spend convivial evenings at their friends' houses. Walter and Adam Monek, brothers, visit the house of their friend Agnes White in Brackley, Northamptonshire, one evening in 1299, and two years later, Henry Curteis visits his friend Luke Havering, a rope-maker, at his home on Roperestrete ('Roper Street', now part of Thames Street) in London.[12] Centuries before television, cinema and Netflix, medieval people often entertain themselves by hiring minstrels, who are performers of every description: the majority are musicians or singers, but others are actors, dancers, acrobats and tumblers, jugglers, conjurors, storytellers, and much else. In Middle English, they are often called *pleyers* or 'players'. In 1312, a man called John Colon, who comes from Lombardy, performs some kind of act in Dover that involves snakes, and a few years later two squires perform an act with fire and manage to burn their arms and legs quite badly.[13]

Musical instruments of the late Middle Ages include the psaltery, which is a kind of zither, different kinds of stringed instruments such as the vielle, tabor drums, horns, harps, trumpets, and the crwth, a Welsh instrument similar to a violin. Rather remarkably, there is a *scola menstralcie* or 'school of minstrelsy' in London in the mid-fourteenth century, though as Latin has no definite or indefinite articles, it is not clear whether this means 'the school of minstrelsy' or 'a school of minstrelsy'. Edward III's mother Isabella of France pays one mark (13 shillings and 4d) to send Walter Hert, one of her household minstrels, there not long before her death in 1358.[14] Minstrels frequently travel around Europe, and are sent from royal court to royal court. In Yorkshire in 1316, Edward II hosts a vielle-player, Robert Daverouns, sent to him by his kinsman Philip of Taranto, king of Albania and prince of Achaea and Taranto.[15] Because they travel from country from country so often, minstrels make excellent spies. In the late 1330s, after her husband Edward III claims the French throne, Philippa of Hainault, queen of England, sends a minstrel called Gerard to the Continent to report the movements of the king of France, Philip VI (who happens to be her own uncle), to her. This appears in the queen's accounts as 'to investigate secretly the actions of Lord Philip de Valois', and Gerard is paid the huge sum of 18d a day.[16]

Much medieval humour tends to be bawdy, and Geoffrey Chaucer's 'Miller's Tale', where a man kisses a woman's behind in the dark by mistake and then is farted on by another man as he tries to get his revenge on her, is a prime example. A fragment of a farcical play first performed around 1300 is called 'The Interlude of the Clerk and Damsel' (*Interludium de clerico et puella* in Latin, though the text is in English). It deals with a clerk unsuccessfully practising his seduction techniques on a young woman, and the line *Bot his hers ly wituten dore*, 'but his arse lay outside the door', is part of the extant fragment.[17] In the late fifteenth century, a text known as 'A Talk of Ten Wives on their Husbands' Ware' is written. A group of ten female friends, because they are bored and have nothing else to talk about, discuss their husbands' private parts while they sit in a tavern ('lett us tell of owre hosbondes ware'). The second wife states that she met her husband 'when he was in his moste pryde', i.e. in his greatest glory, 'the lenghte of thre bene' (length of three beans). Another woman's husband's penis is the 'lenghte of a snayle' (snail), and another complains that her husband 'pysses his tarse every yere', i.e. only ejaculates once a year. The sixth wife's spouse is impotent and his penis *lythe styll* despite her efforts to arouse him, and the seventh's is a 'sory pyne [sorry pin] that schuld hengge bytwen his leggis' but instead is 'a sory laveroke satt on brode opon two adyll eggis', a sorry lark sitting on a nest upon two addled eggs.[18]

In the fourteenth century, 'mystery plays' become popular, especially in York, Lincoln, Chester, Coventry and Wakefield (in Yorkshire), and are performed for 200 years. The rather confusing name has nothing to do with modern mysteries in the Agatha Christie sense, but derives either from the medieval word for a guild of craftsmen or tradesmen, 'mistery' (itself from the Italian *mestiere* or 'trade'), or from 'mystery' in the sense of 'miracle'. Each guild in a town performs a particular scene from the bible; the *neyleres* or nail-makers might perform the Crucifixion, for instance. As most people in the late Middle Ages are illiterate, literature is almost always heard rather than read, and in 1306, one of the minstrels performing for the more than 250 new knights in Westminster Hall is called Reynald le Mentour. This literally means 'the liar', though is probably intended in the sense that he makes up and recites stories or fables.

Books and manuscripts are startlingly expensive and only owned by the wealthiest people in the country, mostly the nobility and royalty, but also successful merchants and a few clerks. Towards the end of the Middle Ages, literacy starts to become more widespread and books become less pricy, and William Caxton brings the printing press to England in the 1470s. Saints' lives are massively popular, as are biblical stories. William Thorneye, a rich pepperer and alderman of London, originally from an impoverished background in Lincolnshire, leaves his book *The Proverbs of Solomon* to his 2-year-old son John in 1349.[19] William Walworth, mayor of London in 1374/75 and 1380/81, owns a 'book of romance of King Alexander in rhyme, well and curiously illuminated' (in the Middle Ages, a romance means any kind of fictional story, not necessarily a love story). Sir James Audley owns four 'books of romance' in 1352.[20] Benet or Benedict Fulsham, sheriff of London in 1324/25, has a valuable item stolen from his home on Sunday, 8 July 1341: a breviary, i.e. a small, easily portable book containing religious texts, called a *portehors* or *portifory* in the fourteenth century. The breviary is worth 240d.[21] The former mayor of London John Gisors mentions a number of religious tomes in his will of 1350: a missal in two volumes, a breviary with musical notation, and a psalter (a book containing the psalms).[22] Psalters (*sawters*) are very popular, especially illuminated ones bound with silver clasps.[23] In his will of 1361, goldsmith Robert Walcote mentions *tres libros coloris*, literally 'three coloured books', presumably meaning manuscripts with colourful illustrations.[24] The deservedly famous and lavishly illustrated Luttrell Psalter, which still exists, is commissioned by Sir Geoffrey Luttrell of Irnham in Lincolnshire (1276–1345).

In 1337, John Bokelond of London accuses one John Writele of stealing his 'book written in English' called *Legends of the Saints*. Bokelond claims that the book is worth 40s; the jury who convict Writele value it at 30s. Thomas Carleton, a *brouderer* or embroider who runs the tavern called the *Lyon in the Hope* in London (see Chapter 8 above) with his wife Joan, also owns a copy of the *Legends of the Saints*.[25] Another book-owner, and evidently a man with a taste for learning, is Thomas Giles of Fleet Street. In his will of early 1348, Thomas leaves to his and his wife Diamanda's son Thomas the younger, whom he wishes to be educated as a clerk, 'all his books bound and unbound, on the canon and civil law, grammar, dialectic, theology, geometry and astronomy'. Henry Graspays, a fishmonger, makes his will in early December 1348, and leaves his son Henry his 'books of *romanse* and others'. A few weeks later in January 1349, the vintner Robert Felstede bequeaths 'a book called *Byble*' to John Heurle and 'a psalter written in Latin and English' to John Foxton.[26] Men of religion are far more likely to be able to read than the general population, and in the early 1380s, a London chaplain called William Causby owns a psalter worth half a mark or 6s 8d, as well as 'another large book containing grammatical treatises'.[27]

Eleanor de Bohun, duchess of Gloucester and countess of Essex (b. 1366), dies in her early thirties in 1399, and leaves a long will. To her eldest daughter Anne (b. 1383), countess of Stafford, Eleanor leaves a book called *Legenda Aurea* or 'Golden Legend', a compilation of the lives of the saints, and to her youngest daughter Isabel (b. 1386), who is professed as a nun in 1402 and is already living at the London convent of the Minoresses in 1399, Eleanor leaves a large number of books including a two-volume bible with gold clasps, a psalter, St Gregory's *Pastoral Rule*, and the *Lives of the Fathers*. To her 17-year-old eldest child Humphrey, who in fact dies a month before her, Duchess Eleanor bequeaths an illuminated psalter, a manuscript of a poem called 'The History of the Knight and the Swan' in French, and 'a book of vices and virtues', also in French. Eleanor's husband Thomas of Woodstock (b. 1355), youngest son of Edward III, owns no fewer than 123 books, which are confiscated and inventoried after he is murdered in 1397 on the orders of his nephew Richard II. They include the famous French poem 'Roman de le Rose', a manuscript of Arthurian tales, and 'a new book of the Gospels, glossed into English'. Thomas and Eleanor also own a bible in English which they commission themselves and for which they pay 40 shillings.[28] Eleanor's niece-in-law Joan Beaufort (d. 1440), countess of Westmorland, a granddaughter of Edward III, owns several psalters which once belonged to 'the illustrious lady, my mother, Lady Katherine, duchess of Lancaster', better known as Katherine Swynford (d. 1403), long-term mistress and third wife of Edward III's son John of Gaunt, duke of Lancaster. Joan bequeaths 'a great book about *Fisica*' (*librum magnum de Fisica*), most probably meaning a book containing medical advice and about the human body, to her four secular sons Richard, William, George and Edward Neville. It will pass from the eldest to the second eldest and so on in succession.[29]

A letter sent in April 1372 by John of Gaunt, duke of Lancaster, reveals that there are 'grammar schools' (*escoles de grimoire* in the French original) in the Northamptonshire town of Higham Ferrers. The duke appoints Henry Barton of Billing Magna to run them for the benefit of 'scholars and children wishing to study the subject of grammar'. John also appoints John Bradley to teach in the grammar schools of Crofton, near Wakefield in Yorkshire, in August 1372.[30] In the late 1300s, William Admastre is one of the 'masters of the grammar schools' (*magistri scolarum grammaticalium*) in Nottingham, and is also known as William Scolemayster or 'schoolmaster'. A John Scholmayster lives in Tiverton in Devon in the first half of the fifteenth century.[31] In July 1301, an 8-year-old boy named Richard Mason sadly drowns on his way to school in London: he is larking about while crossing London Bridge, and falls into the Thames. He dies before any of the crowd of shocked onlookers can help him.[32]

Nicholas Picot, an alderman of London, states in his will of *c.*October 1312 that his sons Nicholas and John are 'to study and attend school' and to learn how to write, and the fishmonger Richard Gubbe leaves £10 to his nephew and godson, Richard Gubbe the younger, in April 1335 'for his maintenance at school'.[33] When a clerk is taught how to write in 1326, a feather, to make a quill pen, and an inkhorn for storing his ink are purchased for him at a cost of 6d. In the fifteenth century, inkhorns are called *enke hornes*, and pencils for drawing lines on a piece of *parchemyn* or parchment – to keep your writing straight and neat – are called *poyntels*.[34] William Hanington, a skinner, dies in 1313 leaving two sons named John and Richard and a daughter named Rohese. Laurence Hanington, probably William's brother, becomes John's guardian, but seven months after William's death, a complaint is made to the mayor and aldermen of London that John has not been 'decently maintained'. The mayor orders Laurence 'to provide him yearly whilst at school with a furred gown, a coat of Alemayne [Germany] with tunic to match, four pairs of linen cloths, sufficient shoes and a decent bed', and 10d a week for expenses. The reference to the bed implies that John Hanington sleeps at the school, and the 'coat of Germany' with matching tunic might imply a kind of school uniform.[35] Some English schools have a remarkably long history and are already ancient in the late Middle Ages, such as the King's School in Canterbury, founded at the end of the 500s, the King's School in Rochester, founded at the start of the 600s, and St Peter's School in York and Thetford Grammar School in Norfolk, also founded in the 600s.

Chapter 15

How Moche Cometh It To? Going Shopping

The Middle English words *chepe* and *cheping* mean 'market' and 'trading' respectively. The modern London street name Cheapside (called Chepe in the late Middle Ages), has nothing to do with the modern adjective 'cheap' but reveals that the street is the main trading area of medieval London, and the names of towns like Chipping Sodbury and Chipping Norton come from the same root. The word *evecheping* or *evynchepyng* means trading or selling in the evening, which is forbidden by the authorities in medieval towns. In the darkness of a world without electricity, with only the dim light of a guttering tallow candle, it is all too easy to sell unsatisfactory goods to your unsuspecting customers, and instead you must sell them between sunrise and sunset, i.e. during daylight hours when customers are able to inspect the items properly. This applies to all traders, not only those who sell food. In 1349, for example, the regulations of the guild of glovers in London state that members must not sell their wares in their own homes by candlelight, 'seeing that folks cannot have such good knowledge by candlelight as by daylight' and are therefore unable to tell 'whether the wares are made of good leather or bad'.[1]

Most traders are not allowed to open their shops on Sundays. Butchers are an exception, though only until 10.00am, and in London in June 1416, a proclamation is made that it is forbidden to sell food and drink after 9.00pm and before 6.00am on any day of the week.[2] Cutlers are also included in the general prohibition on opening shops on Sundays, though if someone urgently needs a knife or blade, it is permitted to sell him or her one from a private house without opening the shop. In 1413, barbers in London are also ordered not to work on Sundays and are informed that they will have to pay a fine of half a mark (6s 8d) for every time they are found to have done so.[3] Shops in medieval towns are often tiny: one on the corner of Cheapside and Sopereslane (now Queen Street) in London in the early 1300s that sells buttons and other small clothing items measures just 5.8 feet (1.76 metres) long and 5.4 feet (1.64 metres) wide. It is 8 feet (2.4 metres) high on the Sopereslane side and 8.75 feet (2.66 metres) high on the other side.[4] In 1348, Joan Sautemareys gives her daughter Isabella and Isabella's husband Roger Love a shop in Bath, with a solar above and a cellar below. The shop is 11.5 feet long and 14 feet wide.[5]

Traders and shops cluster together, and the names of streets which still exist in modern London show what is sold there in the fourteenth and fifteenth centuries: Milk Street, Bread Street, and Poultry, for example. Medieval Nottingham has a Street of the Lorimers, written in Latin as *Vicus Lorimeriorum*. A lorimer is a maker of small metal objects, e.g. for horses' harnesses; they are either *copresmythes* (coppersmiths) or *irensmythes* (ironsmiths). Nottingham also has an area of drapers' shops, i.e. cloth-sellers.[6] In the fourteenth century, an area of Leicester is called *Satirdaymarketh*, i.e. 'Saturday market', and another, near Leicester's east gate, is called *Swynesmarket*. While John of Gaunt, duke of Lancaster and earl of Leicester, visits the town in August 1375, he arranges that 'new shopping stalls' will be constructed in the *Satirdaymarketh*. The word 'shop' appears in English in the middle of the French in which the duke's letter is written, *shoppe*.[7] Medieval Nottingham also has a *Seterdaymarket* as well as a *Womenmerkeyth*, 'women's market', and a *Wykedaymerkeyth*, 'weekday market'.[8]

The late medieval world is, for the most part, a world where the written word is not used in public, because this would be pointless. Instead, shopkeepers and traders hang a pole outside their shop or stall which will have something hanging from it to make clear which products they sell, or which services they provide. A barber, for instance, will have basins hanging from his, and a person who runs a tavern from their house might have branches and leaves hung outside their front door, signifying wine.[9] Haggling over the price of goods in medieval shops and markets is acceptable and expected, as is expressing your incredulity at the excessive amount the seller asks for at first. When the seller has totted up the total cost of your purchases, ask 'Now, dame/sire, how moche cometh it to, this that I have of you?'[10]

As medieval England is a place where starvation is an ever-present danger, there are considerable anxieties around the availability of basic foodstuffs. In some towns such as Leicester, it is forbidden for anyone to buy more corn than their household needs, and the corn-sellers at the Saturday market are not allowed to sell any before 10.00am, the official opening time of the market. Getting the timing just right, when the *cornmongere* has not yet sold out of his wares but might be willing to sell to you for a little less as the day grows long, is a good idea to ensure that you *hath not of the dere chepe*, i.e. have made a good bargain.[11] The prices of foodstuffs are strictly regulated, and it is illegal to sell your produce for more than the official price. All these regulations are in place to ensure that everyone has a fair chance of buying sufficient corn and that people do not go hungry because others have selfishly bought more than they really need or because traders have sold their goods at a higher price to certain privileged customers before shops and markets officially open (this is called 'forestalling' and will be severely punished).

Many English towns hold a weekly market after they are granted a charter to do so by the king, and throughout the Middle Ages numerous English landowners are given royal permission to hold an annual fair in the towns or villages which they own. They mostly take place on three days: on the feast day of a saint and the day before and after. Fairs are usually, though not always, held during the warmer months of the year. In February 1227, for example, Sir Hugh Despenser (d. 1238) is granted an annual fair at Loughborough in Leicestershire 'on the vigil, the feast, and the morrow of St Peter ad Vincula', i.e. on 31 July, 1 and 2 August.[12] Occasionally, as a special royal favour, fairs are allowed to be held twice a year and to last longer than three days. Edward III gives John Stratford, archbishop of Canterbury, permission to hold two fairs a year in his Sussex manor of Cliffe Hill in May 1345. One is to take place on 'the feast of the Decollation of St John the Baptist', 29

August, and the eight days following, and the second on the feast of St Katherine, 25 November, and the eight days following.[13] In a charter dated 12 February 1284, Edward I gives the town of Nottingham permission to hold, in addition to the existing fair held for eight days at the feast of St Matthew the Apostle (21 September), a second to last for fifteen days 'on the eve, the day, and the morrow of the feast of St Edmund the King and Martyr, and for the twelve days following'.[14] The feast day of St Edmund, the king of East Anglia murdered by the Danes in 869, is 20 November. Sir Roger Lestrange (d. 1382) holds two fairs every year at his Middlesex manor of Uxbridge, on the feasts of St Margaret and St Michael, i.e. 20 July and 29 September.[15] In 1318, it is said that the bailiffs of Great Yarmouth have held an annual fair 'from a time whereof memory exists not'.[16]

An agreement is reached around 1300 between the prior of Lenton, a very wealthy and influential religious house just outside Nottingham, and the burgesses of Nottingham. Lenton Priory has its own annual fair which began the day before the feast of St Martin, i.e. on 10 November, and strife has arisen on account of this fair and the two which are held annually in Nottingham itself. Cloth merchants, mercers and apothecaries use the Lenton fair, and pay 12d to the prior for each stall during the eight days of the fair. Merchants of other products only pay 8d. Stalls are, in the usual medieval fashion, grouped together, with the merchants selling the best cloth in one area, the middling cloth merchants together, and the cheapest kind together as well. Each booth measures eight feet by eight feet. During the Lenton fair, no markets are held in the town of Nottingham, and only essentials, meaning food, drink, and leather, can be sold at all, and only from the sellers' houses.[17]

John and Isabel Brudeport hold a fair at their manor of Bere (later called Bere Regis) in Dorset, which in or shortly before October 1325 is attacked by Sir John Maltravers (b. *c.*1266), lord of nearby Lytchett Matravers, and over two dozen of his retainers. The Brudeports have deputed three men, Richard and John Turbervill and Ralph Chidiok, to 'collect the customs and other profits of the fair' but the three are assaulted by Maltravers and his men, who steal the money. The couple have also hired men to 'keep the peace' at the fair, but they are attacked as well. Edward II orders an investigation.[18] Edward I forbids the holding of a fair in London called *Neue Feyre* or 'new fair' in 1297, on the grounds that it is a hive of cutpurses (thieves) and murderers, though evidently the prohibition has little effect, as his son Edward II bans it again a few years later.[19]

A great international fair is held every summer at Boston in Lincolnshire, then called the 'town of St Botolph'. The fair begins on 17 June, the feast day of St Botolph. In 1330, Edward III's queen Philippa of Hainault (*c*.1314–69) buys large quantities of fine Flemish and Italian cloth, including green silk decorated with griffins' heads, from this fair.[20] So many London merchants travel to Boston that the Court of Husting in the city closes for a month every year. Other annual fairs frequented by numerous merchants are held at Stamford also in Lincolnshire, Salisbury in Wiltshire, Winchester in Hampshire, St Ives in Huntingdonshire (which takes place just after Easter) and Bury St Edmunds in Suffolk. *Seint Bartilmews faire* or 'Saint Bartholomew's fair', a large and important cloth fair, is held in Smithfield in London on the feast of St Bartholomew and the day before and after every year, that is, 23 to 25 August.[21]

Chapter 16

Medieval Misteries: Working

If you are a boy, you will, in many cases, begin an apprenticeship at age 12 or 13, though if you do not, there is also work for labourers without a particular skill. Girls are also sometimes taken on as apprentices, especially in the cloth trades, and weaving, brewing ale, baking bread, fishing, and driving carts are also popular occupations for women. If you prefer not to follow in your father's profession and learn it from him, your parents or guardians will pay a master craftsman or tradesman a sum of money somewhere between 12 shillings (144d) and 5 marks (800d) for instructing, feeding, and clothing you for the duration of your apprenticeship. It will last a minimum of seven years, sometimes ten or even fourteen years, and you will be paid between 1½d and 3d a day throughout. You will be at least 19 or 20 when you finish your apprenticeship and perhaps in your mid-20s. Bear in mind that you will not be allowed to marry until it is completed, and furthermore, you will find yourself in deep trouble if you commit what is called 'fornication' in your master's house.[1]

Valentine Hamond, aged 13, becomes an apprentice skinner (i.e. a person who prepares and deals in animal skins) with Richard Hudy in Winchester, Hampshire in 1334, and in 1343, 42-year-old William Ward of the Lincolnshire village of Thurlby sends his teenage son Robert to learn goldsmithery with William Goldsmyth of Lincoln.[2] A few decades later in September 1402, Robert Grave of Redbourne in Lincolnshire also moves to Lincoln and becomes an apprentice saddler for seven years with Henry Sadeler. In 1411, John Bakham moves the 30 miles from Marlborough to Salisbury to be apprenticed to Walter Shirley, a merchant.[3] After Hamo Palmer of London dies in 1306, his 12-year-old son Nicholas is taken on as an apprentice by William

Causton, a mercer. Nicholas, now aged 20, completes his eight-year apprenticeship in July 1314. Ralph Mymmes is also 12 when he begins to train as a carter in 1339.[4]

Marion Lymeseye begins a seven-year apprenticeship with Roger Oriel, a paternostrer, in 1276. Her mother Christine acknowledges that she owes Roger 14 shillings (168d), to be paid in instalments of 6d four times a year for the seven years, and is lucky to be allowed to do so, as many master tradesmen and craftsmen will demand full payment upfront. Elizabeth Forster, an orphan in the care of her stepfather John Munstede, is placed as an apprentice with John and Joan Appelby in 1387, who will teach her 'the art of a *thredwomman*', i.e. a woman who sells thread and yarn. Five years later, Marion Walle, daughter of the tailor Nicholas Walle (d. 1389), is placed as an apprentice with another tailor, John Penreth, and his wife Emmote.[5] When the cutler Stephen Page dies in 1340, his sons John and Richard are still underage, and he leaves 'all his implements of the craft of *cotellerie* [cutlery] and the remaining term of Robert and John his apprentices' to his daughter Katherine, along with 640d in cash. In the same decade, the married couple John and Maud Mymmes both work in London as *ymaginours*, image-makers, and Maud, an able and energetic woman, also runs a brewery in their home. They both die in the plague year of 1349, leaving two daughters, Alice and Isabel, who are about 10 and 8 years old that year. Maud divides her 'copies and instruments pertaining to the making of pictures … [and] her best chests for keeping them in' into three parts for her daughters and her apprentice, Thomas.[6]

If you are an apprentice and you are unhappy or dissatisfied for some reason, you may be tempted to run away. Be aware, though, that your master will do his utmost to find you, and the authorities will be on his side. Medieval England is a place where everything is done and made by hand, therefore it is important that there is a constant supply of people with the skills to make everything that needs to be made. Apprenticeships are thus tightly regulated and controlled. Just as the country has no place for people who are unwilling to work very hard, it refuses to tolerate apprentices who run away from their training without a very good reason. Martyn Halscombe, apprentice of the London fishmonger John Crosse (d. 1334), 'suddenly left his service' and makes it as far as Exeter, 180 miles away, while John Tesdale, apprentice to the saddler Thomas Hexham in Newcastle-upon-Tyne, flees to London, 280 miles away. Despite the distances involved, both young men are located and ordered to return, because, as noted in Chapter 6 above, it is very difficult to disappear for good in medieval England.[7] The 1349 Ordinance of Labourers prescribes imprisonment for apprentices or labourers who leave their service without an excellent reason, and your 'indentures of apprenticeship' are a binding contract which can only be breached in extreme circumstances. In 1376, the apprentice pie-baker John Boys is imprisoned after running away from and refusing to serve his master, John Pygeon. It is also forbidden for anyone to attempt to lure you away from your master to work for them instead during your apprenticeship.[8]

The indentures of apprenticeship are binding on both sides, and you have recourse to the courts if your master ill-treats you or does not instruct you or feed you properly; the urgent importance of training the next generation of craftsmen and tradesmen does not mean that masters have carte blanche to abuse their young charges. The chaucer Thomas Kydemenstre appears before the mayor of London's court in 1305 after he takes on Thomas Beverle as an apprentice, but fails to clothe, feed, or instruct him. Kydemenstre beats young Thomas after the boy lends two pairs of shoes to someone without his permission, whereupon poor Thomas, frightened and distressed, runs away to his father. Kydemenstre is ordered to pay 40d in damages to Thomas's father, and to feed and instruct his young charge properly.[9] Although Thomas has run away, the court acknowledges that he had good reason to do so, and he is not punished or reprimanded.

In 1369, John Catour, father of Alice Catour of Reading, takes the London *brouderer* (embroider) Elis Mympe to court 'for beating and ill-treating the girl and failing to provide for her'. Elis pays John Catour one mark (13s 4d) in compensation, and Alice is allowed to leave her apprenticeship without penalty or censure.[10] If your master does not instruct you properly but instead makes you perform menial tasks unrelated to the trade which you wish to practise, you also have a legal right to be released from your apprenticeship, because he is wasting your time and your parents' money, and is also failing to ensure that there will be sufficient people in the future skilled and trained in his particular trade. Richard atte Welle, a goldsmith, gets into trouble in 1365 for sending his apprentice John in the Lane 'into the country to thresh his corn', and the following year Nicholas Salman sues his master, Robert Leddered, for making him do 'mean tasks both within and outside his house' rather than teaching him how to be a draper.[11]

If your master gets into trouble with the law in some way and is therefore unable to instruct you, you will be officially released from the apprenticeship. In 1383, apprentice mercer John Penreth – who probably comes from the town of Penrith in Cumberland, in the far north of England – complains that his master William Reynald has been imprisoned for debt for the last eight weeks and his London shop is sealed up. John is, he says, 'wasting his time treading the streets', and is therefore allowed to leave his apprenticeship.[12] At Easter 1391, John Shynguler of Birmingham is taken on as an apprentice by the master draper Roger Grymston for eight years. Only seven months later, however, John reports his master to the authorities, as Roger has 'absconded for debt' and has left poor John, only at the start of his teens, 'destitute and homeless' in the mean streets of London, a city he barely knows. He is forced to beg for food and drink, which a few kindly people give him 'for the love of God'. John is released from his apprenticeship, as he has more than reasonable cause to be allowed to do so.[13] Members of a mistery will often look out for you and intervene if something goes wrong during your apprenticeship. The father of Robert Fraunceys of Maltby in Yorkshire pays 20s to the Fleet Street spurrier Nicholas Beaubelot in 1305 to instruct and feed his son, but Nicholas fails to do so. His neighbour Hugh Strubby steps in and takes young Robert into his own service, 'lest he should perish of hunger'.[14]

Once you are fully qualified in your trade, you will be paid 3d or 4d a day until you become a master craftsman, when you will receive 5d or 6d a day. Unskilled labourers will be paid 1½d or 2d. When you are hired for a job, food and drink will either be provided on top of your daily wages or you will be given extra money to pay for it, and this payment is called *nonschenche*.[15] Given how expensive food is, this is a real bonus. If you manage to work hard and long enough to save up some money, you will have to decide where to keep it safely, given that banks and safes will not exist for hundreds more years. Wealthy people often leave their cash in religious houses, where it is mostly, though not completely, safe from thieves. Others bury it in the ground or under a tree, where it is less safe. By the late thirteenth century, companies from Florence such as the Bardi and the Peruzzi are operating in England, and are proto-banks who look after their clients' money, pay it out to them on demand, and offer credit. You will need to be very rich indeed to avail yourself of their services, however.

Some women take on the trade of their late father or husband. Rohese Burford (born *c.*1286) is, with her younger sister Margery Weston, co-heir to her parents Thomas Romeyn and Juliana Hauteyn, and inherits properties in London, Kent, Surrey and Sussex. Sometime before December 1312, Rohese marries John Burford, a pepperer from Southampton. They have two daughters, Joan and Katherine, and a son, James Burford, who is probably born in 1320. Not long after she gives birth to James, Rohese is widowed. She has her own business exporting wool, and is a talented seamstress to boot: Edward II buys a cope which she has embroidered as a gift for the new pope, John XXII, in 1316, and pays Rohese 100 marks (£66.66) for it. As well as her own successful businesses, Rohese runs her late husband's spice business until her death in 1329, and is wealthy enough to lend a man 1,000 marks (£666) in 1325.[16]

In 1310, there is a rather remarkable reference in London to a young man who has recently completed a ten-year apprenticeship with 'Henry the Surgeon and Katherine, wife of the same'.[17] It seems as though there is a medically trained woman in London in the early fourteenth century, though sadly there is no more information about Katherine and her life and work. Women are economically active in late medieval

England, and they often run businesses and make and sell their own produce. In the 1320s, Eleyne Glaswreghte ('glasswright') has her own successful glassmaking business in London, Alice Coleman of Byfleet in Surrey runs a brewery, Isabel Lynne of King's Lynn and Cecile Maar of Lenton near Nottingham make leather goods, and Agnes of Kimbolton in Huntingdonshire, Alice Lely of Nottingham, and Eleyne Lambley also of Nottingham all work as carters. Half a century later, Isabel Gerland is one of the masters of the London guild of *hurers*, who make and sell caps.[18]

For the overwhelming majority of people, your working day begins very early: around sunrise in the lighter months of the year, and otherwise around Prime or 6.00am. If you are a person who enjoys a lie-in, you have come to the wrong place. In 1362, masons, carpenters, plasterers and tilers are to be paid 6d a day from Easter until St Michael's day (29 September) but only 5d a day from St Michael to Easter, because of the shorter hours of daylight and, therefore, the shorter working time. They are not paid on feast days when they do not work. Shops are open Mondays to Fridays, mornings to afternoons, and on Saturday until mid-afternoon.[19] Sundays and feast days are rest days, as is Tuesday, 14 November 1312, at least in London; the future king, Edward III, eldest child of Edward II and Isabella of France, is born at Windsor Castle on 13 November, and a proclamation is made early the following day that no one in the city needs to work that day. In fact, Londoners take the whole week off 'for joy at the birth' of their future king.[20]

Feast days are known either as *chirchehalydayes* ('church holy days') or *hye dayes* ('high days'). The most important ones in late medieval England, in addition to Christmas (*Cristemasse*), Easter (*Estre*) and Pentecost/Whitsuntide (*Whitsontid*), are: the feast of the Circumcision of Jesus Christ on 1 January; the Epiphany, usually known as the feast of the Three Kings (*Thre Kynges*), on 6 January; the Purification, also known as Candlemas, on 2 February; the Annunciation on 25 March; the Nativity of St John the Baptist on 24 June; the Translation of St Thomas the Martyr on 7 July (the date in 1220 on which the remains of Thomas Becket, murdered in 1170 and canonised in 1173, were moved or 'translated' to a new shrine in Canterbury Cathedral); the Assumption of *Mayde Marie*, the Virgin Mary, on 15 August; the Nativity of the Virgin Mary on 8 September; the feast of St Edward the Confessor, the king of England who died at the start of 1066 and was canonised a century later, on 13 October; All Saints (*All Halowes*) on 1 November; and the feast of Thomas Becket, usually known to medieval English people as St Thomas the Martyr, on 29 December, the date on which he was murdered in 1170.[21] Passion Week or Holy Week is called the *Paynful Weke* in Middle English. Numerous other saints' days are commemorated as well, such as the feast of St Michael, also often called Michaelmas, on 29 September, St Matthew the Evangelist on 21 September, St Luke the Evangelist on 18 October, St Laurence on 10 August, St Martin on 11 November, St Katherine on 25 November, and St James on 25 July.

The days before and after a feast day are called 'the vigil' and 'the morrow' and are also important, and the special mass said by priests on the day after the feast is called the *Morowemasse*. Some medieval misteries specify that their members cannot sell goods on the vigil or morrow of important feast days as well as on the feast day itself.[22] On Thursday, 23 June 1306, the vigil of the Nativity of St John the Baptist,

> the tailors of Oxford and other townsmen with them kept vigil in their shops all night, singing and making their solace with harps, vielles and other diverse instruments, as is the custom to do, both there [Oxford] and elsewhere, by reason of the observance of that feast. And after midnight ... they went forth from their shops, and began to dance in the high street.[23]

As noted in Chapter 4 above, it is proclaimed in London in the early 1400s that lanterns must be hung outside people's houses on certain special feast days, which are specified as the period between Christmas and Epiphany and the vigil of the Nativity of St John the Baptist.[24]

Other than having time off on the important feast days, in late medieval England you will have to work very hard. Joining the royal household may be your best bet for a comfortable life, though as is the case with all great households in late medieval England, almost all royal servants are men. If you are a woman, you will have far fewer opportunities, though in the 1320s Edward II hires two women, who are married to two of his existing servants, to work in his chamber. Rather remarkably, he even pays them the same rate as the men, 3d a day, though women usually only receive half of what men are paid.[25] Rates of pay in the royal household are higher than average, all your food, drink, clothes, shoes and accommodation will be provided on top for free, and there will be little real work to do; the king surrounds himself with hundreds of servants to increase his magnificence and splendour, not because there is a genuine amount of work for so many people – the king's household consists of around 400 to 500 servants – to undertake.

Although you are not allowed to have your wife and children living at court with you, they are allowed to visit, and you may leave court and go home to see them several times a year, armed with money from the king. This represents your missing wages, travel costs, and what amounts to holiday pay. If you are too ill to work or are injured in royal service, you will continue to be paid, and will be accommodated at a royal manor if you wish, or sent home to recuperate if you prefer that. In March 1326, John Dene, one of the ushers of Edward II's chamber, falls ill. He is sent to his own home to Canterbury and given the huge sum of £5, the equivalent of a few months' sick pay in advance. More than two months later, John is still ill, and the king, passing through Kent, visits him at home and gives him another £5. If you receive news that a spouse or parent is dying, or that something unpleasant has befallen a relative, you are given permission to leave court and go home. Edward II gives his servant Richard 'Hick' Mereworth permission to travel to his native Henley-on-Thames in Oxfordshire in 1326 when Hick receives word that thieves have broken into his and his pregnant wife Joan's house and stolen their goods. Hick departs with a generous gift of 20 shillings (£1) from the king. Another servant, Syme Lawe, informs Edward in 1324 that his father Roger is very ill in Henley-on-Thames, and Syme and his brother Henry, who also works in the royal household, are sent home to visit Roger for a while, armed with 10 shillings to buy medicines for him.[26]

On the other hand, one big disadvantage of working in the royal household is that it is constantly on the move. Unlike later centuries, the medieval kings do not spend most of the year in their palaces and castles in and around London, but move in a never-ending circuit around the south and Midlands of England. You will have to walk for miles along the dirt tracks of medieval England several times a week, or every day if the king is feeling particularly restless, regardless of the weather. For much of the year, rain will drip down your neck as you tramp along, you will have to splash through puddles and wade through flooded streams and rivers, you will be knee-deep in mud, and you will be expected to lend a shoulder whenever a cart's wheels get stuck in the mud, as they often will. On freezing days, you will slip about all over the ice or trudge through snow, and on hot days you will bake and burn in the sun. You know that you have another 12 or 15 or 18 miles of this torment to endure until you reach Nottingham, or wherever the king has decided to spend the night, and even when you get there, it is not as though you can turn the central heating on or have a hot shower to warm up, or take a cool shower to wash off the sweat and grime.

Work is perhaps the only arena where those of common birth have something of an advantage over their nobly born contemporaries. The earl of Arundel is unlikely to react well if his eldest son tells him that he would like to train as a carpenter; young men in noble families have no such choice, and will undergo military training from early childhood, apart from a small minority who will be given to the Church and expected to live a celibate life. On the other hand, if your father is a chandler and you tell him that you think you would like to learn the skills to make a living as a carpenter, this is likely to go down a lot better. The English elite have more comfortable, easy and privileged lives than everyone else, but the price they pay for this privilege is having little if any freedom of choice as to how they would like to conduct those lives.

In a world where everything is made by hand, crafts and trades are highly valued. Guilds, or misteries as they are often known in the Middle Ages, begin to form in the twelfth century, and between the thirteenth and the fifteenth centuries many of them develop codes of conduct. Strict regulations clarify how much a guild member will be paid and how often, how much you can charge for your goods or services, the level of quality that the goods must reach, and so on. The dimensions of your goods and materials you must use when making them, if applicable, will also be specified. Regulations usually also state that workers cannot be paid in advance except in exceptional circumstances. What is known as 'rebellious conduct' towards the masters of each mistery will be punished by ten days' imprisonment and a fine of 10 shillings for the first offence, and twenty days' imprisonment and a fine of 20 shillings for the second.[27]

Chapter 17

Olifaunts, Sothseyers and Storms: Oddities and Intense Weather

You live or are staying in London sometime in the second half of the thirteenth century or in the fourteenth. As you settle down to sleep one night, you can hear voices, laughter, and horses whinnying outside in the streets. So far, so normal. But what on earth is that other noise? It sounds terrifyingly like the roar of a lion, startlingly loud and echoing through the city in the chilly night air.

It is, in fact, the roar of a lion. In the 1230s, Henry III receives gifts of lions and leopards from his brother-in-law Frederick II, Holy Roman Emperor, and twenty years later takes possession of an elephant from another brother-in-law, Louis IX, king of France. Not to be outdone, the king of Norway, Haakon IV, sends Henry a gift of a polar bear, and thus the Tower of London menagerie is born. Lions and leopards are kept in the Tower for many more years, and they have a keeper who earns 1½d a day, a rather small amount. Each lion and leopard, by contrast, is provided with 6d worth of food per day. In the 1310s, the keeper is a Frenchman, Pierre Faber of Montpellier, and in the 1330s, Berengar Couder or Caudrer of Aragon, who is Spanish, holds the position. Berengar is then taking care of two lions and two leopards, and his wages have declined to a rather pitiful 1d a day, though he does have his accommodation, food and drink provided for free, and has the huge Tower complex on his doorstep and is allowed to wander around at will.[1]

If you live in a provincial English town rather than in London, you will still have an occasional opportunity to see the exotic animals kept by the king and other members of the royal family. Edward II, as prince of Wales and heir to the throne in the early 1300s, takes his pet lion, which has its own keeper and is kept on a silver chain, around the country with him, and at his favourite residence of Kings Langley (then called 'Childerlangele') in Hertfordshire, stables a camel alongside his horses. In 1317, he receives a gift of another two camels from an Italian friend, Antonio di Pessagno. Edward's son Edward III owns at least two lions, three leopards, a wildcat, and a bear.[2] By 1364, he has also acquired 'a beast from the land of Egypt called *Oure*'. This is a Middle English word meaning either an Egyptian buffalo or a wild ox, presumably the former in this instance. The king's barber Roger Ewerye is, whether willingly or not, placed in charge of the animal.[3] Medieval English people know of elephants (*olifaunts* in Middle English) as well as lions and leopards (*lupardis*), though how many people will ever have laid eyes on these animals is another matter.[4]

In 1300, a rector named William is hauled before the mayor of London's court for bringing the bodies of four dead wolves to the city.[5] William is curious about a disease he calls 'Wolf', perhaps the condition we now know as lupus, which means 'wolf' in Latin, and believes that it can be cured by the application of wolf flesh. He therefore orders a cask of dead wolves to be sent to his church from the Continent, though unfortunately, where exactly on the Continent is not specified. By the time the dead animals arrive in London, their corpses have become 'putrid', and William is ordered to explain himself to the mayor's court. This situation reveals several things: that a man in England somehow manages to contact a person on the Continent who is willing and able to send him dead wolves (in England by this time, wolves are close to extinction); that officials are aware that the welfare of the general public in a crowded city might be worsened by the presence of decaying animal corpses; and that a person in 1300 is deeply interested in a particular disease and cares about its victims, and therefore attempts, albeit in a comically misguided way, to find a cure for it.

Alongside matters which raise a knowing chuckle among people who have vastly more advanced knowledge of medicine than their forebears, there are things in late medieval England that feel surprisingly modern and that still exist many hundreds of years later. To take a random example, you might not have known that auditors already exist in the late Middle Ages, but they do. Thomas Romeyn (d. 1312), a merchant of Italian origin who serves as mayor of London in 1309/10, is often appointed as an auditor in the early 1300s. In July 1307, he and some colleagues carry out an audit on the accounts of two trading partners, John Trumpeshale and William Conele, at *Coldhakber* or Coldharbour, a famous London mansion.[6] A few years later in the mid-1320s, Edward II falls out with the English-born archbishop of Dublin, Alexander Bicknor (d. 1349), and declares that auditors have found 'diverse falsities' in the archbishop's accounts.[7] An accusation of cooking the books; how very modern.

At other times, you will feel most decidedly alien. If you happen to be in the Yorkshire town of Pontefract in 1382, you will hear that a man has been arrested for 'casting the evil eye on the horse of his neighbour, John Hirn'.[8] And if you visit Coventry in 1324, you will hear of the arrest of one John of Nottingham. John is a necromancer who has been hired, at great cost, by a group of disgruntled men in Coventry to assassinate the king, the prior of Coventry and four other important men by 'his necromancy and arts', or *sa nigromancie et ses artz* as it appears in the medieval French of the indictment. John and his assistant Robert Mareschal purchase 7 pounds of wax and 2 ells (i.e. 90 inches) of canvas to make wax figures of the six men they have been hired to kill, and make a seventh figure of a local resident named Richard Sowe as a test case. One night in September 1324, in an 'old house' half a league (i.e. about half an hour's walk) outside Coventry, they drive a sharpened feather into the forehead of Richard's wax figure. The next day, Robert Mareschal goes to Richard's house, and discovers that the unfortunate man has lost his memory and can do nothing but howl and cry out '*Harrou!*', an expression of distress in Middle English. Some days later, John of Nottingham and Robert Mareschal plunge the feather into the place where Richard Sowe's heart would be on the wax figure, and supposedly the unfortunate Richard dies soon afterwards. Before the necromancer can attempt to murder the king and the other men, however, his assistant Robert suffers an attack of conscience and gives the game away to the authorities.[9]

Sothseyers or *sothseggers*, i.e. 'soothsayers' or truth-tellers, people who claim to know the future and will tell you your fortune, are a feature of late medieval English towns, and an alliterative poem from the fifteenth century is called *Mum and the Sothsegger* or 'silence and the soothsayer' ('mum' in the sense of silence still exists in the modern expression 'keep mum'). Thomas Forde of Canterbury, a sawyer and a *sothseyer*, is condemned to the pillory in 1418. He has told Jonet, widow of Janyn Cook, that he knows where her late husband buried £200 – a sum equivalent to hundreds of thousands today – underground, and that he will tell her where it is if she pays him 40 shillings.[10] Robert Berewold, also a soothsayer, is hired to discover who has stolen a mazer (a drinking vessel made of maple-wood) from Maud Eye in London in 1382. Robert sticks a wooden peg in a loaf of bread, fixes four knives around the loaf, and does 'soothsaying and magic over them'. He accuses one Joan Wolsy of being the thief, whereupon the indignant Joan sues him for defamation. She wins, and Robert is locked in the pillory for an hour with the loaf, the peg and knives still stuck in it, hanging around his neck. Also in London in 1382, Henry Pot accuses Christina Freman of stealing a mazer lost by Stephen Gardiner. Henry has determined her guilt by making thirty-two balls of white clay, 'and over them did sorcery, or his magic art'. Christina is proved innocent, and Henry is condemned to the pillory for defaming her good name and because sorcery 'manifestly redounds against the doctrine of sacred writ'.[11]

No less a person than Henry V's stepmother Juana of Navarre, dowager queen of England and widow of Henry IV, is accused of witchcraft and sorcery in 1419. The accusation is also levelled at Eleanor Cobham, duchess of Gloucester, wife of one of Henry V's brothers, a few years later. Queen Juana is accused of trying to kill her stepson the king by magic, and though she is never put on trial, she is held under house arrest for several years. Duchess Eleanor, meanwhile, is convicted of 'treasonable necromancy' and sentenced to life imprisonment. Her astrologers have informed her that her husband's nephew, Henry V's son Henry VI, will suffer from a life-threatening illness in the summer of 1441.[12] Predicting the death of the king is a decidedly unwise move, especially as Eleanor would benefit hugely from it: her husband Humphrey, duke of Gloucester, as the only living brother of Henry V and uncle of the currently childless Henry VI, would succeed to the throne if the young man died, and Eleanor would become queen of England.

Even soothsayers cannot accurately predict the weather, and you are at its mercy far more than will be the case for your modern descendants. You have no reliable way of knowing what the weather will be like tomorrow or in a few days' time, and you also have no way of knowing what the temperature is, as the scales of Fahrenheit and Celsius will not be invented until the 1700s. Even if you are not fluent in Middle English, however, you will have little problem describing the weather, as the words are so similar to modern English: *it thondreth and lyghtneth, it rayneth and haylleth* (it thunders and lightnings, it rains and hails).[13]

The weather feels more intense in the late Middle Ages than it will be a few centuries later. Around 1300, the Medieval Warm Period begins to give way to the start of the centuries-long Little Ice Age, and winters of the late Middle Ages are often bitterly cold, even during the Warm Period. A London chronicler states that on 28 December 1256, there is 'a great tempest, with thunder and lightning' in the city, and that the winter of 1262/63 is a particularly bad one: the River Thames freezes solidly, and there is a 'great frost and thick ice' for many weeks. Even this is beaten by the winter of 1282/83, which sees 'such an abundance of frost, cold and snow' that even the oldest English people have never experienced before, and five arches of London Bridge are destroyed 'by the violence of the ice'. The *French Chronicle of London* confirms that 'London Bridge was broken by the great frost'. In the winter of 1305/06, snow and ice lie on the ground from 15 December to 27 January, and again from 13 February until as late as 13 April.[14]

The winter of 1308/09 is another harsh one, and in 1309/10, the Thames freezes solidly and Londoners are able to walk over it to

Southwark on the south bank of the river. In 1316, there is a hard frost during Christmas week, snow lies on the ground for most of the first three months of 1322, and there is a reference in the Assize of Nuisance on 6 December 1325 to the prevailing 'wintry conditions' that are making outside work impossible.[15] Wintry weather sometimes persists into spring. When Thomas, earl of Lancaster, is taken from York to his own castle of Pontefract to be executed shortly before 22 March 1322, onlookers throw snowballs at him, and nearly a century and a half later, the almost unbelievably bloody battle of Towton in Yorkshire is fought on 29 March 1461 during a blinding snowstorm. The freezing cold is not the only problem inhabitants of medieval English towns have to endure: in the winter of 1294, the Thames floods so badly that 'it drowned a great part of the lands of Bermundeseye [Bermondsey] and of all the country round about'.[16]

In January 1257 and again throughout January and into early February 1259, there are many references to the 'excessive wind and changeable weather', and the wind is strong enough to destroy buildings across the south of England, especially on the latter occasion. Even the walls of the great stronghold of Dover Castle on the Kent coast are badly damaged, while buildings in the royal manors of Kennington near London and Woodstock near Oxford, and towers, battlements and other buildings in the castles of Oxford, Winchester, Gloucester and Salisbury, are unroofed by the fierce wind.[17] In 1286/87, terrible storms wash away the Sussex port of Winchelsea and the Suffolk port of Dunwich, and there is a truly horrendous storm and consequent widespread flooding in January 1362 (see also Chapter 2 above) which affects Germany, Scandinavia, the Low Countries and Ireland as well as England, Wales and Scotland. This storm and its deadly consequences remain famous, or infamous, even in the twenty-first century, and the event is often known as St Marcellus's Flood and in the Netherlands as *Grote Mandrenke*, the 'great drowning of men'.

The St Paul's annalist says that a terrific storm with much thunder and lightning takes place in London on 15 July 1315, and that a bolt of lightning causes a conflagration at Woburn Abbey 40 miles away.

Six days later, a storm in London around midday is supposedly so bad that it sweeps up a boy of 14 and strips the clothes from him, but deposits him back in the same place, whereupon he excitedly relates that he has seen 'many wonderful things'.[18] In July 1317, another terrific thunderstorm and heavy rain cause havoc in London; people are swept away and drowned.[19] Around 1 August 1341, a summer storm causes a 'great inundation of the sea' on the Lincolnshire coast, and in and around Lyme Regis and Bridport in Dorset, another awful storm occurs on 1 November 1401. A little boy present at a baptism supposedly loses his senses when there is 'a great peal of thunder' which is horrifically, violently loud, and a little girl playing in the street loses her vision thanks to a flash of incredibly bright lightning. A few years later, during the night of 9 April 1413, there is a terrible flood that destroys the North Bridge in Colchester, which is made of stone. Thomas Colchestre, who lives nearby, is kept awake half the night by the noise and by fear.[20]

In the early summer of 1383, the 16-year-old king, Richard II, is passing through Ely a few miles from Cambridge when a sudden and violent storm causes him and his large household to seek urgent shelter. A bolt of lightning strikes Sir James Berners, a knight of the royal chamber and a friend of the young king, and leaves him half-blind and in shock. Supposedly, however, the young man is cured and restored to full vision when he visits the shrine of St Etheldreda the Virgin in Ely Cathedral. Richard II makes a grant to the cathedral on 3 August 1383, and talks of how he 'saw many wonders wrought by the divine power of that glorious virgin, among others, the bestowal of sight upon a knight of the king, who was blinded by lightning in the night-time'.[21] As well as a belief in the power of miracles, something else of the medieval mentality is captured in one chronicler's magnificent description of a thunderstorm in July 1293: 'We beheld in the east a huge cloud blacker than coal, in the midst whereof we saw the lashes of an immense eye darting fierce lightning into the west … and demons were heard yelling in the air'.[22]

Medieval winters are often harsher and storms more overwhelming than they will be in the modern era, though conversely, it may be that summers of the 1300s and 1400s are rather hotter than in the twentieth and twenty-first centuries. In the summer of 1305, the 'burning heat ... oppressed mankind', and the consequences of the long hot months are, supposedly, drought and pox, so that many children and young people are 'afflicted with freckles and spots' and die.[23] The summer of 1326 is a particularly long, boiling hot and intensely dry one, and there are droughts that year and in 1324, 1344 and 1345. England experiences more boiling hot summers in 1375, 1377 and 1390.[24] On the other hand, the summers of 1327, 1330, 1350 and 1351 are chilly and wet. The year 1348, when the Black Death arrives in England for the first time, is a year without a summer, and it pours down relentlessly for many months. A chronicler named Ranulph Higden, based in Chester, states that 'scarcely a day passed without it raining during the day or night' between the Nativity of St John the Baptist, i.e. 24 June, and Christmas that year. Thomas Walsingham, a monk of St Albans, also writes that 'there was a great downpour which lasted from Midsummer to Christmas' in 1348.[25] In fact, most of the period from the autumn of 1347 until the spring of 1350 is wet. The winter of 1347/48 sees lots of flooding, the rainy summer of 1348 is followed by another very wet winter in 1348/49, and the autumn of 1349 and the spring of 1350 are, yet again, wet.[26]

An earthquake (recorded as *terre motus* in Latin by contemporaries) takes place in England on 11 September 1275, early in Edward I Longshanks' reign, and makes enough of an impression that four decades later in 1315, the year 1275 is still referred to as 'the time of the general earthquake'. Another earthquake, 'with great sound and much noise', takes place on 1 December 1319.[27] Two chronicles record a curious phenomenon on 31 October 1322, when the sky is 'of a colour like blood', or 'the sun turned into blood', from early in the morning until sunset. Finally, the year 1361 – when the Black Death returns to England and there is another terrible pandemic – is an odd one which sees a drought in England and northern France, and around late May that year, before the long dry spell begins, a rain 'almost like blood' falls. People claim to have seen apparitions in the sky, including a cross made of blood, and in England, France and other countries, supposedly two castles appear in the air from whence two armies of men, one dressed in black clothes and the other in white, sally forth and do battle before vanishing again.[28]

Chapter 18

Frenzy and Next Friends: Medieval Kindness

Thanks in large part to novelists and filmmakers, there is an abiding modern image of the Middle Ages as an era of superstition, ignorance, hateful bigotry and wanton cruelty, and not a great deal else. Medieval people, meanwhile, are often viewed as a parade of grotesque, overly religious freaks who are filthy all the time and produce little of value. In Connie Willis's hugely popular and still widely read 1992 novel *Doomsday Book*, myths and exaggerations about the Middle Ages abound. One of the main medieval characters, an undersized 12-year-old girl, is about to be forced into marriage to a man who is old enough to be her grandfather or even her great-grandfather. Although in the Middle Ages it is reasonably common for people at the higher end of the social scale to marry as children, they almost always marry other children. In some cases, girls in their teens are married to men ten or twelve years their senior, but for an adolescent girl to be married off to a man a few decades older is vanishingly rare if it ever happens at all, and marriage before adolescence is also extremely rare for anyone who is not of noble birth.

The medieval characters in *Doomsday Book* are depicted as somewhat primitive and dirty and are bitten constantly by fleas, as they do not have the wit to keep themselves clean or know how to keep their clothes and furnishings dirt and flea-free. The viewpoint character, a young woman from the middle of the twenty-first century who travels back 700 years in time (supposedly to 1320, though she arrives in 1348 by accident), is afraid of being burned at the stake as a witch for much of the first half of the novel. A professor of medieval history tells her before she leaves that witches are 'still burned alive' in the England of 1320, though the era of witch-burning does not in fact begin until the fifteenth century and is at its height in the seventeenth, three centuries after the novel is set, and nobody in England is burned for heresy until the early 1400s. Michael Crichton's 1999 novel *Timeline*, later made into a film, is a work of science fiction set mostly in France in the 1350s, with modern American characters. The medieval people are constantly trying to kill the modern time travellers for no particular reason, because killing people randomly or finding an excuse to drag them off to the stake to burn them alive is just something that they apparently do for fun in the Middle Ages.

Karen Maitland's 2008 *Company of Liars*, set in 1348, is another novel for which the expression 'relentlessly grim' might have been invented for its depiction of medieval life, and includes a scene where a man is forced to eat stinking, green-tinged pork in the belief that he might be Jewish, not Christian. He vomits because the meat is rotten, and is therefore dragged off to be slowly and agonisingly burned alive as a non-believer – more than half a century before this punishment for heresy was actually applied in England – because we cannot possibly have a novel set in the Middle Ages without someone being sent off to the stake or at the very least frightened that they might be. You would never know from modern fiction that burning people alive in the Middle Ages is exceedingly rare; novels tend to give the impression that it happens all the time. In *Company of Liars*, the unfortunate man's tormenters claim they are burning heretics to demonstrate that 'the Church has got everything under control' after the arrival of the Black Death, because presenting medieval Christians as murderous, hateful bigots and zealots is another essential feature of modern fiction.

The novel also includes a bizarre invention called the Cripples' Wedding. Two mentally and physically handicapped youngsters are forced to marry each other, then are subsequently coerced into attempting to copulate in front of their entire village, who find sadistic amusement in their plight and believe that this grim spectacle will protect them from the plague and divine wrath. Fourteenth-century people are, it seems, such unfathomably horrible people that even their entertainment is cruel and revolting, and kindness and empathy barely exist in this strange fictional world. Fantasy novels often present this same distorted idea of the Middle Ages. George R.R. Martin's *A Song of Ice and Fire* novels, made into the enormously popular television series *A Game of Thrones*, are set in a fantasy world that is predominantly based on late medieval Europe. In Martin's creation, rape, torture, murder and constant cruelty are an everyday part of life.

Such novels are frequently praised for their historical accuracy, though they are probably not really accurate; instead, they portray an image of what modern people think the Middle Ages must have been like. It is, admittedly, true that late medieval England is indeed a violent and corrupt place a lot of the time. Its homicide rate is orders of magnitude higher than it will be in later centuries, and those with power often squash those further down the social scale. This is, however, far from being the full picture. Although no one would argue that late medieval England is a place known for equality and liberty, it can, in fact, sometimes be a surprisingly progressive and tolerant place. Medieval English people, or Europeans more generally, are often assumed to be religious bigots who cannot tolerate other religions, and for sure many of them are, but in 1351 Edward III's eldest son Edward of Woodstock, prince of Wales (b. 1330), has two 'Saracen', i.e. Muslim, children whose names are recorded as Sigo and Nakok living in his household. He purchases coats, hats, and cloaks for them. A few decades earlier, the prince's grandfather Edward II accommodates six 'Saracens' at Dover Castle and gives them expenses of 6d a day each.[1] Sixpence is the daily wage paid to master craftsmen with many years' experience, and is thus a very generous amount. It is clear, therefore, that the Saracens, whoever they might be, are honoured guests of the king, not his prisoners.

Although late medieval justice can often be swift and harsh, and you can be executed for stealing items worth as little as 12½d, compassion is shown for those who commit crimes – even murder – while suffering from madness or what is called *frensy* in Middle English and *frenesia* in Latin. An investigation is held after a murder to determine whether the perpetrator killed feloniously or 'in a frenzy'. If the killing is found to be felonious and of malice aforethought, the killer is executed, but if s/he was deemed to be in a frenzy at the time, his/her life is spared. In 1270, something tragic and awful happens in Norfolk. While Richard Cheddestan and his wife (whose name is not recorded) are coming home from the market, Richard tries to drown himself in a water-filled pit, but his wife pulls him out and saves him, and they go home. Sometime later, his wife has to go out to buy some necessities, leaving Richard at home with their two children. Richard kills them. His wife returns home and cries out with grief at seeing what has happened, and Richard kills her then tries to hang himself. Neighbours, hearing the commotion, rush in, and though they are too late to save the woman's life, they prevent Richard from taking his own. Richard is imprisoned in Norwich and pleads not guilty when it comes to trial. The jurors find that he committed these awful crimes while in a frenzy, and he remains in prison rather than being executed. Six years later, John Lovetot, the judge at the trial, is charged with finding out whether it is now safe for Richard Cheddestan to be released. John discovers that Richard is currently sensible, but that 'it cannot be said that he is so far restored to sanity as to be set free without danger, especially in the heat of summer'.[2]

In the early 1300s, Agnes Birley of Derbyshire kills her daughter Rohese, and is imprisoned in Nottingham. Agnes is released and pardoned in July 1306 after the local justices determine that 'she killed her in a fit of frenzy'.[3] Katherine Ronges of Messing in Essex kills Alice Charles of Maldon in July 1371. The two women are strangers, and when they encounter one another, Katherine kills Alice by throwing 'great tiles and sea-coal' at her head. She is found to be insane and is not punished, and the word 'felonious' is not used to describe her killing of Alice.[4] Those who commit suicide are also sometimes deemed to have been suffering from *frensy*. In the summer of 1285, John Chepman of Taunton in Somerset drowns himself in the River Tone, and an inquisition finds that he has been 'afflicted with frenzy at times in summer in the three preceding years'. William atte Childerne of Kent, who has been ill for a long time, gets out of bed and drowns himself in a well in 1297, and is deemed to have been in a state of frenzy at the time. Henry Bordesle of Oxford, who 'has long been sick with diverse diseases', stabs himself in the stomach in his friend Richard Coke's house in March 1343, 'for he was, as it were, mad'.[5]

Nicholas Pays, elected as one of the two wardens of the guild of joiners in London in 1376, is 'deprived of his natural senses' in or before 1386, and is placed in the care of his son-in-law Peter Feriby, as he is unable to look after himself or his possessions. The London authorities place Nicholas's money and goods in Peter's custody, and Peter is enjoined to provide Nicholas with all his food, clothes, shoes, and bedding for as long as Nicholas is unable to live alone and take care of himself. Peter must render account for his actions yearly until such time as, 'by the mercy of God', Nicholas recovers.[6] In the early 1380s, Alice, widow of Henry Smale, undertakes to provide food, clothes, shoes, and a bed for her elderly father John atte Wode, 'and to give him 14d a week to spend as he liked'.[7] People who cannot look after themselves are not left alone to fend for themselves but are assigned a carer whose actions are scrutinised regularly to ensure that they are not taking advantage of the vulnerable person. Their carer is not a random person but someone who is close to them, preferably a relative by blood or marriage, and if they recover and are deemed fit to look after themselves and their own affairs, they will be regranted possession of their own money and goods.

Many medieval people care about the sick, poor, and needy, and do what they can do to help them. People from humble backgrounds who succeed in their careers and become well-off often help those in their native village or area. William Thorneye from Whaplode Drove in Lincolnshire, who moves to London at the age of about 12 and becomes a wealthy pepperer and alderman, bequeaths large sums of money to his 'poor kinsfolk' in his native Whaplode Drove and nearby Crowland in his will of 1349. Thorney Abbey is a Benedictine house not far from where William grew up, and he leaves money to the 'poor and maimed' who live on the waste ground around the abbey and to the *bedemen* of the abbey, i.e. those who rely on the Thorney monks' charity. William

Macchyng, son of Richard and Christina Macchyng, comes from the Essex village of Matching in Epping Forest. In the early 1310s at the age of about 12 or 13 – he is an almost exact contemporary of William Thorneye – he moves to London, where he becomes an apprentice to the master draper James Botiller. Successful in his career, on his death in 1361 William leaves money to 'six of the poorest of his family' in his native Matching, and gives further sums to people in London who suffer from leprosy.[8]

The wealthy goldsmith John Walpol instructs in 1349 that after his death, one of the houses that he owns should be sold and the proceeds divided. Part of the money is to be given to 'the poor members of the goldsmithery' and the rest is earmarked 'for marriage portions [dowries] for poor girls of the same handicraft'.[9] A man known as 'Elias the Priest' instructs in 1289 that the property and lands he owns in London should be sold after his death and divided into three parts: one to be 'devoted to Masses', one to buy clothes and shoes for the poor, and one to provide 'marriage portions' for poor girls and apprenticeships for poor boys.[10] Some people, including William Macchyng in 1361, leave money to those who are suffering from leprosy, or *laseres* (lazars) as they are often known, and King Edward II founds the *Loke* or 'Lock', a hospital for lepers near Bermondsey, around 1321.[11] In the early 1370s, a chaplain called Robert Denton founds a 'house of charity' in London for people who have lost their memory (*existentes extra memoriam suam*).[12] As noted above, many people give alms to prisoners who might otherwise starve to death or die of cold, and in the early 1390s people give food and money to the apprentice John Shynguler, barely even into his teens and abandoned to his own devices on the streets of London. Late medieval towns are not merely a dog-eat-dog world where the rich and powerful trample on the poor and vulnerable; many people show genuine concern and compassion for those less fortunate than themselves. When the young Londoner John Lyncoln is robbed, stabbed in the stomach and left for dead on Blackheath in May 1322, the man who finds him lifts him onto his cart and takes him to Greenwich, 'for charity's sake'. A group of boatmen agree to take John from Greenwich to a wharf in central London, where yet more people carry him a few hundred yards to the Cornhill home of Agnes St Neot, a relative or friend of John's.[13] All of these people are willing to help a stranger in dire need, and go out of their way to ensure he reaches a place of safety.

Another feature of the late Middle Ages that you might not have expected to find is that safeguarding of children is an unexceptional, common thing. When a child is orphaned, a new guardian is found for him or her, and the person must be someone who can be expected to take an interest in the child's welfare, so would never be a stranger. A blood relative is preferred, or failing that, a friend, executor, close associate, or former apprentice of the child's late parents, or at the very least someone who works in the same guild as the child's father and knew him well. Agnes Stokwell of London loses her father Walter and mother Joan, her aunt Isabel and uncle William, and all four of her older siblings in the Black Death pandemic of 1349, when she is just 7 years old. Having survived the horror of seeing her entire family succumb to a terrible disease within mere months, Agnes is placed in the care of her late father's apprentice Thomas Bournham, a young man who already lived in her household before the pestilence and whom she knows well.[14]

If the new guardian is a relative, a strictly enforced rule holds that s/he must not be someone to whom the child's inheritance would pass after the child's death. Medieval people recognise the potential risks inherent in sending a child to live with someone who would benefit financially if the child died. If the child inherits money and/or property from his or her late father, it is acceptable to send him or her to live with relatives from the maternal side of the family, such as grandparents or an aunt and uncle. A child would not be sent to live with his or her father's brother or sister or niece or nephew if that person would be next in line to receive the inheritance if the child died, though the father's brother's widow would be considered safe, as she would not be a blood relative and so would not inherit. If there is absolutely no one else who might reasonably be expected to look after and care for a child, a trusted official will be appointed as their guardian. Andrew Horn, the city chamberlain of London, becomes the guardian of 1-year-old orphan William Fullere in August 1315, and five years later also takes over custody of the 'vagrant orphan' Walter Cook.[15]

Some adults intervene to help orphaned and vulnerable children who have been taken advantage of in some way by other adults. Paulin Turk, a fishmonger, dies in 1325 and leaves two silver dishes and £6 10s in cash to pass one day to his four underaged children. Six years later in 1331, the late Paulin's friend and fellow fishmonger, Walter Mordon, calling himself the 'next friend of the children of Paulin Turk', contacts the authorities. He tells them that after the death of the children's mother Emma, their stepfather and legal guardian John Comptone has 'wasted their property' and has absconded. Comptone is finally captured and imprisoned in early 1335; his theft is not dismissed or ignored but taken very seriously, and although years pass, justice catches up with him in the end. Sadly, two of Paulin and Emma's four children have died in the meantime, though the remaining two inherit the possessions that once belonged to their father, thanks in great part to the concern for them shown by their father's friend Walter Mordon.[16]

Even in the plague year of 1349, while one of the greatest pandemics in human history is raging, people intervene to protect children's interests. On 26 August 1349, the mayor and sheriffs of London order three men to be imprisoned 'on a charge of withholding from children moneys left to them by their father'. The children in question are Margery and Juliana, daughters of the late John Sellyng, a victim of the Black Death who has left £10 worth of possessions including a set of silver spoons, silver rings, and silver cups with his executor Henry Asshebourn to be given to his daughters when they come of age. Henry also dies in the pestilence, and three of his own executors admit to unlawfully detaining the Sellyng children's goods. Henry Asshebourn's two other executors are John Pampesworth and Amy Rokesbourgh, who help to uncover their fellow executors' theft, and a couple named William and Margery Stokes, acting as the 'next friends of Margery and Juliana' Sellyng, bring the matter to the attention of the authorities. The goods are restored to the children.[17] Ellen Parmenter is a young child from York who loses both her parents and all her siblings in the Black Death, and her father John Parmenter's executor Robert Haugham dies too. Robert's own executor, Robert Wodham, is charged with the theft of £30 in cash, a signet ring, and other items which belonged to the Parmenters and which should have passed to their only surviving child, Ellen. A couple named William and Joan Spershore, one of whom is perhaps a relative or friend of John Parmenter or his wife, take the matter to the authorities, and in December 1349 the Spershore couple are appointed as Ellen's guardians.[18] It is interesting to note that all these children, the Sellyng siblings and Ellen Parmenter, are female; although late medieval England is certainly not a place of sexual equality, women and girls are by no means excluded from inheritance and ownership of property.

As noted above, although many modern people think that the marriage of children is normal and unexceptional in the Middle Ages, this usually only holds true for those or royal and noble birth. There is a recorded instance when concerned adults intervene to prevent a child-marriage. A couple named Maud Laurence and Simon Burgh marry in London in or before April 1315. They each have children from a previous marriage: Maud has an 8-year-old daughter, Agnes Laurence, and Simon has a 10-year-old son, Thomas Burgh. Maud and Simon 'contrive to marry' the two children, who are stepsiblings, and the couple's plans advance as far as having the banns of marriage published, making the children's wedding clothes, and preparing the wedding feast. Their plan is to ensure that Agnes's inheritance of 40 marks from her late father John Laurence (d. 1311) will remain within the family and will benefit her stepbrother and putative husband Thomas one day when the children come of age. However, a group of adults, calling themselves 'certain friends of the said Agnes', take the girl to the mayor, chamberlain, and aldermen of London after they 'discovered the plot' to marry the children, as they call it. The adults go as far as removing the child from the custody of her mother and stepfather. The mayor, Stephen Abingdon, brings the matter to the personal attention of Edward II, who decides there is insufficient reason for Agnes to have been removed from her home and orders her to be restored to her mother Maud and stepfather Simon. Showing that some medieval people take children's welfare very much to heart, the mayor and aldermen bravely announce their dissatisfaction with the king's pronouncement and state that Maud and Simon should not have custody of her daughter.[19]

Even in an age when child mortality is horrifically and heartbreakingly high, the sudden and unexpected deaths of children are investigated. In London, the deaths of 1-day-old Dionise Snowe at sunrise on 15 June 1339, 7-day-old Joan Parlepott on 17 May 1340, and 9-day-old John Russell on 19 July 1340, are investigated by the local coroner, assisted by a group of jurors. In all three cases, there is a suspicion that the infant 'lay dead of a death other than her/his rightful death', but the jurors ascertain that in fact, the three tiny infants have all died natural deaths.[20] In the late Middle Ages, clearly there are anxieties around the deaths of children, despite the tragic fact that they are very common, and there is an instinct to make sure that the deaths are natural. A sad case is investigated in Oxford in May 1343 when the body of an infant girl, believed to be just half a day old, is found in the river near the convent of the Franciscan friars by a *waynepayn* (servant or labourer) named William Sweyn. Despite the efforts of a sizeable number of jurors, the little girl's identity remains unknown, though the jurors remark that they believe she was not baptised, 'by the sign that the navel was not tied'.[21] Coroners' investigations into the sudden deaths of children reveal that in almost all cases, they happen by accident; usually by drowning in a well or a pond, or in a fire at their parents' house. The murder of children in the late Middle Ages is, thankfully, extremely rare.

John Staunford, aged 9, dies in the village of Padbury near Buckingham on 29 September 1321 while being looked after and educated by his uncle, William Offynton, the vicar of Padbury. The boy's death raises sufficient concern that nearly three years later in May 1324, Edward II orders the sheriff of Buckinghamshire to investigate it. The sheriff does so, and finds that John Staunford 'fell ill, but his uncle did not notice this at first and continued to teach him'. John's condition worsens, so William takes him home to his mother Margery – either the vicar's sister or sister-in-law – elsewhere in Padbury, where, sadly, the boy dies soon afterwards. The young boy is buried in Padbury church, a wake is held for him, and masses are sung for his soul (this being the fourteenth century, concern for John's eternal soul is paramount, and so this fact is emphasised in the sheriff's report). William Offynton is cleared of any wrongdoing.[22]

Late medieval England is not a place where people shrug their shoulders when children die or when they are taken advantage of in some way; it is a place where people care very much, and wish to investigate and make sure that vulnerable children have not been hurt, abused or killed. Late medieval England is a place that is much kinder than you might ever have expected, and though there is much in a medieval town that will be alien to you, and though there are many things from the modern era that you will definitely miss (perhaps coffee, chocolate, toothpaste and antibiotics to name but a few), there is also much for you to like, admire and enjoy.

Abbreviations

BB:	*The Babees' Book: Medieval Manners for the Young*
CChR:	*Calendar of Charter Rolls*
CCR:	*Calendar of Close Rolls*
CIM:	*Calendar of Inquisitions Miscellaneous*
CIPM:	*Calendar of Inquisitions Post Mortem*
CLB A/B/C/etc:	*Calendar of Letter-Books of London*, Letter-Book A/B/C, etc.
Coroner:	*Calendar of Coroners Rolls of the City of London 1300–1378*
CPR:	*Calendar of Patent Rolls*
Dialogues:	*Dialogues in French and English by William Caxton; Adapted from a Fourteenth-Century Book of Dialogues in French and Flemish*
EMCR:	*Early Mayor's Court Rolls, 1298–1307*
LAN:	*London Assize of Nuisance 1301–1431*
Leicester 1:	*Records of the Borough of Leicester, vol. 1, 1100–1326*
Leicester 2:	*Records of the Borough of Leicester, vol. 2, 1327–1509*
MLLF:	*Memorials of London and London Life in the 13th, 14th and 15th Centuries*
Nottingham 1:	*Records of the Borough of Nottingham, vol. 1, 1155–1399*
Nottingham 2:	*Records of the Borough of Nottingham, vol. 2, 1399–1485*
RMO:	*Records of Medieval Oxford: Coroners' Inquests*
SAL MS 122:	Society of Antiquaries of London, *Manuscript 122*
SCCR:	*Select Cases from the Coroners' Rolls 1265–1413*
SPMR:	*Calendar of Select Plea and Memoranda Rolls of the City of London*
TNA:	The National Archives
Wills, vol. 1:	*Calendar of Wills Proved and Enrolled in the Court of Husting, London, vol. 1, 1258–1358*
Wills, vol. 2:	*Calendar of Wills Proved and Enrolled, vol. 2, 1358–1688*

Notes

Introduction

1. *Records of Medieval Oxford: Coroners' Inquests*, 55; *Calendar of the Select Plea and Memoranda Rolls*, vol. 2, 153, 166.
2. Ian Mortimer, *The Time Traveller's Guide to Medieval England*, 36.
3. *Calendar of Coroners Rolls of the City of London A.D. 1300–1378*, ed. R. R. Sharpe, 37, 47; *Records of the Borough of Nottingham*, vol. 1, ed. W.H. Stevenson, 1155–1399, 255. Edward II's clerks often described an axe or a ship or another object the king had purchased as 'very beautiful'.

Chapter 1: Arriving in a Medieval Town

1. H.T. Riley, *Memorials of London and London Life in the 13th, 14th and 15th Centuries*, 247, 266, 438; *Coroner*, 170; *Calendar of Letter-Books of London: Letter-Book G*, 150; *Letter-Book H*, 338.
2. Constance Bullock-Davies, *Menestrellorum Multitudo: Minstrels at a Royal Feast*; *Calendar of Patent Rolls 1321–24*, 210.
3. *Calendar of Early Mayor's Court Rolls, 1298–1307*, ed. A. H. Thomas, 220.
4. Robert Shepherd, *Westminster: A Biography*, 73; *Calendar of Close Rolls 1302–07*, 486.
5. *Chronicles of the Mayors and Sheriffs of London*, ed. H. T. Riley, 251.
6. *CCR 1346–49*, 509.
7. *CPR 1307–13*, 38; *London Assize of Nuisance, 1301–1431: A Calendar*, ed. Helena M. Chew and William Kellaway, no. 200.
8. *MLLF*, 223–24.
9. *MLLF*, 279–280; *Dialogues in French and English by William Caxton; Adapted from a Fourteenth-Century Book of Dialogues in French and Flemish*, ed. Henry Bradley, 46 ('*with sayme of heryngs*').
10. *London Sheriffs Court Roll 1320*, ed. Matthew Stevens, 63; *EMCR, 1298–1307*, 110, 168, 170; *Calendar of Wills Proved and Enrolled in the Court of Husting, London*, vol. 1, 1258–1358, ed. R. R. Sharpe, 54, 127, 211, 269; *CLB B*, 29, 132, 198; *CLB E*, 177; *MLLF*, 78; *LAN*, no. 183; *CPR 1321–24*, 8–9; *Calendar of Inquisitions Post Mortem 1365-69*, no. 275; *SPMR*, vol. 3, 1381–1412, 11. Francis Vilers/Villiers was murdered in 1324: *Coroner*, 91–92. For medieval tavern names, including the *Swerd in the Hope*, see Chapter 5.
11. Caroline Barron, *London in the Later Middle Ages*, 4, 10.
12. Peter Ackroyd, *The History of England, Volume 1: Foundation*, 138; Mortimer, *Time Traveller's Guide*, 10–11, 293–294.
13. *MLLF*, 6–7; *Coroner*, 33–34; *The London Eyre of 1276*, ed. Martin Weinbaum, no. 44.
14. *SPMR*, vol. 2, 140–141.

15. *Wills*, part 2, 528, and see *MLLF*, 20, 267, 458, 488, 535.
16. *Dialogues*, 42.
17. *Wills*, vol. 1, 581 (London); Bristol Archives P.St JB/D/2/24 and 25, P/AS/D/PH A 6, available at https://archives.bristol.gov.uk; TNA C146/5690 (Northampton); *Calendar of the Manuscripts of the Dean and Chapter of Wells*, vol. 2, nos. 154, 162, 172, 180, 195; Keith Briggs, 'OE and ME *cunte* in place-names', *Journal of the English Place-Name Society*, 41 (2009), 28–29 (the other towns).
18. *Coroner*, 235–236; *CLB C*, 198; *CLB D*, 187; *Dialogues*, 43.
19. *Coroner*, 235–236. A resident of London in the mid-1270s is called Andrew le Sarazin, 'the Saracen': *London Eyre of 1276*, no. 257.
20. *EMCR*, 112; *Calendar of Charter Rolls 1257–1300*, 202.
21. *Wills*, 529.
22. *Wills*, vol. 1, 572; vol. 2, 23.
23. *CIPM 1336–46*, no. 576; *CPR 1334–38*, 229; *CCR 1339–41*, 21; *CPR 1343–46*, 613; *CCR 1346–49*, 353; *CCR 1364–68*, 398.

Chapter 2: Vagrant Pigs and Obnoxious Fumes

1. *Coroner*, 46–47.
2. *LAN*, nos. 97, 327, 396, 577.
3. Cheshire Archives and Local Studies, ZA/F/1, f.3, available on TNA website; *Records of the Borough of Leicester*, vol. 2, 1327–1509, ed. Mary Bateson, 290–291.
4. *CLB G*, 33; *CLB H*, 301, 355, 372; *SPMR*, vol. 2, 93–94, 151; *MLLF*, 67–68, 295–296, 298–299, 356–358, 367–368.
5. *Coroner*, 44–46, 198–199.
6. *LAN*, nos. 140–142, 186, 300, 369.
7. *MLLF*, 35; *LAN*, p. xxviii, nos. 234, 547–548, 574; *CLB A*, 217.
8. *Calendar of Inquisitions Miscellaneous 1308–48*, no. 144.
9. *CLB H*, 355; *Coroner*, 62.
10. *CLB A*, 216; *CLB E*, 116; *CLB G*, 33; *CLB H*, 355; *Leicester 2*, xxxvii, 292–293.
11. Canterbury Cathedral Archives and Library, CC/JQ/237/2, available on TNA website.
12. *Nottingham 1*, 358–359.
13. *CIPM 1219–1307*, no. 2316; *Coroner*, 56–57; *Records of Medieval Oxford: Coroners' Inquests, the Walls of Oxford, Etc*, ed. H.E. Salter, 46.
14. *MLLF*, 46–47, 116; *CLB E*, 39.
15. *MLLF*, 308–309; *CLB G*, 138.
16. *SPMR*, vol. 2, 237.
17. *MLLF*, 65–66; *CLB C*, 165; *Wills*, vol. 1, 237.
18. *CIM 1219–1307*, no. 170.
19. *CIM 1219–1307*, nos. 494, 2317; *Wills*, vol. 1, 53, 122, 332, 405, 478, 563–65; *CLB F*, 85; TNA BCM/B/2/5/1.
20. *LAN*, no. 326.
21. *CIM 1219–1307*, nos. 1770, 1889; *EMCR, 1298–1307*, 120.
22. *CIM 1219–1307*, no. 1099.
23. *LAN*, nos. 340–341, 362–366, 492, 528; *SPMR*, vol. 1, 36.
24. *Dialogues*, 6.
25. *LAN*, no. 255.
26. *LAN*, no. 381; *Wills*, vol. 1, 30, 397–398.

27. *LAN*, nos. 312, 654; *Wills*, vol. 1, 251, 581.
28. Society of Antiquaries of London, Manuscript 122, p. 77, *xij fenestres de verre*.
29. *CIM 1219–1307*, no. 238; *SPMR*, vol. 2, 165–166.
30. *LAN*, nos. 14, 30, 31, 129, 340–41, 359, 361–66, 407, 410, 549 (John Haukyn), 652 ('thick glass' quotation).
31. *LAN*, nos. 361–366; *Wills*, 253, 349.
32. *LAN*, no. 609.
33. TNA C 146/4461, E 210/7883.
34. *CIPM 1405–13*, nos. 211, 379.
35. *LAN*, nos. 110, 485, 510, 644.
36. *EMCR*, 247; *SPMR*, vol. 2, 237–238; *MLLF*, xvi, xlvi, 67; *Coroner*, 43, 62.
37. *Leicester 2*, 60–62. Henry's letter is written in medieval French, and the word for 'latrine' or 'privy' is *longayne*.
38. *LAN*, nos. 222, 378, 500–502, 566.
39. *LAN*, no. 214.
40. *LAN*, nos. 12, 270–271; *SPMR*, vol. 3, 153–154.
41. TNA C 131/2/9.
42. *CLB C*, 237–238; *Wills*, vol. 1, 175.
43. *CLB F*, 38.
44. *SPMR*, vol. 2, 62.
45. *SPMR*, vol. 2, 150, 172, 179.
46. *CIPM 1317–27*, nos. 588, 665.
47. *CIPM 1347–52*, no. 229.
48. *CIPM 1307–17*, no. 470.
49. Elisabeth van Houts and Julia Crick, *A Social History of England 900–1200*, 405 (*saltum, siffletum, pettum*).
50. *CIPM 1347–52*, no. 108; *CIPM 1506–09*, no. 366.

Chapter 3: Godday, Ich Highte Johan (Hello, I'm Called John)

1. *Two Early London Subsidy Rolls*, ed. Eilert Ekwall, 34–43.
2. *CLB I*, 6; *MLLF*, 553–554.
3. SAL MS 122.
4. The Middle English Dictionary, available online at https://quod.lib.umich.edu/m/middle-english-dictionary/dictionary.
5. *The Three Earliest Subsidies for the County of Sussex, 1296, 1327, 1332*, ed. William Hudson, 115, 117, 147, 240, 258, 261.
6. *MLLF*, xl; *CLB F*, 8, 146, 150; *Wills*, vol. 1, 676.
7. *Three Earliest Subsidies for the County of Sussex*, 82, 148.
8. *Leicester 2*, 389.
9. *Ancient Deeds Belonging to the Corporation of Bath*, ed. The Rev. C.W. Shickle, 11.
10. *Wills*, vol. 1, 427.
11. *Wills*, vol. 1, 463, 514, 519.
12. *Coroner*, 41–42; *Wills*, vol. 1, 516.
13. *Wills*, vol. 1, 382–383, 465, 679; *SPMR*, vol. 1, 54–55; *Feet of Fines for Essex*, vol. 2, no. 740, p. 98; *CPR 1343–45*, 238.
14. *Wills*, vol. 1, 465, 679; *SPMR*, vol. 1, 54–55.
15. *CLB C*, 123; *CPR 1317–21*, 569.

16. *Select Cases from the Coroners' Rolls 1265–1413*, ed. Charles Gross, 129; *CLB I*, 25.
17. *Leicester 2*, 447.
18. TNA SC 8/50/2489.
19. Lister M. Matheson, 'Chaucer's Ancestry: Historical and Philological Assessments', *The Chaucer Review*, 25 (1991), 171–189. Isabel Malyn's father was named Walter Aurifaber, which means 'goldsmith' in Latin.
20. *Coroner*, 10–11, 27–28, 34–35; *CLB B*, 266; *Wills*, vol. 1, 284; Middle English Dictionary, accessed 8 August 2024. There are numerous references in the chancery rolls, plea and memoranda rolls and so on to Hamo Godchep, alderman of Bread Street ward; see also *Wills*, vol. 1, 251, 581, 704.
21. *Nottingham 1*, 370, 376.
22. Edward Charlton, *Memorials of North Tyndale and Its Four Surnames*, 22–23.
23. *Three Earliest Subsidies for the County of Sussex*, 78, 178, 293; *CCR 1349–54*, 145.
24. *SPMR*, vol. 1, 125.
25. https://quod.lib.umich.edu/m/middle-english-dictionary/dictionary/MED9133; https://languagehat.com/new-words-in-the-oed; https://whynow.co.uk/read/susie-dents-introduction-to-swearing-the-c-word, all accessed 21 August 2024.
26. *Leicester 1*, 356; *MLLF*, 235, 663; *Staffordshire Historical Collections*, vol. 7, part 1, ed. George Wrottesley, 197.
27. SAL MS 122.
28. *CLB C*, 111; *Coroner*, 111, 267; *SPMR*, vol. 1, 161; SAL MS 122; *Wills*, vol. 2, 330; *SCCR*, 128, 131.
29. *CPR 1317–21*, 363; *CPR 1324–27*, 72; *CPR 1330–34*, 497; *CPR 1354–58*, 63, 386–387.
30. David Scott-Macnab, '*The Names of All Manner of Hounds*: A Unique Inventory in a Fifteenth-Century Manuscript', available on Academia.edu, www.academia.edu/44222801/THE_NAMES_OF_ALL_MANNER_OF_HOUNDS_A_UNIQUE_INVENTORY_IN_A_FIFTEENTH_CENTURY_MANUSCRIPT, accessed 2 October 2024.
31. C. M. Woolgar, *The Great Household in Late Medieval England*, 190; Jennifer Ward, *Elizabeth de Burgh, Lady of Clare (1295–1360): Household and Other Records*, 33–35, 61; George Frederick Beltz, *Memorials of the Garter from Its Foundation to the Present Time*, 384; Martyn Lawrence, 'Too Flattering Sweet to be Substantial? The Last Months of Thomas, Lord Despenser', 157.
32. Ward, *Elizabeth de Burgh, Lady of Clare*, 62.
33. SAL MS 122; *SPMR*, vol. 1, 76, 149; *SPMR*, vol. 2, 114; *CLB A*, 133; *Calendar of Memoranda Rolls (Exchequer): Michaelmas 1326–Michaelmas* 1327, no. 892; *CIM 1308–48*, no. 1728; *CIM 1348–77*, no. 14.

Chapter 4: Common Nightwalkers and Curfews

1. *Leicester 1*, 352; *Leicester 2*, 292.
2. *CIM 1348–77*, no. 425.
3. *CLB C*, 85.
4. *CIPM 1392–99*, nos. 150, 481, 877, 1250; https://co-curate.ncl.ac.uk/newcastle-city-walls; https://twsitelines.info/SMR/1549, accessed 2 October 2024.
5. CIPM 1418-22, no. 371; www.visitchurches.org.uk/visit/church-listing/st-john-on-the-wall-bristol.html, accessed 2 October 2024.
6. *CIM 1308–48*, no. 1903; *CIM 1348–77*, no. 3.

7. *Nottingham 2*, 265; *SPMR*, vol. 1, 109, 111–112; *SPMR*, vol. 2, 43; *MLLF*, 129–130, 133, 139–141, 173, 193, 272.
8. *SPMR*, vol. 3, 1; *Nottingham 2*, 265.
9. *CLB I*, 44–45, 93.
10. *Leicester 2*, 287.
11. *CLB B*, 1–2; *CLB C*, 16, 85; *CLB E*, 136, etc.
12. *RMO*, 16–17.
13. *CPR 1416–22*, 205; TNA SC 8/302/15089 and SC 8/176/8781.
14. *SPMR*, vol. 1, 126.
15. *MLLF*, 91–93.
16. *Leicester 1*, 379.
17. *Oxford Dictionary of National Biography*.
18. *Le Livre de Seyntz Medicines: The Unpublished Devotional Treatise of Henry of Lancaster*, ed. E.J. Arnould, 22–23 (*...je puisse veoir comme longement jeo puisse dormir, et si jeo faille de Messe, jeo en orroie demeyn diaux*).
19. *Foedera, Conventiones, Litterae et Cujuncunque Generis Acta Publica*, vol. 2.1, 1307–1327, ed. Thomas Rymer, 216–217.

Chapter 5: At Whiche Hande Shall I Take My Way? Travelling

1. Hilda Johnstone, *Edward of Carnarvon 1284–1307*, 23.
2. *Calendar of Papal Registers Relating to Great Britain and Ireland: Papal Letters*, vol. 2, 1305–41, ed. W.H. Bliss, 498–499.
3. *Leicester 1*, 353.
4. TNA SC 8/192/9597; *Calendar of Chancery Warrants 1244–1326*, 439.
5. *Coroner*, 87–90.
6. *Dialogues*, 49.
7. *CLB D*, 291; *MLLF*, 98–100.
8. *RMO*, 50; *SCCR*, 60–61, 64.
9. *CLB F*, 228; *MLLF*, 263–264.
10. *Coroner*, 84, 130–131.
11. *London Sheriffs Court Roll 1320*, 50; *MLLF*, 19; Ward, *Elizabeth de Burgh, Lady of Clare*, 48; *SPMR*, vol. 2, 37–38; *Leicester 1*, 74.
12. *SPMR*, vol. 2, 37–38.
13. *SPMR*, vol. 1, 54–55.
14. SAL MS 122, 26, 31, 41, 55, 68, etc.
15. Ward, *Elizabeth de Burgh*, 3.
16. SAL MS 122, 9, 56; TNA E 101/379/4, E 101/380/4, fo. 20v.
17. Martyn Lawrence, 'Too Flattering Sweet to be Substantial?', 156–157 (*ove rouge velewet stods ove pynnapples de latoun*).
18. *Calendar of Documents Relating to Scotland*, vol. 2, 1272–1307, ed. Joseph Bain, no. 1403; *Leicester 1*, 303; TNA E 101/379/4; *SPMR*, vol. 2, 174, 235.
19. There are numerous examples of broken arms and legs in the Calendars of Inquisitions Post Mortem.
20. Ward, *Elizabeth de Burgh*, 146; *A Collection of All the Wills, Now Known to be Extant, of the Kings and Queens of England, Princes and Princesses of Wales, and Every Branch of the Blood Royal*, ed. J. Nichols and Richard Gough, 35 (*mon grant char ove les houces, tapets et quissyns*).

21. Lawrence, 'Too Flattering Sweet', 156–157.
22. TNA E 101/310/24.
23. *The War of Saint-Sardos (1323–1325): Gascon Correspondence and Diplomatic Documents*, ed. Pierre Chaplais, 227.
24. *Coroner*, 58.
25. *CIPM 1336–46*, no. 57; *CIPM 1352–60*, nos. 265, 274, 395, 454; *CIPM 1361–65*, no. 552. There are many dozens of other examples of visits to Santiago in the Inquisitions Post Mortem.
26. *CIPM 1352–60*, no. 479.
27. *CLB E*, 206–07; *CPR 1324–27*, 145–146.
28. *MLLF*, 323–324; *SPMR*, vol. 2, 174, 235; *Dialogues*, 5, 49–50.
29. *SPMR*, vol. 1, 220.
30. *SPMR*, vol. 2, 261; *SPMR*, vol. 3, 11.
31. *CLB G*, 217; *Wills*, vol. 2, 342.

Chapter 6: Faitours, Bocardo and the Thewe: Crime and Punishment

1. Cheshire Archives and Local Studies, ZCHD/2/1, on TNA website.
2. *CPR 1405–08*, 69.
3. *A History of the County of Somerset*, vol. 6, ed. R.W. Dunning and C.R. Elrington, 306–08.
4. *MLLF*, 671–672; *CLB K*, 16.
5. *MLLF*, 318; *CLB G*, 173; *CLB H*, 110.
6. *MLLF*, 315–316, 460; *CLB G*, 176; *CLB H*, 181.
7. *Leicester 1*, 104.
8. *SPMR*, vol. 1, 256.
9. *CLB H*, 154; *MLLF*, 445–446; *SPMR*, vol. 3, 5.
10. *The Babees' Book: Medieval Manners for the Young*, trans. Edith Rickert and L.J. Naylor, 12, 21, 24; *Dialogues*, 3.
11. *Statutes of the Realm*, vol. 1, 308.
12. *Leicester 2*, 291; *SPMR*, vol. 1, 274.
13. *MLLF*, 319, 324, 367–368, 375, 385, 525–526; *CLB H*, 10, 271–272, 363.
14. *MLLF*, 319–320; *SPMR*, vol. 2, 14, 16, 19.
15. *CLB I*, 273–287.
16. *MLLF*, 484–486; *CLB K*, 17.
17. *CLB A*, 120–121.
18. *MLLF*, 119–120, 316.
19. *Coroner*, 7–8; *London Eyre of 1276*, no. 197.
20. *SPMR*, vol. 1, 50; *CLB E*, 276–278; *MLLF*, 230.
21. *Nottingham 1*, 94–95.
22. *MLLF*, 89; *CLB D*, 277.
23. *CLB F*, 126.
24. *MLLF*, 484–486.
25. *SPMR*, vol. 2, 139.
26. *Coroner*, 46–47; *SPMR*, vol. 2, 297.
27. *Leicester 1*, 103–104; *Dialogues*, 36. A few years later in 1300, a new pillory is built in Leicester: *Leicester 1*, 227–228.
28. *Dialogues*, 43.

29. *CPR 1313–17*, 40; *CPR 1324–27*, 47.
30. *SCCR*, 86–87.
31. *Coroner*, 64, 87–89.
32. *Leicester 1*, 371.
33. www.medievalgenealogy.org.uk/inquests/abstracts_113.shtml; www.medievalgenealogy.org.uk/inquests/abstracts_116.shtml; www.medievalgenealogy.org.uk/inquests/abstracts_119B.shtml, accessed 23 August 2024; see also *Leicester 1*, 358.
34. *RMO*, 12, 46.
35. *SCCR*, 68, 103.
36. *SPMR*, vol. 1, 54–55.
37. *Coroner*, 34–35; *CPMR*, vol. 1, 137.
38. *SCCR*, 75–77.
39. *Leicester 1*, xxvi, 342, 358; *CCR 1307–13*, 167.
40. *Coroner*, 53–54, 67.
41. www.medievalgenealogy.org.uk/inquests/abstracts_110.shtml, accessed 24 August 2024; *RMO*, 42; *SCCR*, 79–81.
42. *Coroner*, 53–54, 67; *CLB K*, 124–127.
43. *Wills*, vol. 1, 609, 640, 645, 648, etc.; *Wills*, vol. 2, 32, 127, 129, 140, etc.
44. *SPMR*, vol. 3, 158–159.
45. *CPR 1313–17*, 237; *CPR 1330–34*, 442–443; *CLB K*, 124–127.
46. *SPMR*, vol. 2. 119.
47. *SPMR*, vol. 3, 157.
48. *RMO*, 24.
49. *CLB K*, 124–127.
50. *CLB I*, 49–50; *CLB K*, 124–127, 183, 189.
51. *CPR 1313–17*, 270; *CPR 1324–27*, 86; *CPR 1327–30*, 20; *Coroner*, 130–31.
52. *CIM 1348–77*, no. 315.
53. *CPR 1354–58*, 20; *CCR 1354–60*, 3; *CIM 1348–77*, nos. 138–139.
54. *RMO*, 17.

Chapter 7: Tallow Candles and Penny Loaves: Sleeping, Washing and Eating

1. *BB*, 24, 34, 66, 74.
2. *Coroner*, 51, 183; www.medievalgenealogy.org.uk/inquests/abstracts_119C.shtml, accessed 4 October 2024; *RMO*, 7–8.
3. *RMO*, 23, 48–49.
4. *SCCR*, 52, 106–107.
5. *SPMR*, vol. 2, 153, 166; *Dialogues*, 47.
6. *BB*, 33, 50, 110.
7. *SPMR*, vol. 2, 58; *Wills*, vol. 2, 207; *A Collection of All the Wills*, 156–157.
8. *BB*, 34; Chris Given-Wilson, *Henry IV*, 132.
9. 'Account of the Expenses of John of Brabant and Thomas and Henry of Lancaster, 1292–3', ed. Burtt, 2; *BB*, 34.
10. *CPR 1324–27*, 72; TNA SC 8/18/863.
11. *BB*, 12, 32, 73–74; *Dialogues*, 8.
12. *BB*, 14, 32, 62–63, 66, 74.
13. *CIPM 1399 1405*, no. 310.

14. SAL MS 122, 9; *Dialogues*, 13.
15. www.medievalgenealogy.org.uk/inquests/abstracts_113.shtml, accessed 23 September 2024.
16. *Coroner*, 59, 127; *RMO*, 14, 27–28, 51. Just outside Gloucester in November 1396, Robert Hendy drowned while he was drinking water from a river and fell in: *SCCR*, 51.
17. *BB*, 27, 68.
18. *Leicester 2*, 287; *Wills*, vol. 1, 175; *MLLF*, 122, 323; *CIM 1348–77*, no. 959; *SPMR*, vol. 2, 69.
19. *CLB A*, 208, 213; *CLB B*, 13; *MLLF*, 162–65; *SPMR*, vol. 2, 1.
20. *Foedera 1307–27*, 266; *Calendar of Documents Relating to Scotland 1272–1307*, no. 1403; *Leicester 1*, 261.
21. *MLLF*, 312–313, 426, 438.
22. Ruth Carroll, '*Utilis Coquinario* and its Unnamed Author', 45–48.
23. *Dialogues*, 41.
24. *MLLF*, 120, 536–537; *CLB H*, 412. William Whitman was sentenced to the pillory with the 'false powders' that he had sold burnt beneath him.
25. *Dialogues*, 10, 19–20, 42; TNA E 101/379/4.
26. *MLLF*, 240–241.
27. *Coroner*, 198–199.
28. *Leicester 1*, 180–181; *MLLF*, 141–142.
29. *Nottingham 1*, 269ff.
30. *Dialogues*, 9–12.
31. *CPR 1321–24*, 425–426; *CPR 1364–67*, 5–6; *CLB D*, 281–282; *CLB E*, 179–180; *MLLF*, 179–180, 222–223, 226.
32. *Dialogues*, 14, 20, 41; Middle English Dictionary; Anglo-Norman Dictionary at www.anglo-norman.net/entry.
33. *MLLF*, 247, 266, 438, 508; *Coroner*, 14–15, 170; *CLB G*, 150; *CLB H*, 338.
34. *SPMR*, vol. 2, 163.
35. TNA E 101/379/4 is the account; Maggie Black, *The Medieval Cookbook*, 45–47, for *Blawmanger*.
36. *Coroner*, 170; *Calendar of Documents Relating to Scotland 1307–57*, no. 234.
37. *Leicester 1*, 304.
38. SAL MS 122, 66 (*iiij vaches achatez ... p' trover let p' la bouche le Roi*).
39. *MLLF*, 228–229.
40. *Dialogues*, 8–10, 13.
41. *Dialogues*, 13.
42. SAL MS 122, 15.
43. *BB*, 3, 6–9, 13–14, 40–41, 69–70, 96.
44. *Foedera 1307–27*, 204.
45. *BB*, 69.

Chapter 8: Water, Wine and Ale: Drink and Taverns

1. *Dialogues*, 14.
2. *MLLF*, 225.
3. *Coroner*, 100, 178, 253; *Dialogues*, 7.
4. *CPR 1324–27*, 234; *CPR 1327–30*, 12, 182.

5. *Nottingham 1*, 332–334.
6. www.medievalgenealogy.org.uk/inquests/abstracts_106.shtml, accessed 2 October 2024. There are numerous other examples.
7. *Coroner*, 100–101.
8. *RMO*, 31, 48.
9. *CLB D*, 240; *CLB E*, 71, 131; *CLB F*, 27; *MLLF*, 78, 137; *Dialogues*, 7; *BB*, 28.
10. *Dialogues*, 13–14; Middle English Dictionary.
11. *Croniques de London*, ed. J. G. Aungier, 50; *Annales Paulini 1307–1340*, in ed. W. Stubbs, *Chronicles of the Reigns of Edward I and Edward II*, vol. 1, 312–313.
12. *SPMR*, vol. 2, 199.
13. *SPMR*, vol. 2, 147.
14. *MLLF*, 665–666.
15. *CLB K*, 205, 270; *Dialogues*, 14.
16. *MLLF*, 181; *CLB F*, 83, 246; *CLB G*, 4, 137; CLB H, 214; CLB K, 16; *SPMR*, vol. 1, 120, 204, 219; *SPMR*, vol. 2, 235; *SPMR*, vol. 3, 41; *Dialogues*, 14.
17. *SPMR*, vol. 2, 234, 258.
18. *CIPM 1352–60*, no. 523.
19. *BB*, 69–70: 'Temper thyself with drink, so keep thee from blame/It hurteth thine honesty and hindereth thy good name/A pint at a draught to pour in fast, as one in haste/Four at a mess is three too many, in such I think waste'.
20. Alice Quernbetere is drunk in London in the late summer of 1301 (*Coroner*, 29), and Maud Coffeur also of London is drunk shortly before Christmas 1276; see Chapter 12.
21. *CLB A*, 216; *CLB G*, 4; CLI, 131, 191; *MLLF*, 264; *SPMR*, 125.
22. *MLLF*, 181–83; *CPR 1321–24*, 8–9; *Wills*, vol. 1, 269, 394, 450; *CIPM 1365–69*, no. 275; *SPMR*, vol. 2, 198.
23. *Nottingham 1*, 201–205.
24. *Leicester 2*, 267–268, 343–348.
25. *CIM 1219–1307*, nos. 1713, 2151, 2168; *CIPM 1418-22*, no. 371.
26. *CIM 1219–1307*, no. 2127; *CLB I*, 86–87, 115.
27. *Annales Paulini 1307–1340*, 267.
28. *EMCR*, 253.
29. *Leicester 1*, 261, 266.
30. *CIM 1219–1307*, nos. 2138, 2394; *Coroner*, 77–88.
31. *SPMR*, vol. 1, 109; SPMR, vol. 2, 249; *CLB H*, 12.
32. *CLB I*, 110, 251; *SPMR*, vol. 1, 43; *SPMR*, vol. 3, 261, 272; *CPR 1321–24*, 1; *CCR 1360–64*, 288; *Wills*, vol. 1, 241, 445, 699; *Wills*, vol. 2, 217, 324, 378–379, 515, 521, 536, 600–601; *CIPM 1365–69*, no. 282; *Coroner*, 50; *MLLF*, xl, 264, 599; 'The Register: Accounts, 1432–41 (126–30)', *Parish Fraternity Register: Fraternity of the Holy Trinity and SS. Fabian and Sebastian (Parish of St. Botolph without Aldersgate)*, ed. Patricia Basing, nos. 128–130.

Chapter 9: Surcotes and Scrimpyn: Clothes

1. *Dialogues*, 40.
2. *Dialogues*, 20, 34.
3. *Dialogues*, 8, 16; *BB*, 32–33.
4. SAL MS 122.

5. *MLLF*, 254–255.
6. *Leicester 1*, 361–364.
7. *CLB C*, 79–80; *CLB E*, 232–4; *MLLF*, 153–54; *Dialogues*, 2, 46.
8. *Wills*, vol. 2, 220–221.
9. TNA E 101/380/4.
10. SAL MS 122; *Dialogues*, 41.
11. *Collection of All the Wills Now Known to be Extant*, 24–25; Ward, *Elizabeth de Burgh, Lady of Clare*, 141–142; TNA PROB 11/1/56.
12. William Rees, *Caerphilly Castle and Its Place in the Annals of Glamorgan*, 109–21; Walter E. Rhodes, 'The Inventory of the Jewels and Wardrobe of Queen Isabella (1307–8)', 518–521; Mortimer, *Time Traveller's Guide*, 105–106.
13. *Leicester 1*, 364.
14. *John of Gaunt's Register 1371–75*, nos. 931, 1133, 1343.
15. *CIM 1219–1307*, no. 2305.
16. Vincent Ilardi, *Renaissance Vision from Spectacles to Telescopes*, 70–71. Ilardi points out that *spectaculum* certainly means spectacles rather than a mirror; the bishop also owned a mirror, and it appears in the inventory as *speculum* and was worth 1d.

Chapter 10: Eme, Mome and Cousyns Germain: Family Relations

1. *BB*, 43, 62, 65–66; *Dialogues*, 9.
2. *Dialogues*, 6–7, 29, 33.
3. *A Collection of All the Wills Now Known to be Extant*, 35–36, 40; *Testamenta Vetusta: Being Illustrations From Wills*, vol. 1, ed. Nicholas Harris Nicolas, 158, 174–175.
4. *Wills*, vol. 1, 614; *CIPM 1317–27*, nos. 181–182, 632.
5. *CIPM 1352–60*, no. 564; *CIPM 1361–65*, nos. 516, 545; *CCR 1360–64*, 455.
6. *CIPM 1272–91*, no. 743; *CIPM 1291–1300*, no. 623.
7. *CIPM 1327–36*, no. 709; *CIPM 1336–46*, no. 672; *CIPM 1352–60*, no. 124.
8. *CIPM 1327–36*, no. 535; *CIPM 1361–65*, no. 71; *CIPM 1374–77*, no. 157; *CIPM 1399–1405*, no. 979.
9. *CPR 1358–61*, 337, 571–572, 582–83; *CPR 1361–64*, 1, 6–8; *CIM 1348–77*, no. 460; *CIPM 1352–60*, no. 412; *CCR 1369–74*, 506–07; *CIPM 1370–73*, no. 153.
10. *CIM 1348–77*, no. 126; *CCR 1349–54*, 604.
11. *Calendar of Papal Letters 1431–47*, 579; *Calendar of Papal Letters 1447–55*, 607–608.
12. *Wills*, part 1, 213; *CLB D*, 184–186.
13. *SPMR*, vol. 3, 151.
14. *CIPM 1370–73*, no. 313; *CIPM 1432–37*, no. 272.
15. *CIM 1219–1307*, no. 359.
16. *Wills*, vol. 1, 604–605, 635; vol. 2, 86–87, 109; *CLB F*, 222; *CLB G*, 261.
17. *Wills*, vol. 1, 342; *CIPM 1327–36*, no. 223; *CLB E*, 239, 250; *CLB F*, 75; *SPMR*, vol. 1, 168; *CPR 1324–27*, 1; *CFR 1327–37*, 119.
18. *Wills*, vol. 1, 354–355, 689; *CCR 1354–60*, 43; *CCR 1360–64*, 525; *CLB E*, 250, 256.

Chapter 11: Midovernone and Right Grete Gramercy: Time and Talking to People

1. *Leicester 1*, 377.
2. Ian Mortimer, *The Perfect King: The Life of Edward III, Father of the English Nation*, 287–288.
3. *CLB H*, 27; *Dialogues*, 30; *Leicester 2*, 287.

4. *CIPM 1307–17*, no. 156.
5. *CIPM 1300–07*, no. 328.
6. *CIPM 1399–1405*, no. 316.
7. *BB*, 12, 45, 74–75; *Dialogues*, 4–6, 29, 49; https://d.lib.rochester.edu/teams/text/salisbury-trials-and-joys-interludium-de-clerico-et-puella, accessed 21 August 2024.
8. *BB*, 1–2, 6, 43, 62, 67; *Dialogues*, 5, 9–10, 18, 28–29.
9. *Staffordshire Historical Collections*, vol. 7, part 1, ed. George Wrottesley, 44–56; *CIM 1308–48*, no. 458; *CPR 1324–27*, 153.
10. *CIM 1308–48*, no. 776.
11. *Leicester 1*, 377–378.
12. *SPMR*, vol. 2, 15, 224, 265.
13. *EMCR*, 261.
14. *SPMR*, vol. 1, 122–129; *Coroner*, 266–269; *CPR 1340–43*, 226–227.
15. *CCR 1377–81*, 1–5.
16. *BB*, 30–31, 35–37.
17. Jennifer Jahner, *Literature and Law in the Era of Magna Carta*, 224.
18. *Annales Londonienses 1195–1330*, in ed. W. Stubbs, *Chronicles of the Reigns of Edward I and Edward II*, vol. 1 (1882), 201.
19. *Statutes of the Realm*, 376–377.

Chapter 12: Tisik, Apostomes and Quinsy: Health

1. *MLLF*, 11; *Coroner*, 63–64; *CIPM 1365–69*, no. 255; *CIPM 1413–18*, no. 807.
2. *Leicester 1*, 361.
3. *Coroner*, 2, 231–232.
4. *RMO*, 47.
5. *Coroner*, 5–6, 16, 177–178; *SCCR*, 109; *Dialogues*, 41–42.
6. *CLB F*, 131.
7. Sara M. Butler, *Forensic Medicine and Death Investigation in Medieval England*, 229.
8. *Coroner*, 22–25, 215.
9. *Coroner*, 11–12, 16; Butler, *Forensic Medicine*, 227, 229.
10. *Dialogues*, 41–42; *Coroner*, 209–210; Middle English Dictionary.
11. *Dialogues*, 11.
12. *Calendar of Documents Relating to Scotland 1307–57*, no. 766.
13. *CLB G*, 204.
14. *MLLF*, 273–274; *CLB G*, 21.
15. *CLB H*, 184.
16. *London Sheriffs Court Roll 1320*, 63.
17. *SPMR*, vol. 2, 236.
18. *Coroner*, 90–91; *CLB B*, 272; *MLLF*, 14.
19. *CIPM 1377–84*, no. 656; *CIPM 1374–77*, no. 161.
20. *SCCR*, 18–19, 21–23.
21. *Coroner*, 116–117.
22. *SCCR*, 24.
23. *Coroner*, 23–24; *CPR 1301–07*, 256.
24. *SCCR*, 68–69.
25. *SCCR*, 62.
26. *MLLF*, 393–394, 606–609; *CLB K*, 11, 14, 17, 29–30; Middle English Dictionary.

27. *Coroner*, 256–257; *CLB B*, 275.
28. www.medievalgenealogy.org.uk/inquests/abstracts_119C.shtml, accessed 4 October 2024.
29. *Coroner*, 15–16.
30. SAL MS 122, 56, 64, *qest tout malades de lune coste.*
31. *SCCR*, 17.
32. *Chronicles of the Mayors and Sheriffs of London*, 249 (*'graunt maladie des oelz'*).
33. *London Eyre of 1276*, nos. 25, 136.
34. T.W.E. Roche, *The King of Almayne*, 148–149.
35. *RMO*, 36; *SCCR*, 12.
36. *CLB G*, 270, 285, 310.

Chapter 13: Foteball and Penypryk: Having Fun (1)

1. *Munimenta Gildhallae Londoniensis*, vol. 3, ed. H. T. Riley, 439–441.
2. *SPMR*, vol. 2, 152.
3. *MLLF*, 561–562, 571; *CLB I*, 72, 85; *SPMR*, vol. 3, 291.
4. *CIPM 1432–37*, no. 272.
5. *CIPM 1219–1307*, nos. 2121, 2241.
6. SAL MS 122, 21–22, 65.
7. *CIM 1219–1307*, no. 2209; *CPR 1272–81*, 223. In two records of the early 1400s, football is called *ad pilam pedalem* in Latin: *CIPM 1422–27*, nos. 189, 360.
8. Paul Donnelley, *Firsts, Lasts and Onlys of Cricket*.
9. Allen Guttmann, 'From Ritual to Record', *Sport: Critical Concepts in Sociology, Volume II: The Development of Sport*, ed. Eric Dunning and Dominic Malcolm, 16–17.
10. *Leicester 2*, 317–318; *Nottingham 2*, 265.
11. *CIM 1219–1307*, nos. 2233, 2273, 2282.
12. *Leicester 2*, 317–318; *CIM 1219–1307*, no. 2394.
13. www.medievalgenealogy.org.uk/inquests/abstracts_113.shtml, accessed 23 September 2024.
14. *MLLF*, 3–4.
15. TNA E 101/380/4.
16. *CCR 1360–64*, 534–535; *CCR 1364–68*, 181–182; *CLB I*, 125–126.
17. *Coroner*, 213; *CLB F*, 10.
18. *SPMR*, vol. 1, 36; *SPMR*, vol. 2, 218; *ECMR*, 205.
19. *SPMR*, vol. 2, 172–173.
20. Although the Oxford English Dictionary states that 'chop-cherry' is first recorded in 1561, a coroner's inquest taken in Oxford in 1389 records *choppecherye* as a watchword (*waccheword*) among a gang of thieves: *RMO*, 55.
21. *London Eyre of 1276*, no. 151.
22. *Coroner*, 17–18; *MLLF*, 395–396, 455–457; *SPMR*, vol. 2, 210–211.
23. *Leicester*, vol. 2, 290; *SPMR*, vol. 2, 93.
24. *MLLF*, 86.
25. *Coroner*, 38–39; *SPMR*, vol. 1, 113, 257.

Chapter 14: Wrastleng, Mommyng and Romanse: Having Fun (2)

1. *CIM 1219–1307*, no. 2099.
2. *CCR 1302–07*, 355.

3. *MLLF*, 269.
4. TNA E 101/380/4; W. Mark Ormrod, *Edward III*, 103.
5. TNA E 101/380/4; SAL MS 122.
6. *London Eyre of 1276*, no. 116; *SCCR*, 62.
7. *MLLF*, 580.
8. *MLLF*, 88; *CLB C*, 16; *Munimenta Gildhallae Londoniensis*, vol. 3, 440.
9. *SPMR*, vol. 2, 58.
10. Kenneth Fowler, *The King's Lieutenant: Henry of Grosmont, First Duke of Lancaster 1310–1361*, 106–110.
11. *MLLF*, 193, 669; *CLB G*, 3; *CLB H*, 54, 157, 293; *CLB I*, 38, 209.
12. www.medievalgenealogy.org.uk/inquests/abstracts_120.shtml, accessed 7 October 2024; *Coroner*, 2, 12–13.
13. *Dialogues*, 2; Constance Bullock-Davies, *A Register of Royal and Domestic Minstrels 1272–1327*, 32; TNA E 101/380/4.
14. Edward A. Bond, 'Notices of the Last Days of Isabella, Queen of Edward the Second, drawn from an Account of the Expenses of Her Household', 468.
15. Thomas Stapleton, 'A Brief Summary of the Wardrobe Accounts of the Tenth, Eleventh and Fourteenth years of King Edward the Second', 342; Bullock-Davies, *Register of Minstrels*, 39.
16. Richard Rastall, 'Secular Musicians in Late Medieval England', University of Manchester PhD thesis, 87.
17. https://d.lib.rochester.edu/teams/text/salisbury-trials-and-joys-interludium-de-clerico-et-puella, accessed 21 August 2024.
18. https://d.lib.rochester.edu/teams/text/salisbury-trials-and-joys-talk-of-ten-wives-on-their-husbands-ware, accessed 21 August 2024.
19. *Wills*, vol. 1, 649–651.
20. *SPMR*, vol. 3, 11; *CIM 1348–77*, no. 109.
21. *CLB F*, 255.
22. *Wills*, vol. 1, 643–644.
23. *Dialogues*, 39.
24. *Wills*, vol. 2, 24–25.
25. *SPMR*, vol. 1, 145; *Wills*, vol. 2, 272–273.
26. *Wills*, vol. 1, 557, 627, 636.
27. *SPMR*, vol. 3, 17.
28. *A Collection of All the Wills Now Known to be Extant*, 177–185; Jeanne E. Krochalis, 'The Books and Reading of Henry V and his Circle', 50–52.
29. *Historiae Dunelmensis Scriptores Tres*, ed. James Raine, cclviii–cclx.
30. *John of Gaunt's Register 1371–75*, nos. 244, 259.
31. *Nottingham 1*, 246–247; *CIPM 1422–27*, no. 530.
32. *Coroner*, 25.
33. *Wills*, vol. 1, 233–234, 403–404, 435–436, 669–670.
34. SAL MS 122, 62; *Dialogues*, 21.
35. *Wills*, 237–238; *CLB E*, 17–19.

Chapter 15: How Moche Cometh It To? Going Shopping

1. *MLLF*, 33, 245–247, 339, 440, 532; *SPMR*, vol. 1, 1–3; *CLB E*, 156–157.
2. *MLLF*, 141–142; CLB I, 151; *CLB K*, 10, 220–221.

3. *MLLF*, 216–219; *CLB I*, 115–116.
4. *LAN*, no. 206.
5. *Ancient Deeds Belonging to the Corporation of Bath*, ed. Shickle, 11.
6. *Nottingham 1*, 377, 395.
7. *John of Gaunt's Register 1371–75*, nos. 389, 1707, 1713; there are numerous references to both markets in the *Records of the Borough of Leicester*, vols. 1 and 2.
8. *Nottingham 1*, 154–155, 282, 298–301, 314–315, 409.
9. *Nottingham 1*, 218–219; *SPMR*, vol. 2, 249.
10. *Dialogues*, 15–17.
11. *MLLF*, 332–333; *Leicester 2*, 291; *Dialogues*, 35.
12. *Calendar of Charter Rolls 1226–57*, 4.
13. *CChR 1341–1417*, 38.
14. *Nottingham 1*, 57–59.
15. *CIPM 1377–84*, no. 841.
16. *CPR 1317–21*, 290.
17. *Nottingham 1*, 61–66.
18. *CPR 1324–27*, 232.
19. *CLB B*, 236; *CLB D*, 236; *CLB E*, vii; *MLLF*, 33, 75.
20. Ormrod, *Edward III*, 128.
21. *MLLF*, 637–638; *CLB A*, 3, 6; *CLB C*, 9–10; *Dialogues*, 19.

Chapter 16: Medieval Misteries: Working

1. *EMCR*, 47–48, 52, 158, 166, 169–171, 190–192; *CLB D*, 97ff, 167; *Wills*, vol. 1, 194–195, 431, 445; *MLLF*, 227; *Munimenta Gildhallae Londoniensis*, vol. 3, 254; *SPMR*, vol. 1, xxxi; vol. 3, 126.
2. *CIPM 1352–60*, nos. 330, 475.
3. *CIPM 1422–27*, nos. 827–828.
4. *Wills*, vol. 1, 175–176; *EMCR*, 239; *CLB C*, 200–201, 216; *Coroner*, 219–220.
5. *CLB A*, 227; *CLB H*, 185–186, 340–341.
6. *Wills*, vol. 1, 439–440, 558, 560–561.
7. *Letters from the Mayor and Corporation of London, circa 1350–1370*, ed. Reginald R. Sharpe, 25, 34, 38–39, 46, 64–65, 70; *Wills*, vol. 1, 395.
8. *Statutes of the Realm*, 308; *SPMR*, vol. 1, 231; *SPMR*, vol. 2, 220.
9. *EMCR*, 166.
10. *SPMR*, vol. 2, 107.
11. *SPMR*, vol. 2, 18, 58.
12. *SPMR*, vol. 3, 69, 120–121. John Penreth is perhaps the same person as the man of this name who marries a woman called Emmote and takes on Marion Walle as an apprentice in 1392.
13. *SPMR*, vol. 3, 180.
14. *EMCR*, 168, 170.
15. *MLLF*, 265; *CLB G*, 6.
16. *Wills*, vol. 1, 238, 352, 609; *CIPM 1317–27*, no. 696; *CIPM 1327–36*, no. 229; Stapleton, 'Brief Summary of the Wardrobe Accounts', 322; *CCR 1323–27*, 336, 582–585; TNA SC 8/178/8894; *Calendar of Memoranda Rolls 1326–1327*, nos. 445, 630.
17. *CLB D*, 47.
18. SAL MS 122; *SPMR*, vol. 2, 229.

19. *CLB G*, 115–118, 148, 301; *MLLF*, 216–219, 253–258.
20. *MLLF*, 105–107; *CIPM 1327–36*, no. 542.
21. In the Middle Ages, women were churched or purified thirty or forty days after giving birth, and the feast of the Purification on 2 February falls forty days after Christmas Day. The Annunciation falls nine months before Christmas Day and commemorates the Archangel Gabriel telling Mary that she is pregnant with Jesus Christ. The Assumption commemorates Mary's body being taken, or 'assumed', into heaven to be reunited with her soul.
22. *CLB K*, 17 (*Morowemasse*); for the misteries, see for example *MLLF*, 354.
23. *RMO*, 18.
24. *CLB I*, 44–45, 93.
25. SAL MS 122, 54, 63, 65, 70, 78, 88; Ian Mortimer, *Time Traveller's Guide*, 100.
26. SAL MS 122, 56, 62, 64, 68; TNA E/101/380/4.
27. *SPMR*, vol. 2, 13; *CLB G*, 174.

Chapter 17: Olifaunts, Sothseyers and Storms: Oddities and Intense Weather

1. *CCR 1313–18*, 249, 389, 502; *CCR 1333–37*, 412–413, 611; *CCR 1337–39*, 67.
2. Hilda Johnstone, *Edward of Carnarvon*, 30, 86; Stapleton, 'A Brief Summary of the Accounts', 344; Mortimer, *Perfect King*, 290.
3. *CLB G*, 178–179; *SPMR*, vol. 2, 18; *MLLF*, 320; Middle English Dictionary.
4. *Dialogues*, 11.
5. *EMCR*, 51.
6. *EMCR*, 130, 136, 228, 232, 238, 261.
7. Niav Gallagher, 'The Audit of Alexander Bicknor's Accounts', 1997, formerly available at www.ucd.ie/pages/97/gallagher.html.
8. *CIPM 1399–1405*, no. 854.
9. *Select Cases in the Court of King's Bench Under Edward II*, ed. G.O. Sayles, vol. 4, 155–157; *A Contemporary Narrative of the Proceedings Against Dame Alice Kyteler*, ed. Thomas Wright, xxiii–xxix.
10. *CLB I*, 196–197.
11. *MLLF*, 462–463, 472–473; *SPMR*, vol. 2, 188.
12. *Oxford Dictionary of National Biography*.
13. *Dialogues*, 50.
14. *Chronicles of the Mayors and Sheriffs of London*, 26, 44, 54, 240, 249; *The Flowers of History, Especially Such As Relate to the Affairs of Britain, From the Beginning of the World to the Year 1307, Collected by Matthew of Westminster*, vol. 2, ed. and trans. C.D. Yonge, vol. 2, 476, 582.
15. *Chronicles of the Mayors and Sheriffs of London*, 208; *LAN*, no. 281.
16. *Chronicles of the Mayors and Sheriffs of London*, 243.
17. *Calendar of Liberate Rolls 1251–60*, 349–350, 445–447, 450, 452–453, 455, 463, 496, 500, 529; Frederick Devon, ed., *Issues of the Exchequer: Being a Collection of Payments Made Out of His Majesty's Revenue*, 68–69; *The Flowers of History*, ed. Yonge, 337.
18. *Annales Paulini 1307–1340*, 278.
19. *Chronicles of the Mayors and Sheriffs of London*, 252.
20. *CIPM 1361–65*, no. 544; *CIPM 1422–27*, nos. 223, 830.
21. *Calendar of Charter Rolls 1341–1417*, 288–289.
22. *The Chronicle of Lanercost 1272–1346*, ed. Herbert Maxwell, 103.

23. *Flowers of History*, vol. 2, 582.
24. SAL MS 122, 66; *CPR 1324–27*, 295; *Annales Paulini 1307–1340*, 312–313; John M. Stratton, *Agricultural Records A.D. 220–1977*, 27–30.
25. *Polychronicon Ranulphi Higden Monachi Cestrensis*, vol. 8, ed. Joseph Rawson Lumby, 344–346; *The Black Death*, ed. and trans. Rosemary Horrox, 65–66.
26. Derek Vincent Stern, *A Hertfordshire Demesne of Westminster Abbey*, 100, 166.
27. John Carmi Parsons, 'The Year of Eleanor of Castile's Birth and Her Children by Edward I', 262; *CIM 1308–48*, no. 230; *Le Livere de Reis de Brittaniae e le Livere de Reis de Engletere*, ed. John Glover, 336–337.
28. *Le Livere de Reis*, 347; *The Brut or the Chronicles of England*, ed. Friedrich W.D. Brie, 228, 313–314.

Chapter 18: Frenzy and Next Friends: Medieval Kindness

1. *Register of Edward the Black Prince Preserved in the Public Record Office*, ed. M. C. B. Dawes, vol. 4, p. 10; *CCR 1307–13*, 537.
2. *CIM 1219–1307*, no. 2202.
3. *CPR 1301–07*, 458.
4. *SCCR*, 46–47.
5. *CIM 1219–1307*, nos. 1384, 1767; *CCR 1296–1302*, 152; and see also *CIM 1219–1307*, nos. 1136, 1296, 1375, 1422, 2220, 2261, 2275–76, 2279; *CPR 1292–1301*, 81; *Coroner*, 36–37, 249; *RMO*, 26, 37. A horse-thief dies while imprisoned in Leicester in 1323, and the cause of death, rather obscurely, is also given as 'frenzy': *Leicester 1*, 377.
6. *SPMR*, vol. 3, 104–105; *CLB H*, 43.
7. *SPMR*, vol. 2, 294.
8. *Wills*, vol. 1, 603, 649–651; *Wills*, vol. 2, 57–58; *CLB D*, 161; *CLB G*, 256–257.
9. *Wills*, vol. 1, 563–565.
10. *Wills*, vol. 1, 87–88.
11. *Wills*, vol. 1, 654, 688, 694; *Wills*, vol. 2, 3, 13, 24–25, 45, 57, 75, 103, 114, etc.
12. *SPMR*, vol. 3, 23.
13. *Coroner*, 52–53.
14. *Wills*, vol. 1, 640; *CLB F*, 229.
15. *CLB E*, 52, 136; *MLLF*, 117–118.
16. *CLB E*, 208, 293–295; *Wills*, 317; *MLLF*, 149.
17. *SPMR*, vol. 1, 226, 228.
18. *CLB F*, 199; *SPMR*, vol. 1, 227.
19. *CLB E*, 47–48; *Wills*, vol. 1, 217. A man named Thomas Burgh, perhaps this same Thomas, dies in 1379, and though he has a daughter named Agnes, his wife is called Isabella: *Wills*, vol. 2, 211.
20. *Coroner*, 222–223, 254–255, 260–261.
21. *RMO*, 27.
22. *CIM 1308–48*, no. 777.

Bibliography

Primary Sources

'Account of the Expenses of John of Brabant and Thomas and Henry of Lancaster, 1292–3', *Camden Miscellany*, second volume, ed. J. Burtt (1853), 2–11

A Descriptive Catalogue of Ancient Deeds, six vols., ed. H.C. Maxwell-Lyte (1890–1915)

Ancient Deeds Belonging to the Corporation of Bath, XIII–XVI Cent., ed. The Rev. C.W. Shickle (1921)

Annales Londonienses 1195–1330, in ed. W. Stubbs, *Chronicles of the Reigns of Edward I and Edward II*, vol. 1 (1882)

Annales Paulini 1307–1340, in ed. W. Stubbs, *Chronicles of the Reigns of Edward I and Edward II*, vol. 1 (1882)

The Babees' Book: Medieval Manners for the Young, trans. Edith Rickert and L.J. Naylor (2000)

The Brut or the Chronicles of England, ed. Friedrich W.D. Brie (1906)

Calendar of Chancery Warrants, one vol., 1244–1326 (1927)

Calendar of the Charter Rolls, six vols., 1226–1517 (1906–27)

Calendar of the Close Rolls, fifty-four vols., 1227–1454 (1982–1941)

Calendar of Coroners Rolls of the City of London A.D. 1300–1378, ed. R. R. Sharpe (1913)

Calendar of the Manuscripts of the Dean and Chapter of Wells, vol. 2 (1914)

Calendar of Documents Relating to Scotland, vol. 2, 1272–1307, and vol. 3, 1307–57, ed. Joseph Bain (1884–87)

Calendar of Early Mayor's Court Rolls, 1298–1307, ed. A. H. Thomas (1924)

Calendar of the Fine Rolls, eighteen vols., 1272–1461 (1911–39)

Calendar of Inquisitions Miscellaneous, three vols., 1219–1377 (1916–37)

Calendar of Inquisitions Post Mortem, twenty-five vols., 1235–1447 (1904–2009)

Calendar of Letter-Books of the City of London, Letter-Books A to K, 1275–1457, ed. R. R. Sharpe (1899–1911)

Calendar of the Liberate Rolls, six vols., 1226–72 (1916–64)

Calendar of Memoranda Rolls (Exchequer): Michaelmas 1326–Michaelmas 1327 (1968)

Calendar of Papal Registers Relating to Great Britain and Ireland: Papal Letters, eight vols., 1198–1455, ed. W.H. Bliss and J.A. Twemlow (1893–1909)

Calendar of the Patent Rolls, forty-nine vols., 1216–1461 (1891–1916)

Calendar of the Select Plea and Memoranda Rolls of the City of London, vol. 1, 1323–64, vol. 2, 1364–81, and vol. 3, 1381–1412, A. H. Thomas (1926–32)

Calendar of Wills Proved and Enrolled in the Court of Husting, London, vol. 1, 1258–1358, and vol. 2, 1358–1688, ed. R. R. Sharpe (1889–90)

The Chronicle of Lanercost 1272–1346, ed. Herbert Maxwell (1913)

Chronicles of the Mayors and Sheriffs of London, ed. H. T. Riley (1863)

A Collection of All the Wills, Now Known to be Extant, of the Kings and Queens of England, Princes and Princesses of Wales, and Every Branch of the Blood Royal, ed. J. Nichols and Richard Gough (1780)

Croniques de London, ed. J. G. Aungier (1844)
Dialogues in French and English by William Caxton; Adapted from a Fourteenth-Century Book of Dialogues in French and Flemish, ed. Henry Bradley (1900)
Early Lincoln Wills: An Abstract of All the Wills and Administrations Recorded in the Episcopal Registers of the Old Diocese of Lincoln, 1280–1547, ed. Alfred Gibbons (1888)
Feet of Fines for Essex, vol. 2, 1272–1326 (1913)
The Flowers of History, Especially Such As Relate to the Affairs of Britain, From the Beginning of the World to the Year 1307, Collected by Matthew of Westminster, vol. 2, ed. and trans. C.D. Yonge (1853)
Foedera, Conventiones, Litterae et Cujuncunque Generis Acta Publica, vol. 2.1, 1307–1327, ed. Thomas Rymer (1818)
Historiae Dunelmensis Scriptores Tres, Gaudfridus de Coldingham, Robertus de Graystanes, et Willielmus de Chambre, ed. James Raine (1839)
Issues of the Exchequer: Being a Collection of Payments Made Out of His Majesty's Revenue, ed. Frederick Devon (1837)
John of Gaunt's Register, vol. 1, 1371–1375, two vols., ed. Sydney Armitage-Smith (1911)
John of Gaunt's Register, vol. 2, 1379–1383, ed. Eleanor C. Lodge and Robert Somerville (1937)
Le Livere de Reis de Brittaniae e le Livere de Reis de Engletere, ed. John Glover (1865)
Le Livre de Seyntz Medicines: The Unpublished Devotional Treatise of Henry of Lancaster, ed. E.J. Arnould (1940)
Letters from the Mayor and Corporation of London, circa 1350–1370, ed. Reginald R. Sharpe (1885)
Life-Records of Chaucer, parts 1 to 4, ed. Walford D. Selby, F.J. Furnivall, Edward A. Bond and R.E.G. Kirk (1900)
Lincoln Wills, vol. 1, 1271–1526, ed. C.W. Foster (1914)
London Assize of Nuisance, 1301–1431: A Calendar, ed. Helena M. Chew and William Kellaway (1973)
The London Eyre of 1276, ed. Martin Weinbaum (1976)
London Possessory Assizes: A Calendar, ed. Helena M. Chew (1965)
London Sheriffs Court Roll 1320, ed. Matthew Stevens (2010)
Munimenta Gildhallae Londoniensis, vol. 3, ed. H. T. Riley (1862)
The National Archives records
Parish Fraternity Register: Fraternity of the Holy Trinity and SS. Fabian and Sebastian (Parish of St. Botolph without Aldersgate), ed. Patricia Basing (1982)
Polychronicon Ranulphi Higden Monachi Cestrensis, vol. 8, ed. Joseph Rawson Lumby (1882)
Records of the Borough of Leicester, vol. 1, 1100–1326, and vol. 2, 1327–1509, ed. Mary Bateson (1899–1901)
Records of Medieval Oxford: Coroners' Inquests, the Walls of Oxford, Etc, ed. H.E. Salter (1912)
Records of the Borough of Nottingham, vol. 1, 1155–1399, and vol. 2, 1399–1485, ed. W.H. Stevenson (1882)
Register of Edward the Black Prince Preserved in the Public Record Office, ed. M. C. B. Dawes, vol. 4 (1933)
Select Cases from the Coroners' Rolls 1265–1413, ed. Charles Gross (1896)
Select Cases in the Court of King's Bench Under Edward II, ed. G.O. Sayles, vol. 4 (1957)
Society of Antiquaries of London, Manuscript 122
Staffordshire Historical Collections, vol. 7, part 1, ed. George Wrottesley (1886)
Statutes of the Realm, vol. 1, 1101–1377 (1810)
Testamenta Vetusta: Being Illustrations From Wills, vol. 1, ed. Nicholas Harris Nicolas (1826)

The Three Earliest Subsidies for the County of Sussex, 1296, 1327, 1332, ed. William Hudson (1910)

The War of Saint-Sardos (1323–1325): Gascon Correspondence and Diplomatic Documents, ed. Pierre Chaplais (1954)

Two Early London Subsidy Rolls, ed. Eilert Ekwall (1951)

Selected Secondary Sources

Ackroyd, Peter, *The History of England, Volume 1: Foundation* (London, Pan Macmillan, 2011)

Anglo-Norman Dictionary, https://anglo-norman.net

Barron, Caroline, *London in the Later Middle Ages* (Oxford, Oxford University Press, 2004)

Beltz, George Frederick, *Memorials of the Garter from Its Foundation to the Present Time* (London, William Pickering, 1841)

Black, Maggie, *The Medieval Cookbook* (London, British Museum Press, 1992)

Bond, Edward A., 'Notices of the Last Days of Isabella, Queen of Edward the Second, drawn from an Account of the Expenses of Her Household', *Archaeologia*, 35 (1854), 453–469

Briggs, Keith, 'OE and ME *cunte* in Place-Names', *Journal of the English Place-Name Society*, 41 (2009), 26–39

Bullock-Davies, Constance, *Menestrellorum Multitudo: Minstrels at a Royal Feast* (Cardiff, University of Wales Press, 1978)

Bullock-Davies, Constance, *A Register of Royal and Domestic Minstrels 1272–1327* (Woodbridge, The Boydell Press, 1986)

Butler, Sara M., *Forensic Medicine and Death Investigation in Medieval England* (New York, Routledge, 2014)

Carroll, Ruth, '*Utilis Coquinario* and its Unnamed Author', *Cooks & Other People: Proceedings of the Oxford Symposium on Food and Cookery 1995*, ed. Harlan Walker (1996), 45–51

Charlton, Edward, *Memorials of North Tyndale and Its Four Surnames* (Newcastle-upon-Tyne, J.M. Carr, 1871)

Donnelley, Paul, *Firsts, Lasts and Onlys of Cricket* (London, Hachette, 2010)

Dunning R.W., and C.R. Elrington, eds., *A History of the County of Somerset*, vol. 6 (London, Victoria County History, 1992)

Fowler, Kenneth, *The King's Lieutenant: Henry of Grosmont, First Duke of Lancaster 1310–1361* (New York, Barnes & Noble, 1969)

Given-Wilson, Chris, *Henry IV* (New Haven and London, Yale University Press, 2016)

Guttmann, Allen, 'From Ritual to Record', *Sport: Critical Concepts in Sociology, Volume II: The Development of Sport*, ed. Eric Dunning and Dominic Malcolm (2003), 5–40

Rosemary Horrox, ed. and trans., *The Black Death* (Manchester and New York, Manchester University Press, 1994)

Houts, Elisabeth van, and Julia Crick, *A Social History of England 900–1200* (Cambridge, Cambridge University Press, 2011)

Ilardi, Vincent, *Renaissance Vision from Spectacles to Telescopes* (The American Philosophical Society, 2007)

Jahner, Jennifer, *Literature and Law in the Era of Magna Carta* (Oxford, Oxford University Press, 2019)

Johnstone, Hilda, *Edward of Carnarvon 1284–1307* (Manchester, Manchester University Press, 1946)

Krochalis, Jeanne E., 'The Books and Reading of Henry V and his Circle', *The Chaucer Review*, 23 (1988), 50–77

Lawrence, Martyn, 'Too Flattering Sweet to be Substantial? The Last Months of Thomas, Lord Despenser', *Fourteenth Century England V*, ed. Nigel Saul (Woodbridge, The Boydell Press, 2008), 146–158

Matheson, Lister M., 'Chaucer's Ancestry: Historical and Philological Assessments', *The Chaucer Review*, 25 (1991), 171–189

Middle English Dictionary, https://quod.lib.umich.edu/m/middle-english-dictionary/dictionary

Mortimer, Ian, *The Perfect King: The Life of Edward III, Father of the English Nation* (London, Vintage, 2006)

Mortimer, Ian, *The Time Traveller's Guide to Medieval England* (London, The Bodley Head, 2008)

Mount, Toni, *How to Survive in Medieval England* (Barnsley, Pen & Sword, 2021)

Ormrod, W. Mark, *Edward III* (New Haven and London, Yale University Press, 2011)

Oxford Dictionary of National Biography, online edition, www.oxforddnb.com

Parsons, John Carmi, 'The Year of Eleanor of Castile's Birth and Her Children by Edward I', *Mediaeval Studies*, 46 (1984), 245–265

Rastall, Richard, 'Secular Musicians in Late Medieval England', University of Manchester PhD thesis (1968)

Rees, William, *Caerphilly Castle and Its Place in the Annals of Glamorgan* (Caerphilly, Caerphilly Local History Society, 1971)

Rhodes, Walter E., 'The Inventory of the Jewels and Wardrobe of Queen Isabella (1307–8)', *English Historical Review*, 12 (1897), 517–521

Riley, H. T., ed., *Memorials of London and London Life in the 13th, 14th and 15th Centuries* (London, Longmans Green, 1868)

Roche, T.W.E., *The King of Almayne* (London, John Murray, 1966)

Shepherd, Robert, *Westminster: A Biography from Earliest Times to the Present* (London, Bloomsbury, 2012)

Stern, Derek Vincent, *A Hertfordshire Demesne of Westminster Abbey* (Abingdon, Bennett and Kerr, 2000)

Stapleton, Thomas, 'A Brief Summary of the Wardrobe Accounts of the Tenth, Eleventh and Fourteenth years of King Edward the Second', *Archaeologia*, 26 (1836), 318–345

Stratton, John M., *Agricultural Records A.D. 220–1977* (London, John Baker, 1978)

Ward, Jennifer, *Elizabeth de Burgh, Lady of Clare (1295–1360): Household and Other Records* (Woodbridge, The Boydell Press, 2014)

Warner, Kathryn, *Living in Medieval England: The Turbulent Year of 1326* (Barnsley, Pen & Sword, 2020)

Warner, Kathryn, *London: A Fourteenth-Century City and Its People* (Barnsley, Pen & Sword, 2022)

Woolgar, C. M., *The Great Household in Late Medieval England* (New Haven and London, Yale University Press, 1999)

Woolgar, C. M., *The Senses in Late Medieval England* (New Haven and London, Yale University Press, 2006)

Wright, Thomas, ed., *A Contemporary Narrative of the Proceedings Against Dame Alice Kyteler* (London, Camden Society, 1843)